PREVENTING
CHILD MALTREATMENT
THROUGH
SOCIAL SUPPORT

PREVENTING CHILD MALTREATMENT THROUGH SOCIAL SUPPORT

A Critical Analysis

Ross A. Thompson

SAGE Publications
International Educational and Professional Publisher
Thousand Oaks   London   New Delhi

For information address:

 SAGE Publications, Inc.
2455 Teller Road
Thousand Oaks, California 91320
E-mail: order@sagepub.com

SAGE Publications Ltd.
6 Bonhill Street
London EC2A 4PU
United Kingdom

SAGE Publications India Pvt. Ltd.
M-32 Market
Greater Kailash I
New Delhi 110 048 India

Printed in the United States of America

Library of Congress Cataloging-in-Publication Data

Thompson, Ross A.
    Preventing child maltreatment through social support: A critical analysis/ Ross A. Thompson.
        p. cm.
    Includes bibliographical references and index.
    ISBN 0-8039-5594-4 (alk. paper).—ISBN 0-8039-5595-2 (pbk.: alk. paper)
    1. Child abuse—Prevention. 2. Abusive parents—Social networks. I. Title.
HV6626.5.T48   1995
362.7′67—dc20   95-7702

This book is printed on acid-free paper.

95 96 97 98 99 10 9 8 7 6 5 4 3 2 1

Sage Production Editor: Tricia K. Bennett

For Janet, Scott, and Brian

Contents

Preface

Among the most challenging contemporary problems in domestic policy is preventing the abuse and neglect of children. Those who seek to protect children as social service caseworkers, law enforcement officials, lawyers, judges, counselors, home visitors, and program administrators must cope with not only the apparent irrationality of child maltreatment but also the daunting complexity of factors that contribute to any adult's proneness to abuse or neglect, and the association between abuse and broader problems of poverty, substance abuse, and family dysfunction. Moreover, they must do so in the spotlight of public concern about maltreated children, indignation over well-publicized failures of the child protection system (including failures to remove children from dangerous homes soon enough, as well as failures of the foster care system), and frustration that the public investment in child welfare does not reap considerably more tangible dividends in protected, secure children.

In this and other areas of domestic policy, the road to despair is paved with not only good intentions but also good ideas that are ineffectively implemented. The 30 years that have passed since the Great Society initiatives of the early 1960s have seen many potentially valuable approaches to strengthening families fail—not primarily because they were based on poor ideas, but because the ideas were operationalized in simple, carelessly designed initiatives that devoted inadequate attention to the specific needs and interests of recipient populations, the social ecology of the neighborhoods and communities to which they were to be applied, and the broader challenges of effectively translating research into programs and policy. Although it is often true that policymakers are not sure what will "work" in domestic policy making and that new and insightful research is always needed, it is also true that underfunded, inadequately developed, and poorly conceived initiatives based on knowledge of "what works" will almost always lead observers to conclude otherwise.

Recently, there has been considerable interest in providing social support to abuse-prone families as a means of preventing child abuse and neglect. It is based on an appreciation of the variety of ways that individuals benefit from the everyday assistance provided by friends, family, and neighbors, and research that suggests that one of the most important characteristics of abuse-prone families is that they are isolated from these supportive social ties. Advancing this idea, several new prevention programs in which social support is a central component have been evaluated recently, with results suggesting that social support (broadly defined) can reduce the likelihood that high-risk families will become abusive or neglectful, and can help parents who are abusive to establish more positive family functioning and improved relations with offspring. Partly because of these program evaluations and the theoretical underpinnings of these initiatives, social support has become the cause célèbre among those who are seeking more effective new avenues to abuse prevention.

Yet social support could join the variety of domestic initiatives that eventually will be deemed a failure not because the underlying idea was a bad one, but because its implementation was not carefully conceived. The view that social support, whether from formal or everyday helpers, can provide a variety of resources that troubled families would find valuable is probably valid, but many important issues must be considered in translating this general idea into effective public policy initiatives related to abuse prevention. What is social support, and what is its potential impact on a parent's proneness to abusive behavior? How does support naturally arise from the social networks of kin, neighborhood, friendship, and workplace, and which network associates are the most reliable sources of support (as well as of stress)? What do we know about the social networks of high-risk families, and how can this inform efforts to mobilize supportive assistance from people within those networks? What potential role can formal helpers, such as social workers, counselors, clergy, and health care providers, assume in efforts to enhance support to abuse-prone families? What factors underlie the impact that social support can have on troubled individuals in general, and on high-risk parents in particular? What do we know about the social isolation of abuse-prone families, and does research concerning their social isolation offer helpful insights into the kind of supportive assistance they are likely to find most helpful? What lessons can be learned from recent efforts to enlist social support into a comprehensive abuse prevention strategy, and how can these conclusions guide the development and implementation of new strategies?

These are important questions that threaten to take us from a simple, straightforward account of the role of social support in alleviating life stress to a more complex—and potentially more vexing—analysis of the role of natural social networks in the life experience of high-risk families, the multifaceted (and sometimes conflicting) functions of social support in abuse prevention, the complex factors underlying the effects of proffered assistance on troubled families, and the social ecology of abuse-prone families in which social support is supposed to aid them. Yet such considerations are essential. The potential benefit of careful thinking about social support and the prevention of child maltreatment is that program planners, caseworkers, and others who are concerned with child protection will approach their task with greater insight into the nature of social support and its potential value, and limitations, as an abuse prevention strategy. The danger of the failure to think carefully about these issues is that premature, ill-conceived initiatives will ultimately lead program evaluators, and the (public and private) administrators who sponsor them, to unduly conclude that social support as an abuse prevention strategy is another of those ideas that simply was inadequate to the task.

The goal of this book, therefore, is to foster the kind of careful, thoughtful reflection about the relevance of social support to the prevention of child maltreatment that is essential to the design of effective interventions. The discussion is organized into seven chapters. In the first, issues of abuse prevention are framed within the broader context of contemporary concerns about the child protection system, and the hope and pessimism that derive (sometimes at the same time) from reflection on the status of children in our society. This chapter also introduces the reader to several issues that frame the discussion of social support and the prevention of child maltreatment: the distinction between primary, secondary, and tertiary prevention; the importance of distinguishing between different forms of maltreatment; and the coordination of the needs of victims as well as perpetrators.

The second chapter is the first of three that critically analyze current research concerning social networks and social support, drawing on studies from community psychology, family sociology, developmental psychology, and related fields. In Chapter 2, the natural social networks created by neighborhood, kinship, friendship, and other ties are explored as they affect adults, children, and families. In particular, the connections between child and parent networks are examined because they have important implications for the coordination of social support to each family member. In Chapter 3, we consider how to describe the organization of social networks and the functions of social support. In each case, it is clear that the natural networks on which individuals rely for support are considerably more complex than we often believe and that social support can assume diverse functions in the lives of most individuals that may, or may not, be consistently interrelated. In Chapter 4, these issues are explored further as we seek to understand the impact of social support on its recipients, including consideration of recipient reactions to aid, the effects of help-giving on helpers themselves, the impact of stress on social support and the stressfulness of social networks, how the recipient's personal characteristics can mediate help-giving, and the general question of whether social support benefits the recipient— and, more specifically, necessarily reduces abuse potential.

The discussion in Chapter 5 begins the transition from theory to application as we consider research concerning the social context of child maltreatment in general and the social isolation of abuse-prone families in particular. In doing so, we draw on the lessons of the research reviewed in the preceding chapters to frame questions concerning the nature of the social insularity that these families might experience and its impact—and then examine the answers provided by research findings. The move to application is further apparent in Chapter 6, when two approaches to the prevention of abuse that entail social support—home visitation and intensive family preservation strategies—are discussed in detail. From the lessons of these programs and the studies that have evaluated them, as well as the research on social networks and social support, we derive suggestions for potentially fruitful new directions in research, policy, and practice in Chapter 7, and also consider social support in the broader context of child welfare reform.

Acknowledgments

I have been exceedingly aided by the generosity of many colleagues and friends who have been willing to discuss these issues with me, share their expertise, and refer me to other materials that I would not have otherwise found. I am happy to acknowledge their contributions: Marcia Allen, Paul Amato, Frank Barry, Urie Bronfenbrenner, Dante Cicchetti, Deborah Daro, Richard Dienstbier, Byron Egeland, Mary Fran Flood, James Gaudin, Robert Halpern, D. Scott Hargrove, Patricia Hashima, Jeffrey Haugaard, Heidi Inderbitzen, Mary Kenning, Michael Lamb, Susan Limber, Gary Melton, Edward Mulvey, D. Wayne Osgood, Diana Prescott, N. Dickon Reppucci, Michael Rutter, Ira Schwartz, Donald Unger, Michael Wald, James Whittaker, Brian Wilcox, and Diane Willis. Jon Conte, Deborah Daro, Mark Fondacaro, Jim Garbarino, Jill Korbin, Jennifer Langhinrichsen-Rohling, Gary Melton, and Jenny Weisz each read an early draft of this manuscript, and their comments and suggestions proved invaluable.

Portions of this manuscript were prepared for the U.S. Advisory Board on Child Abuse and Neglect under a contract with the U.S. Department of Health and Human Services. I am grateful to the advisory board for their support of this work, and also to the authors of other papers commissioned by the advisory board for their helpful comments and reflections on this manuscript: James Garbarino, Jill Korbin, Paul Lerman, Leroy Pelton, and David Wolfe. Other portions of this manuscript were prepared for the Nebraska Department of Social Services through a contract with the Center on Children, Families and the Law of the University of Nebraska, where I served as

Associate Director during the period this manuscript was written. I am grateful to the Nebraska Department of Social Services for their support of this work. The views expressed in this book do not, however, reflect the opinions of either the U.S. Advisory Board on Child Abuse or Neglect or of the Nebraska Department of Social Services.

Finally, my thanks to Terry Hendrix and Dale Grenfell of Sage for unfailing goodwill and tangible assistance and to my family—my sources of support—to whom this book is dedicated.

Ross A. Thompson
Lincoln, Nebraska

1

The Challenges of Child Protection

The current landscape of child maltreatment prevention efforts inspires both despair and optimism. Despair derives from the realization that current efforts to protect children and youth are unequal to the extraordinarily complex causes of child abuse and neglect, provoking the U.S. Advisory Board on Child Abuse and Neglect (1990) to describe the national system as "broken." Optimism derives from creative efforts to design new intervention programs using recent innovative research on the determinants and correlates of child maltreatment, with an emphasis on preventing abuse before it occurs (Wekerle & Wolfe, in press; Willis, Holden, & Rosenberg, 1992). Illustrative of these new approaches are proposals to prevent maltreatment through various kinds of interventions that are intended to enhance social support to high-risk families. It is believed that social support can combat the social isolation of potentially abusive families by enlisting the assistance of either formal or "natural" helpers in the neighborhood who can provide affirmation, information, and instrumental aid that can benefit troubled families in many ways besides aiding in abuse prevention. Furthermore, there is promising initial research evidence that some social support interventions can, indeed, reduce the incidence of maltreatment.

At its (idealized) best, social support can be provided by a neighbor who offers emotional sustenance to troubled parents and counseling about parenting dilemmas and problems, work-related issues, and life stress. It might include the parent's involvement in community programs that provide education, training in job skills, material

1

assistance, and—in the course of doing so—offer an opportunity to strengthen social ties with others in the community. Social support might entail school-based services that enable the victims of child maltreatment to develop social skills, enhance self-esteem, strengthen academic competence, and also develop relationships with supportive peers and alternative adult role models. Informal social support might also be enhanced by church, community, and recreational organizations that have, as part of their explicit mission, the goal of extending their services to troubled families by integrating them into a broader social network through cooperative, mutually beneficial activities. Through the guidance of formal helpers—such as child protection caseworkers, social workers, public health personnel, and even counselors, clergy, and mental health workers—the efforts of such "natural" helpers could be coordinated with the variety of public and private services that needy families often rely on, offering opportunities for social integration in the context of receiving welfare benefits, obtaining treatment for substance abuse, participating in community-based child care programs, or developing educational or job skills. Perhaps most important, at its (idealized) best, social support would provide both emotional support and also monitoring of parental conduct in a manner that is esteem enhancing, nonstigmatizing, and even welcomed by recipient families.

But current enthusiasm for social support interventions to prevent abuse may underestimate the difficulties of enhancing social support to troubled families in a manner that will actually curb child maltreatment. The obstacles to effectively enlisting social support to prevent abuse and neglect are legion. They include the multidimensionality of the natural and formal social networks from which support is to come, and the fact that many potential helpers may be unwilling, or unable, to provide the assistance these families need. They include the deterioration, danger, or lack of resources of the neighborhoods in which many needy families reside, and which provide few opportunities or incentives for social integration. They include the complexity of social relationships with kin, neighbors, and friends, who may be sources of stress as well as support, and who may fail to reduce abuse potential even when they are trying to be emotionally supportive. And they include the problems of the recipients of support themselves, such as substance abuse or mental health problems, resistance to proffered assistance, and poor social skills, that can help to account for their social isolation within the community and the challenges they pose to potential helpers.

Proponents of enhancing social support for abuse prevention must also closely examine the social ecologies of abuse-prone families, their social resources as well as social deficits, and the nature of the social isolation that is believed to beset them. Are abuse-prone families indeed socially isolated, and if so, in what ways? What are the causes of their insularity? Is abuse potential heightened by social isolation, and if so, can interventions designed to enhance social support have a preventive effect? To what extent are the benefits of social support contingent on social skills training, reducing drug dependency, or curbing the danger or deterioration of the neighborhoods in which these families live?

Finally, social support interventions to prevent child abuse must also be based on a thoughtful look at the nature of social support itself. As it is currently conceptualized, social support is a multifaceted phenomenon that entails not only emotional sustenance but also instrumental aid, skill acquisition, and referrals to other sources of assistance, as well as monitoring and sanctioning abusive parental conduct and aiding the victims of abuse or neglect. The breadth of social support raises important issues about how it is accessed. Is social support primarily a matter of the sheer number of helpful partners in the social ecology, for example, or rather the sharing of viewpoints, reciprocity of helping, and expectations of assistance that may characterize a social network of any size? Can the emotionally supportive features of helping relationships be coordinated with the need to monitor and sanction inappropriate parental conduct? Can social support to perpetrators and victims of abuse within the same family be effectively coordinated? How is social support that is designed to prevent abuse in a high-risk family different from (and similar to) social support enlisted to avert the recurrence of abuse in a victimized family?

The purpose of this book is to analyze these challenges—and ideas for addressing them—in a manner that will aid practitioners concerned with child protection, policymakers concerned with child maltreatment, and researchers concerned with the social ecology of abuse-prone families.

The Current Status of Child Protection

Reasons for Concern

It seems that everyone is concerned about child abuse and ne-glect—and with good reason. There were almost 3 million reports of abuse in 1992, which, when prevailing substantiation rates are consid-ered, probably reflects well over 1⅙ million actual incidents of child maltreatment (McCurdy & Daro, 1994). This compares with estimates of the 1970s that about 60,000 children annually were maltreated. Although this increase in abuse reporting is partly due to growing public sensitivity to child abuse and the effects of mandatory report-ing laws, there is also reason to believe that the actual rate of child abuse and neglect has grown significantly during the past 25 years. Family life is increasingly characterized by divorce and single parent-ing, nonmarital parenting, and economic stresses that, in the context of neighborhood dysfunction and limited public assistance, have caused family sociologists to question whether many families can still fulfill their basic functions related to child rearing (e.g., Popenoe, 1993). These changes in the social ecology of the family and its socioeconomic well-being enhance the likelihood of domestic vio-lence in general, and of child maltreatment in particular.

Consequently, abusive families are today multiproblem families, often characterized by poor family income and parent education, which are exacerbated by unemployment, poor housing, welfare reliance, and living in dangerous and/or declining neighborhoods (Daro, 1988; Garbarino & Sherman, 1980a; Polansky, Chalmers, Buttenwieser, & Williams, 1981; Straus, Gelles, & Steinmetz, 1980). Maltreating parents may also have emotional, mental health, or substance abuse problems that add to their continuing difficulties with their children (Daro, 1988; Gaudin & Pollane, 1983). In addition, parents who abuse or neglect their offspring are often characterized as lacking significant social connections to others in the extended family, the neighborhood, the broader community, and to social agencies that can provide assis-tance. As a consequence, their treatment of offspring is likely to remain undetected, and the ways that social connections with support agents can buffer the effects of stress, promote healthy behavior, and socialize parenting are less influential.

These characteristics of abusive families alone pose formidable challenges to the design of effective treatment and prevention efforts.

But in addition, the child protection system is itself beset by a number of difficulties that make surmounting these challenges much harder, and which caused the National Commission on Children (1991) to conclude that

> if the nation had deliberately designed a system that would frustrate the professionals who staff it, anger the public who finance it, and abandon the children who depend on it, it could not have done a better job than the present child welfare system. (p. 293)

This is not an isolated concern. The Select Committee on Children, Youth, and Families (1987) called maltreated children "victims of official neglect," and the U.S. Advisory Board on Child Abuse and Neglect (1990) concluded that "the child protection system lacks a focus on the needs of children" and urged the development of alternative approaches (p. 38). These professional criticisms of the child protection system are consistent with recurrent reports in the popular media of children who are victimized, neglected, or otherwise unaided by local social service agencies that are ostensibly committed to safeguarding their welfare.

The problems of the child protection system are not primarily because the social service caseworkers, program administrators, judges, mental health professionals, police, and other actors within this system are not deeply committed to the children they seek to serve. Rather, they occur for other reasons (Thompson & Flood, in press). The first reason is inadequate resources—and the second is the way that the existing resources are allocated. The growth of the number and complexity of child abuse cases has not been matched by an increased commitment of public funds to effectively address the challenges of reporting, investigating, intervening (and monitoring the effectiveness of interventions), treating (both victims and perpetrators), and preventing child maltreatment in a manner that fosters thoughtful, individualized interventions into families. Consequently, in the spotlight of public concern about abused children, the limited funds of child protection agencies are directed largely toward investigating abuse allegations and supporting out-of-home placements of abuse victims (Pelton, 1989). Investigation and placement satisfy the most essential goals of ensuring that abuse is stopped before it recurs, but it ignores other important, longer term goals of child protection. Treatment and prevention efforts, for example, remain significantly underfunded (U.S. Advisory Board on Child Abuse and Neglect, 1990). As a result, it is much easier to find the funds to remove a child from the home than to provide in-home treatment to the family, or to concertedly prevent abuse from happening in a family that might be prone to maltreatment.

A third reason for concern about contemporary child protection efforts is that the "child protection system" in the United States is a loosely coordinated, somewhat fragmented compilation of diverse agencies that are each concerned with child maltreatment, but are managed with different orientations and agendas. This national "system" actually consists of hundreds of local, independent child protection systems in diverse jurisdictions that are associated with public agencies for law enforcement, public health, social welfare, and education. In each agency, a concern with child protection must necessarily be harmonized with other concerns (e.g., ensuring procedural due process for the accused, fitting a family's diverse needs into existing delivery systems, satisfying federal mandates with a limited budget) that may blunt the effectiveness of child protection efforts. In a sense, the design of the national child protection system—decentralized, involving the coordination of diverse public agencies with different goals, and responsive to local concerns—undermines its effectiveness.

Finally, the child protection system has been buffeted during the past 25 years by the recurrent crisis orientation of public concern about newly discovered forms of child maltreatment, and shifting public sentiment about appropriate solutions to this problem. Institutionalized with the discovery of the "battered child syndrome" in the early 1960s, the child protection system has seen its responsibilities evolve as concerns emerged over the incidence of sexual abuse in the late 1970s and early 1980s, the problems of drug-exposed infants (and the effects of substance abuse more generally on children) in the late 1980s, and renewed attention to the prevalence of homelessness and poverty of children in recent years. Because each new wave of concern about child maltreatment entails new preventive, interventive, and treatment strategies, the child protection system has been stretched in many directions at once. Moreover, the historical growth of this system has also been shaped by changing public sentiment over the appropriate ways of addressing the problem of child maltreatment, including early and continuing concern about the effects of "temporary" foster care placements, a growing emphasis on "permanency planning" in out-of-home placements of abused children, and a concern with "family preservation" in case planning—each of which has been publicly debated as the liabilities as well as benefits of each new policy strategy have become recognized. As a result, the growth of the system has been reactive to the increasingly complex needs of victimized children, and changing public sentiment about how best to intervene, rather than proactive in planning comprehensive and thoughtfully integrated prevention and treatment interventions.

Therefore, concern about child abuse and neglect is warranted not only because it is becoming a more prevalent and complex problem, but because the current child protection system is overtaxed, crisis oriented, and fractionated—and striving mightily to cope with the new demands that continuously emerge concerning its role and mission. Most important, few efforts are devoted to what is perhaps the most important task of all: prevention.

Reasons for Optimism

Because of the seriousness of the problem and the extremity of these challenges, policymakers, practitioners, and researchers have recently devoted renewed attention to formulating new approaches to child protection. Their efforts have resulted in some creative, and potentially useful, strategies that emphasize prevention. The U.S. Advisory Board on Child Abuse and Neglect (1990, 1991, 1993a, 1993b), a congressionally commissioned committee with a broad mandate for proposing reform of the child welfare system, has recommended the creation of a "child-centered, neighborhood-based child protection system" in which federal agencies concerned with child abuse would seek to empower communities to institute formal abuse prevention programs as well as to strengthen informal services and resources within neighborhoods to aid troubled families.

Meanwhile, in many local communities, small-scale programs are enlisting volunteers to visit regularly at home with mothers who are young, single, economically stressed, or otherwise at higher risk for maltreatment, beginning shortly after the baby's birth. Their purpose is to strengthen parenting skills, monitor the child's development, aid with access to social services and other neighborhood resources, and otherwise offer assistance and support to young parents at a time of heightened stress associated with the birth of a new baby. In Hawaii, a statewide home visitation program called Healthy Start seeks to prevent maltreatment by providing developmental guidance, emotional support, and other resources through a home visitor who meets with higher-risk mothers throughout the baby's first 5 years of life. The Hawaii program is similar to other initiatives that are being developed in many other states. In addition, a systematic strategy targeted to abusive families, called *intensive family preservation*, is designed to prevent the recurrence of abuse through several weeks of ongoing counseling, parent education, instruction on home management, vocational counseling, and other assistance through a trained social worker who meets with the family at their home and is on-call the rest of each day. This strategy, pioneered during the early 1970s, is the basis for a variety of intensive intervention programs throughout the country.

These local and national initiatives share in common an emphasis on providing social support to high-risk families. Although social support is never the sole ingredient to these new abuse prevention strategies, each is based on the frequently cited association between the social isolation of high-risk families and child maltreatment. Whereas isolation increases loneliness and depression; diminishes opportunities to obtain emotional sustenance from others (and thus reduces acceptable outlets for the frustration, anger, and anxiety associated with difficult life circumstances); limits the chances to exchange assistance (such as by baby-sitting) that reduces the demands of child rearing; undermines the sharing of knowledge about child development and child rearing; diminishes the family's integration into a supportive neighborhood or community network; reduces access to or knowledge of public resources to assist families economically and in other ways; and limits effective monitoring of parenting behavior, it also potentially heightens the risk of child maltreatment. By integrating a variety of formal and informal support agents into the lives of high-risk families, program planners hope that the affirmative, informational, socializing, and instrumental functions that everyday social support commonly assumes in nonabusive families can help reduce the likelihood of child maltreatment in high-risk families. This can occur not only through the direct services offered by a perinatal home visitor, a social worker in an intensive family preservation program, or a child protection caseworker, but also through this formal helper's mobilization of extended family members, friends, and even neighbors to assist family members in more diverse ways. If programs that incorporate social support can succeed in compensating for some of the problems of social isolation, they can potentially reduce the risk of abuse.

Social support has several additional potential advantages for the child protection system. The benefits of social support are primarily personal and relational and do not necessarily require expensive material resources, administrative bureaucracies, or governmental mandates. Social support provides assistance that most people find helpful, regardless of their economic circumstances, marital status, age, or other conditions, and this versatility suggests that social support interventions might be broadly pertinent to the needs of different kinds of multiproblem families who are prone to abuse, neglect, or other kinds of maltreatment. Social support interventions are noncontroversial in the eyes of policymakers and the public because most people can intuitively appreciate the potential value of social support by reflecting on the assistance they personally receive from neighbors, friends, family, coworkers, and other informal support agents. Depending on the needs of client families, social support agents do not necessarily require extensive training or expertise, whether they are agency representatives (such as social service caseworkers) or are recruited from among the "natural helpers" in the family's neighborhood, because the constituent skills related to counseling, dissemination of information, and instrumental aid are common features of everyday social encounters. The broad and intuitive appeal, inexpensiveness, and local origins of social support interventions are thus attractive features to a child protection system that is frequently frustrated by the problems of administrative coordination, limited funding, and public controversy.

There also exists an extensive research literature documenting the broader benefits of social support to physical and mental health, especially as a buffer of life stress, that adds credence to the view that social support can be enlisted to combat child maltreatment. Clinical researchers have shown, for example, that social support helps to reduce the effects of disease pathology and psychological distress on stressed individuals, and thus contributes to less severe symptomatology, quicker recovery, enhanced coping, and diminished long-term effects of stress. Social support also fosters healthy functioning, they argue, by encouraging and reinforcing healthy behavior in at-risk individuals (cf. Cohen & Wills, 1985). As these conclusions about the potential benefits of social support for physical and mental health coalesced in the mid-1970s (cf. Cassel, 1974a, 1974b, 1976; Cobb, 1976), scholars and practitioners eagerly embraced the value of social support interventions for a broad variety of challenges to physical and psychological functioning (Heller & Swindle, 1983). The President's Commission on Mental Health (1978), for example, enthusiastically endorsed strengthening natural support systems that exist in families, neighborhoods, and communities for the treatment and prevention of mental health problems. The conclusion of Meyer (1985) is representative of this broader enthusiasm for the potential benefits of social support for a range of psychological challenges:

> The research evidence is in: There is a strong relationship between individual physical-social-psychological health and social supports and between social isolation and the breakdown in these areas of functioning. In view of the importance of natural support networks, social workers can do no less than explore the linkages between them and professional intervention. (p. 291)

Reasons for Caution

By 1985, however, other scholars had concluded that "the era of unrestrained enthusiasm that has dominated social support research and interventions for more than 10 years is coming to a close" (Shumaker & Brownell, 1984, p. 11). Although the links between social support and physical and mental well-being remain viable, scholarly enthusiasm for preventive interventions based on this association has become gradually more restrained for several reasons (Vaux, 1988). First, the nature of "social support," and the components of social support that assume stress-buffering and stress-preventive functions, have been vaguely and inconsistently portrayed in both conceptual and empirical analyses (Barrera, 1986). Because social support is not a single phenomenon but rather a variety of complex, loosely connected influences (e.g., emotional nurturance, instrumental aid, information sharing, modeling and reinforcement of healthy practices)—each of which has different consequences for physical and mental health—it has been harder than expected to move from research to applications of social support concepts (Rook & Dooley, 1985). It has been very difficult to determine, in other words, what specific aspects of social support have stress-buffering consequences for distressed individuals, and why, and how to use these features as the basis for social support interventions.

Second, the strength of the effects of social support on stress, symptomatology, and coping has often been unimpressive (Heller & Swindle, 1983). This may occur for many reasons, including (a) the fact that people in one's social networks can be supportive but also demanding and stressful (such as in relationships with kin or coworkers); (b) the realization that the impact of social support may be moderated by the personal skills and characteristics of the recipient (e.g., the recipient's social competence, reaction to aid, or defensiveness), the skills of the helper, and many other factors; and (c) the recognition that there is often a difference between how social support is objectively measured and how it is subjectively perceived, with the recipient's perceptions of being supported a crucial ingredient to its effectiveness (Brownell & Shumaker, 1984; Cohen & Wills, 1985; Heller & Swindle, 1983; Shinn, Lehmann, & Wong, 1984). Third, because of the multidimensional nature of "social support" and the diverse avenues and agents through which it is available, devising social support interventions requires a detailed understanding of the specific needs and conditions of recipient populations that is often unavailable (Shinn et al., 1984). This is because the effects of particular supportive interventions on stressed individuals are often specific to the needs and characteristics of the population requiring aid, but often those characteristics are not considered carefully in the design of generic interventions. Providing social support to an older adult in a residential care center to aid in combating depression is certainly a different task from enlisting social support to enhance the parenting skills of a young adolescent mother.

All of these considerations, and others, are pertinent to evaluating the potential role of social support in the prevention of child maltreatment because they indicate that the nature of social support and its effects are complex, and that the design of interventions that entail social support must be carefully crafted to take these complexities into account. Trying to enhance social support merely by adding additional people to a family's social ecology or encouraging their participation in community groups, for example, may not provide effective prevention, especially without consideration of how family members perceive the roles of these individuals in their lives. Considering how social support interventions can have multiple (and sometimes conflicting) purposes, and how both formal helpers as well as "natural helpers" in the social networks of high-risk families can differentially influence the risk of child maltreatment, can likewise alert program planners to the importance of thoughtfully conceptualizing the needs of maltreating families, and for considering how these needs can be best addressed in the context of social support interventions. These considerations are especially important because, as we shall see, there is evidence that thoughtfully designed, supportive interventions can strengthen children and families against the risk of maltreatment— but there is also the potential that programs that are not carefully conceived will not only fail, but contribute to the mistaken impression that social support is ineffective in preventing abuse. The goal, therefore, is to "unpack" the broad concept of social support to better understand what it is and does in the lives of high-risk families and their children.

Setting the Stage

A preliminary step to such an analysis is to define more clearly its scope and the nature of the problem of child maltreatment that social support is intended to address. Doing so reveals that social support can potentially serve many different goals in diverse contexts, and that distinguishing between these is an essential prerequisite to properly conceptualizing how social support can be enlisted on behalf of maltreated children and their families. These preliminary considerations begin with an analysis of three aspects of the problem of abuse prevention that complicate the potential role of social support as a preventive influence. They concern (a) the distinctions between primary, secondary, and tertiary prevention goals; (b) the differences between various forms of child maltreatment and their correlates; and (c) the distinct but complementary concerns associated with the needs of child abuse perpetrators, and their victims, as part of a broader prevention strategy.

Primary, Secondary, and Tertiary Prevention

Prevention efforts can occur at three levels of intervention. Primary prevention concerns services provided to the general population to reduce or prevent the occurrence of maltreatment. The potential target population is very broad. Secondary prevention concerns services targeted to specially identified high-risk groups to reduce or prevent maltreatment. In this case, the target population is narrower, based on signs of risk for abuse or neglect. Tertiary prevention concerns targeting services to perpetrators and/or victims of maltreatment either to prevent its recurrence or minimize its detrimental consequences. The target population consists of perpetrators and their victims. Primary prevention programs might include, for example, parenting classes in high schools that foster caregiving skills, whereas secondary prevention might focus on developing these skills in teenage parents and other identified groups that are at higher risk for child maltreatment, and tertiary prevention programs might emphasize the development of parenting skills in adults who have already been identified as abusive or neglectful.

Social support interventions can be part of broader primary, secondary, or tertiary prevention efforts to combat maltreatment (Dubowitz, 1989; Helfer, 1982). Primary prevention programs emphasizing social support might seek to strengthen the capacity of neighborhoods and communities to provide social resources that parents can enlist in coping with the demands of caregiving, such as in the design of community family resource centers or respite child care services, in school curricula for adolescents that foster parenting skills, and in hospital and health care programs that provide support to young parents. Secondary prevention programs with a social support component might target specific neighborhoods for such services where the risk of maltreatment is high, as well as providing other targeted interventions, such as school-based programs for teenage parents or perinatal visitation programs for higher-risk parents who are especially likely to be stressed by the baby's birth. Tertiary prevention programs emphasizing social support might intervene with families who have already experienced an abusive episode to either strengthen parent and family functioning (e.g., by providing crisis-intervention "hotline" or stress-management "warmline" services, or offering supervised visitation between parents and children who have been removed from the home) or reduce the detrimental outcomes to children who have been maltreated (e.g., through developmental day care and after-school programs). Thus, the scope of preventive efforts entailing social support is potentially very broad, depending on whether primary, secondary, or tertiary prevention is intended.

It is important to note that the role of social support is not the same in these alternative prevention contexts, even though the consistent goal is the prevention of child maltreatment. One obvious difference is in the nature of the population targeted for prevention efforts and its receptivity to social support interventions. The ease with which social support can be enlisted in the family ecology is much greater for untroubled families (in the context of primary prevention) than for high-risk families (in secondary prevention efforts), and may be most difficult with families who have already experienced child abuse or neglect (tertiary prevention). This is true for several reasons. Families that are troubled and prone to abuse face a greater number of life stresses that are likely to be more severe than those typically encountered by low-risk families, and this can affect their capacities to benefit from social support (especially if substance abuse or mental health problems are involved), their receptivity to such support (not only by heightening perceived need but also by increasing suspicion and defensiveness), and the range and nature of potentially supportive figures in their natural social networks (Ferleger, Glenwick, Gaines, & Green, 1988; Herrenkohl, Herrenkohl, Egolf, & Seech, 1979). Dysfunctional families often live in dysfunctional neighborhoods that offer relatively few natural helpers on whom they can rely, and which are dangerous to adults as well as children. The threats of these neighborhoods may also pose formidable challenges to the safety of formal helpers who are enlisted to aid family members, as well as to their capacity to provide meaningful aid and to enlist others to provide assistance. In addition, the behavioral norms of the residents of these neighborhoods may not only fail to challenge abusive behavior in parents but may reinforce values (such as an emphasis on respect) that may inadvertently contribute to child maltreatment. An emphasis on physical punishment, an acceptance of leaving young children alone for sustained periods, and a tolerance of parental behavior that puts children at risk may be part of the implicit norms of a high-risk neighborhood that can undermine abuse prevention goals. Taken together, the constellation of serious personal, familial, and social-ecological problems that characterize many high-risk families and the neighborhoods in which they live can pose formidable challenges to abuse prevention efforts.

Another important difference between primary, secondary, and tertiary prevention efforts is how social support is offered in the context of other interventions that family members perceive as either voluntary or coercive in nature. Although most social support interventions are more effective when they are voluntarily accepted by recipients, social support in the context of tertiary prevention is more likely to occur in tandem with other, more coercive actions by legal authorities and social service personnel. After all, these agencies also have a responsibility to ensure child protection and to adjudicate child abuse allegations in ways that necessarily enhance their coercive role in family life. Consequently, social support interventions in the context of tertiary prevention are more likely to have the goal of quickly effecting and documenting behavioral change in parents who have already been identified as abusive or neglectful. Parents may be forced, for example, to make mandatory visits to a counselor, participate in required parent education classes, tolerate unannounced home visits by a social worker, and accept other interventions that parents perceive as obligatory and coercive, and thus nonsupportive, even though the outcomes of these interventions are intended to benefit parents and the family as a whole. They may be particularly intolerant of interventions that challenge their preferred modes of family management, child rearing, and other activities, even though changes in these practices may be crucial to preventing further problems in the family. Nevertheless, the fact that parents perceive little support in these interventions because they are obligated to accept them may blunt their intended, beneficial impact.

By contrast, when primary and secondary prevention are involved, public agencies are much less coercive and instead tend to adopt a strategy of encouraging or enabling families to function more successfully, with the offer of services, counseling, and parent education based on the family's interest and willingness to participate. In these contexts, family members are more likely to regard their participation as voluntary and self-initiated, which will likely enhance the perceived supportiveness of these services and the benefits they receive by accepting them. This suggests that apart from the nature of the families that are targeted, it may be more difficult to design effective social support interventions in the context of tertiary than secondary prevention efforts, and that with tertiary prevention, the avenues and agencies of support (in the context of other coercive interventions into the family) and the perceived value of the services that are provided may pose daunting challenges to child protection efforts entailing social support.

Subpopulations of Maltreatment

Although researchers and policymakers commonly refer to child abuse and neglect as if it is a homogeneous phenomenon, child maltreatment assumes diverse forms. Recognizing the different—but overlapping—subpopulations of maltreatment is essential to understanding the potential effects of social support interventions because different goals and strategies are likely to be effective with different kinds of maltreatment perpetrators and victims.

Researchers have sought to distinguish at least four subpopulations of maltreating parents: those who are physically abusive, those who are physically neglectful, those who engage in emotional maltreatment, and those who are sexually abusive (e.g., Daro, 1988, 1994; Herrenkohl, Herrenkohl, & Egolf, 1983). Despite our society's prototypical image of the maltreating parent as a physically abusive adult who is angry or frustrated and lacks self-control, the largest proportion of maltreating parents are identified as neglectful, not physically abusive (National Research Council, 1993). Sometimes their neglect derives from incompetence (especially when a substance abuse problem is involved), but more often it is due to inability: The association between child neglect and poverty is strong, with many parents unable to adequately feed, clothe, shelter, or protect their children in the context of socioeconomic distress and limited public assistance (Pelton, 1994). In a sense, the prototypical image of the abuse-prone situation should be an impoverished family (perhaps with an over-stressed single mother) trying to raise children in the midst of a dangerous housing project from the meager income of a low-paying job.

There are, however, different correlates of various forms of maltreatment, with parents differing in the extent to which socioeconomic stresses (such as poverty and unemployment) figure prominently in maltreatment, in the degree to which abuse derives from the adult's personal problems with impulse control and/or sexual dysfunction, in the nature of the broader family problems that are associated with maltreatment, and in the characteristics of the children who are victimized. These differences are revealed in the findings of a study of 19 federally funded clinical demonstration programs that indicate, not surprisingly, that different intervention strategies work best with different maltreatment subpopulations. A focus on individual and family therapy was found to be most successful with sexual abuse perpetrators, for example, for whom deep-seated psychological problems were paramount, whereas programs involving family counseling and community agency referrals (e.g., for economic assistance) served best those families characterized by neglect. On the other hand, parenting and child development classes were most successful with emotionally maltreating families for whom problems with impulse control and maintaining appropriate expectations of children were involved (Daro, 1988, 1993). There were also differences in the effectiveness of services offered to the child victims of various maltreatment subpopulations.

To be sure, a large number of families are characterized by multiple forms of maltreatment: Physical abuse is often combined with emotional abuse, for example, or with sexual abuse. Thus, it is inappropriate to create sharply delineated distinctions between various kinds of abusive and neglectful parents when, in fact, there is considerable overlap among the typologies one would create. However, distinguishing among different subpopulations of maltreatment is heuristically useful because it sharpens an awareness of how social support interventions can benefit different kinds of abusive families. More specifically, subpopulation considerations are germane to clarifying the goals, agents, and design of social support interventions.

First, the goals of supportive interventions are likely to vary depending on the subpopulation of concern. Because social support can be enlisted to provide many things—including appropriate models of parenting behavior; a buffer against the effects of socioeconomic or other life stresses; enhanced access to skills, services, or information; counseling; or other kinds of assistance—the recipient's specific needs and circumstances are essential to defining the most successful kind of intervention. If neglect is reactive to poverty and limited resources, for example, social support to enhance access to skills and services might be paramount. If maltreatment instead derives primarily from problems in impulse control, social support to provide counseling or appropriate role models may be most important. If abuse or neglect arises partly from inappropriate developmental expectations for offspring, social support in the context of parent education may be valuable.

Second, considerations vary also with respect to the potential agents of support. A neighborhood's or community's standards for parental conduct influence not only kinds of parenting practices that are reinforced but also whether natural helpers in the community will respond helpfully to parents with particular kinds of problems. Widespread condemnation of sexual misconduct with children undermines access to social support in the neighborhood; so also do the strong emotions evoked by the physical abuse of young children. In addition, as we shall see later, many neglectful parents are rejected by community members either because they are manifestly transient or poor, have social characteristics that mark them as "different," or have other problems that evoke negative reactions. In these circumstances, neighborhood-based social support interventions are unlikely to be effective (cf. Garbarino & Crouter, 1978), and the assistance of formal helpers (such as social workers or professional home visitors), self-help groups, or other strategies may be more suitable. Moreover, in some communities, neighbors, extended family members, and other natural helpers may be ineffective not because of their judgments of abusive behavior, but because they are poor role models for appropriate parenting. In these cases, integrating formal assistance into the natural social networks of recipient families may be most valuable. In each case, subpopulation considerations have direct implications for identifying potential sources of social support.

Finally, the design of social support interventions must also take into account different maltreatment subpopulations because of the diverse problems that may be associated with child abuse. Social support interventions may need to be integrated with social skills training and access to community services for some subpopulations, whereas with others, they can be integrated with individual and family therapy or crisis management training. By recognizing that social support alone is unlikely to address the full range of difficulties encountered by maltreating parents or children, program planners can integrate supportive interventions into a constellation of supplementary services that address other needs of these families.

In sum, the consideration of social support interventions is informed by Daro's (1988) admonition that

> if practitioners and policy makers have learned only one thing over the past two decades, it should be that allowing one type of maltreatment to dominate our thinking leaves us with a response system and practice standards inappropriate for the full range of concerns represented by this serious welfare dilemma. (p. 204)

Contributing complexity to these considerations, however, is the influence of other family and community characteristics. A parent's substance abuse problem makes the remediation of child maltreatment considerably more challenging, for example, by making the problem of drug dependency a paramount concern. Consequently, conventional social support programs targeted to these subpopulations may have to be considerably modified and integrated with drug treatment programs, and the enlistment of natural social support networks must take into account the extent to which these networks foster the target individual's substance abuse problem (especially if network associates also experience drug dependency). When child neglect or other forms of maltreatment are associated with the socioeconomic stresses of single parenting, on the other hand, social support programs in the context of guided access to material resources (e.g., affordable child care) may be advisable (cf. Belle, 1982). Adolescent parents present another challenge to the design of social support programs because of the unique constellation of their needs and interests as parents and offspring, as well as the demands and supports that emerge from their families of origin.

Taken together, the design of carefully crafted social support programs for maltreating families must take into consideration not only the characteristics of abuse that require remediation but also other features of perpetrators and victims that help to define the goals, agents, and design of an appropriate supportive strategy.

Victims as Well as Perpetrators

When children are the victims of abuse or neglect, social support should be part of a range of treatment approaches to assist them. However, there are many considerations in devising developmentally appropriate strategies of social support for children.

The child's age is important not only as an index of developing capabilities and needs, but also with respect to addressing the consequences of maltreatment. A number of studies have found that maltreated children show predictable and cumulative developmental losses that are associated with the experience of abuse or neglect (see Aber & Cicchetti, 1984; Cicchetti, 1990; Egeland & Sroufe, 1981; Egeland, Sroufe, & Erickson, 1983; Erickson, Egeland, & Pianta, 1989; Pianta, Egeland, & Erickson, 1989; see also Garbarino, 1989; Toro, 1982). For infants and toddlers, these include the development of

insecure attachments to caregivers and early deficits in the management of emotional arousal in challenging situations. By the preschool
years, maltreated children show less self-control and greater distrac-
tibility in problem-solving situations, and significant problems in
social relationships with peers. Maltreated children are often cogni-
tively delayed by the time of their entry into school, and also show
behavioral problems (such as anxiety and aggression) that are sometimes indicators of emerging psychopathology. During the school
years, these children show impairments in social skills (with adults as
well as peers) and in self-esteem: They are more aggressive, depressed, withdrawn, and impulsive than are nonmaltreated children.
These problems are also apparent in adolescence and are coupled with
greater social deviance and delinquency.

There is considerable evidence that children, like adults, who
enjoy social support from various sources are buffered against some
of the life stresses they may experience (e.g., Dubow, Tisak, Causey,
Hryshko, & Reid, 1991). However, one of the consequences of parental
abuse and neglect is its impact on children's social relationships and
social networks. One research team found that, when compared with
their nonabused classmates, 8- to 12-year-old physically abused children had lower peer status and were rated by their peers as more
aggressive and less cooperative; also, their social networks showed
more insularity, atypicality, and negativity (Salzinger, Feldman,
Hammer, & Rosario, 1993). Because of the impact of maltreatment on
their social skills and self-perceptions, the victims of abuse also have
limited access to the supportive assistance from peers and others that
would most benefit them.

To the extent that tertiary preventive programs involving social
support to victims are designed in a developmentally sensitive manner, they will address the particular problems experienced by maltreated children at different ages. Social support in the context of
therapeutic day care might be used to promote the development of
secure attachments to alternative caregivers for maltreated infants, for
example, and to foster social competence with peers for preschoolers.
For maltreated grade-schoolers and adolescents, social support might
be included in the context of peer counseling and academic tutoring
to enhance self-esteem and buttress perceptions of personal competence. Moreover, given that the deficits of maltreated children are not
only developmentally variable but also cumulative, intervention programs must be flexibly responsive to the changing constellation of

challenges experienced by these children over time. That is, even though maltreatment may have been halted, its consequences for social, emotional, and intellectual functioning may endure and become manifested in different ways as children mature. Treatment requires long-term assessment and monitoring of psychosocial growth, a goal that is seldom accomplished in a contemporary climate of limited public resources.

Developmental concerns are pertinent not just to the goals of social support interventions, but to the actors and agencies by which they are provided. As they mature, children enter into and emerge from different ecological networks that provide different opportunities for enlisting social support, as we shall see in greater detail in the next chapter. In infancy and early childhood, for example, the availability of child care while parents work is a prominent concern for parents (especially in balancing the availability, quality, and affordability of accessible care) and the quality of care can significantly influence children's socioemotional development. Because of this, developmental and/or therapeutic child care services can constitute an important avenue for social support for both maltreated children and their parents, and may assume secondary preventive value with high-risk families by reducing some of their parenting stresses. For older children, school-based and after-school programs may provide the same kinds of joint benefits for parents and offspring.

This suggests that some of the most effective social support interventions are those that offer complementary benefits to parents and children alike. However, this may be more difficult to achieve than it appears because of the complex ways that the natural social networks of children and families grow and change, as well as intersect, over time. Therefore, creating thoughtful social support interventions requires considerable understanding of the natural social networks of families and their offspring. This is the topic we also take up in the next chapter.

Finally, it is important to recognize that maltreated children are often multiproblem children, with developmental challenges that are sometimes independent of the effects of abuse or neglect. In addition to the very serious consequences of maltreatment, these children may have learning disorders, emotional difficulties, attention deficit disorders, and other psychological challenges. Moreover, children who are medically compromised, such as low-birthweight and/or premature infants, are overrepresented among maltreatment populations, as are temperamentally difficult infants and children (Parke & Collmer, 1975). Clearly, interventions that are intended to assist victims as well as perpetrators of child maltreatment must address the diverse needs of child victims, whether or not they stem directly from abuse or neglect. This often requires special educational assistance, psychological therapy and counseling, and other supportive services.

A Complex Calculus

It should be clear that the challenges of conceptualizing the role of social support in a comprehensive abuse prevention strategy are considerably greater than they might first appear. Although social support strategies have the intuitive appeal of drawing on the natural helping networks that most of us enjoy, and of providing many kinds of assistance to multiproblem families, it quickly becomes apparent that social support is a conceptual rubric for a surprisingly complex network of influences whose impact varies depending on the recipient's needs, background, and other characteristics; the relationship between the support agent and recipient; and the manner in which support is provided. The value of social support makes intuitive sense because it is a valued everyday experience, yet intuitions may belie its complexity and the multiple factors that determine its impact.

The considerations discussed here with respect to the distinctions between primary, secondary, and tertiary prevention; the subpopulations of maltreatment; and the distinct but complementary needs of victims and perpetrators only begin to underscore the need for careful thought concerning how best to enlist social support as an abuse prevention strategy. Moreover, although social support approaches— because they are local, relational, inexpensive, and noncontroversial—seem to circumvent many of the problems that have long buffeted the child protection system, this does not guarantee their success. Instead, it is necessary to carefully consider the nature of formal and everyday social networks and the social support that arises from them, the various factors underlying why social support has the consequences it does, and the social needs of abuse-prone families to consider how supportive interventions can best accomplish abuse prevention goals.

It is possible, even likely, that the current enthusiasm for social support interventions among those who are concerned about child maltreatment will, like the earlier enthusiasm of clinical researchers, give way to growing skepticism and discouragement as program planners recognize that social support does not always have the intended benefits and that the problems it is intended to remedy are considerably more complex than were initially expected. Certainly, the long history of child welfare reform suggests that episodes of early enthusiasm, followed by skepticism and ultimate discouragement, have tended to greet each new strategy for child protection. Before this occurs, however, it is worthwhile exploring how careful consideration of the complexity of the problem of child maltreatment, and of social support as a preventive strategy, can lead not only to a dampening of uncritical enthusiasm about the ameliorative effects of supportive interventions, but—more important—to better-designed and potentially more effective interventions. This is the task before us in the chapters that follow.

The Natural Networks
of Social Support

Individuals live within complex social ecologies that begin with their families and extend to the overarching values of the culture and its history (cf. Bronfenbrenner, 1977, 1986, 1989; Bronfenbrenner & Crouter, 1983; Featherman, 1983). They include the institutions of school, church, and government; the relationships associated with one's workplace; associations formed in the neighborhood and community; and the kinship ties that are geographically near or distant. It is from these natural social networks that support is commonly derived.

Because some of the most valuable and meaningful forms of social support occur in the context of close relationships, it is instructive to understand how natural social networks are constituted and maintained by individuals if social support is to be enlisted on behalf of high-risk families. Developing an appreciation of the creation and maintenance of natural social networks accomplishes other goals as well. It enhances our awareness that the experience of social support is based more on how these networks are subjectively perceived and valued by the individual, rather than their more objective characteristics. Social scientists have various ways of objectively measuring social network characteristics—distinguishing them according to their size, geographical dispersion, and stability, for example—but these objective depictions may be far less important to the provision of social support than to how these networks are personally construed as either affirmative, nurturant, and accepting, or as denigrating and inaccessible. Studying the construction and maintenance of natural social networks offers insights into their subjective meaning to individuals.

In addition, understanding how natural networks are conceived enables us to better appreciate the distinctive characteristics of the social networks of families that are at risk for child maltreatment, who have often been characterized as socially isolated. Social isolation can, of course, have many different meanings: It can refer to the sheer number of people in a social ecology; to their frequency of contact with the target individual; or to the subjective qualities of the relationships they share, such as their emotional tone or reciprocity. It is easier to distinguish and evaluate these diverse features of the isolation of maltreating families with an appreciation of what normative social networks look like in nonabusive families.

Finally, an understanding of natural social networks alerts us to the fact that social networks and social support are not at all the same thing. Individuals with extensive social contacts nevertheless may be very lonely people, and it is common to experience stress and turmoil, as well as (or instead of) support, in close relationships. Moreover, a person can have a very small network of friendships but experience considerable support within these intimate ties. Recognizing that social networks and social support are not the same thing cautions against assuming that adding more people to the natural networks of troubled individuals, or encouraging them to spend more time with those they already know, will necessarily assist them. Recognizing that social networks and social support are complexly linked better equips us to consider how the natural networks of troubled individuals might be enfranchised to assist and support them, and the role that formal helpers can potentially assume in providing social support.

A concern with social support in abuse prevention necessarily considers the needs of both perpetrators and victims, as indicated in the preceding chapter. Therefore, this discussion is organized around the natural social networks of adults and their families before considering the natural networks of children. Next, the intersection of parent and child networks is discussed to better understand how each family member shapes, and is influenced by, the social support (or lack thereof) experienced by others in the family.

The Natural Networks
of Adults and Their Families

Who are the potential "natural helpers" that exist within everyday social networks? They may be members of the immediate and extended family, friends who are geographically local or distant, colleagues at the workplace or school, current or former neighbors, employees at businesses in the community (e.g., barbers, grocers, post office personnel, etc.), clergy and other associates within one's religious group, and community and neighborhood leaders. For children, potential "natural helpers" include members of the extended family, peers at school and in the neighborhood, siblings, older children, teachers, and other adult personnel associated with school, recreational programs, or other activities.

For both parents and children, the breadth of natural social networks is influenced by access to transportation (which can significantly extend the boundaries of relational ties), technology (including not only the telephone but also fax and electronic mail), and the availability of time to nurture and cultivate close relationships. Natural networks have thus varied historically—as changes in the ease of transportation and technology have fostered more varied means of contacting and maintaining contact with others—and differed socioeconomically. In the contemporary United States, natural social networks tend to be diverse, and because individuals are also influenced directly and indirectly by the social networks of others in their immediate family, diversity is especially characteristic of the family social network, which is the aggregate of the social networks of its members. As we shall see, for example, children are affected in many ways by the nature and support afforded by their parents' network ties.

Researchers have only recently become interested in mapping and understanding the influence of personal and familial social networks (see especially Cochran, Larner, Riley, Gunnarsson, & Henderson, 1990; Fischer, 1982; Litwak & Szelenyi, 1969). The results of their studies have important implications for enlisting natural networks to support troubled families.

It is clear from this research that natural social networks incorporate but extend far beyond the geographically local neighborhood (Belle, 1982; Cochran & Henderson, 1990; Larner, 1990a). They include, for example, members of the extended family who may live quite some distance away, friends and associates who have moved from the neighborhood and perhaps from the town or city, and colleagues in the workplace or school who usually live outside of one's neighborhood. For children, too, natural networks extend beyond the neighborhood, although school entry focuses many social ties to peers who are attending the same school and/or living in the same neighborhood (Cochran & Riley, 1990; Larner, 1990b). Even so, school-based social contacts are not neighborhood based for many children, such as when they are bused to school, attend a private school, or go to a "magnet" school outside of their neighborhood, and many children participate in recreational, educational, and other activities that extend their social networks significantly beyond the local neighborhood. Children also benefit from other network ties, such as to extended family or former neighbors and friends, that are not necessarily neighborhood based.

There is a high degree of turnover in natural social networks. In a 3-year follow-up study of the personal and familial social networks of a sample of 240 parents in Syracuse, New York, nearly one fourth (22%) of the network members on average were dropped from adults' social networks between the first and follow-up interviews (Larner, 1990a). When these researchers examined the nature of the social relationships that were dropped or retained, they found the highest turnover among nonkin ties (34% turnover); neighbors (32% turnover); and friends, acquaintances, and former workmates (31% turnover). The lowest turnover rate was among kin (only 9% turnover). Consistent with this portrayal of turnover, neighbors did not figure prominently in the social networks of most people in this study, and were readily dropped or added to personal networks with little influence on an individual's or family's primary support systems (Larner, 1990b). This is not surprising given the rather high rates of mobility, job change, educational completion, marital change, and other factors that can alter neighborhood social networks, and the fact that other network associates, such as family members, strive to maintain contact even across great distances. But these findings suggest that different components of natural networks are vulnerable to turnover to different degrees.

In view of this portrayal of instability and change in social networks, on whom do people most rely for support? In most instances, they depend on support from extended kin and others outside the neighborhood (Cochran, Gunnarsson, Grabe, & Lewis, 1990; Gunnarsson & Cochran, 1990; Litwak & Szelenyi, 1969). One reason is that, as we shall see, the enduring, obligatory relationships that develop with extended family members provide a more reliable basis for support than the more casual, voluntary associations formed with neighborhood associates. Moreover, the considerable turnover in neighbors and other local associates makes it more difficult to depend on these individuals for assistance. Indeed, when a person is reliant primarily on neighborhood contacts, it may be an indicator of social insularity in other spheres of social life. In a study of socioeconomically stressed single mothers, for example, Belle (1982) found that the reason these women interacted more frequently with people in the neighborhood was that they felt they had nobody else to whom they could go. Moreover, these contacts did not help them much. The mothers who were in frequent contact with neighborhood associates did not experience greater emotional well-being, receive more tangible assistance, or report more support than did other women who saw their neighbors infrequently, perhaps because these neighborhood associates provided social contact but not social support. The same may be true of many workplace associations, especially those in the kinds of low-paying jobs that these women had.

These conclusions are important in light of recent policy recommendations focused on strengthening neighborhood-based supports for families at greatest risk of child maltreatment (cf. U.S. Advisory Board on Child Abuse and Neglect, 1990, 1991, 1993a, 1993b). In general, an emphasis on supportive neighborhood networks makes sense for several reasons. Neighbors and others in the community are potentially capable of offering troubled families various kinds of assistance because of their day-to-day contact with family members, and they are also uniquely capable of regularly monitoring the family for signs of child abuse or neglect. In addition, neighborhood-based networks do not require travel, a phone, or other resources that may limit access to nonneighborhood associates for economically stressed families. But the research on natural social networks suggests that an exclusive focus on neighborhood social support risks enlisting only a small portion of the social networks on which individuals commonly rely for assistance—and perhaps not even including those individuals who are perceived as most available and supportive when help is needed.

This research also suggests that the distinction between kin and nonkin ties is an important consideration in understanding natural social networks. There are many reasons for this. In contrast with other network ties, relationships with members of the immediate and extended family have a history of interaction that provides a foundation for future assistance and aid (Litwak & Szelenyi, 1969; Tinsley & Parke, 1984). A shared history, socioeconomic background, and geographic origin also commonly contribute to shared core beliefs and values among family members. Family relationships are densely interconnected, with family members knowing many other family members well, which contributes to the mutuality and intercoordination of support. Family members also have greater opportunities for maintaining sociability through various formal events (e.g., holidays, birthdays, anniversaries) and informal occasions that encourage family members to remain in contact even when they are geographically separated. In general, nonkin ties do not have these benefits, especially when they are geographically distant. In a sense, kinship relations are uniquely enduring because they are ascribed relations that emerge from one's birth or marriage, in contrast to the relationships that are sometimes painstakingly achieved with nonkin friends and other associates. In other words, relations with kin are primarily based on *who you are*, whereas nonkin ties are based largely on *what you do*. The former helps to enhance the stability and reliability of kinship ties.

Kinship is also built on strong cultural foundations of respect for family and family integrity that provide added incentives (sometimes obligations) to maintain and support these ties. Consequently, family members figure more prominently in the primary social networks of most individuals than do other partners in the neighborhood, workplace, or broader community. To be sure, individuals usually form intimate relations with only a selected subset of kin (based on age, gender, frequency of contact, and the nature of support required; see Hoyt & Babchuk, 1983), but nevertheless, kin remain preferred sources of primary support for most individuals.

The obligatory, enduring quality of kinship relations is a double-edged sword, however. Although family members may share continuing bonds of support and trust, family relationships may also become characterized by animosity, rivalry, and distrust that also endures. One of the liabilities of kin relations is that because family membership is ascribed, a difficult relationship between family members can endure for a long time and may be hard to break off. In contrast to nonkin ties—when a difficult relationship must either be restored or abandoned—people who cannot or will not get along with relatives nevertheless remain part of the kin network. (Indeed, the ascribed quality of kinship ties undermines some of the incentives to repair relationships because, barring divorce, one remains related regardless of one's congeniality or social skills.) In a sense, the primary role of kinship ties in natural social networks makes them potentially reliable sources of support, but also of stress.

Furthermore, when considering how to enlist natural networks to aid troubled families, it is important to remember that a particular family's difficulties often do not begin with the parents' current problems but are, in part, a legacy of past generations. Concern about the intergenerational transmission of parenting problems among contemporary psychologists alerts us to the possibility that especially in troubled families, extended kin may not only fail to provide supportive assistance to a family member who is experiencing personal or parenting difficulty, but may instead exacerbate maladaptive behavior by humiliating, rejecting, or isolating a troubled parent; denying or minimizing the seriousness of the adult's problems; articulating values that heighten turmoil within the family; allowing or supporting substance abuse, domestic violence, or other practices that enhance the likelihood of child maltreatment; restricting access to extrafamilial sources of support; or otherwise enhancing stress among family members.

Finally, although natural social networks share many commonalities, there are important differences in how networks are constituted and maintained by different subpopulations (Vaux, 1985). For example, there are differences according to socioeconomic status (SES). In general, the personal and familial social networks of lower-SES families tend to be smaller and more kin-based than for middle- and upper-SES families (Cochran, Gunnarsson, et al., 1990; Fischer, 1982; Vaux, 1988). In one large study, these differences by size were apparent for each category of network membership: Higher-SES families had a larger number of social ties with kin, neighbors, and "others" than did lower-SES families (Cochran, Gunnarsson, et al., 1990). One reason is that a higher proportion of higher-SES mothers worked compared to their lower-SES counterparts, which enhanced their work-related network ties. But to Cochran (1990c), Fischer (1982), and other commentators, these differences derive also from the resources, skills, and opportunities to construct and maintain extensive social networks that education and income afford individuals, as well as the constraints imposed by neighborhoods that are impoverished and are thus sometimes dangerous and unpredictable, and that engender suspicion and wariness in contacts with neighbors. In short, it may be more difficult to form extensive social networks within some socioeconomic conditions compared to others.

Single mothers also have smaller personal social networks with higher rates of turnover compared to married mothers (Larner, 1990a; Leslie & Grady, 1985; Weinraub & Wolf, 1983). Single mothers have more frequent contact with network members than do married mothers, and rely on them more for tangible aid, such as child-rearing and child care assistance, as well as emotional support (Belle, 1982; Gunnarsson & Cochran, 1990). However, the natural networks of single White mothers are more focused on nonkin friends and neighbors, whereas single African American mothers place greater emphasis on kin connections (Cochran & Henderson, 1990; Cross, 1990; Fischer, 1982; Gunnarsson & Cochran, 1990; but see Colletta, 1979; Leslie & Grady, 1985). These differences may derive from neighborhood and cultural processes: the importance of kin supports in African American families (McAdoo, 1980; Stack, 1974) and the greater ease of access to same-race neighborhood social networks and supports by White mothers (Cochran, 1990c). However, kin supports are also important to single White mothers, who may especially benefit from a strengthening of kin ties immediately following a divorce (Colletta, 1979; Leslie & Grady, 1985).

Thus, it is apparent that the natural social networks on which individuals commonly rely for support are multidimensional, with the distinctions between neighborhood and nonneighborhood relationships, and between kin and nonkin ties, especially important. These relationships vary in their relative stability, their geographical proximity, in the extent to which they are based on ascribed qualities (related to birth or marriage) or voluntary association, and in the ways that they can develop and are maintained. More important, these relationships vary also in the potential they offer for social support, and in the conditions associated with that support. Kin ties—by virtue of their formality and stability—offer the greatest potential sources of assistance, but extended families may also be sources of stress and may contribute in other ways to the enduring problems of troubled adults and their offspring. The more voluntary associations with neighbors and friends in the community can also provide meaningful support, but these relationships may be transient and thus unreliable. When these considerations are further coupled with the unique characteristics and needs of subpopulations that are demographically at higher risk of maltreatment—such as lower-income families—it is clear that estimating how to enlist the natural networks of troubled families into supportive assistance can be a complex task.

The Natural Networks of Children

To a great extent, similar considerations apply to an understanding of the social networks of children. Yet there are also many unique features of children's natural networks, owing to their developmental capabilities, limited power and autonomy, and their reliance on parents for access to many potential network associates (Belle, 1989; Salzinger, Antrobus, & Hammer, 1988). Understanding these special features of children's social networks is essential to thoughtfully considering how these networks might be enlisted to assist children who are the victims of abuse or neglect, or who potentially may be victimized.

There are, of course, important developmental changes in the nature of children's social networks. In infancy and during the toddler and preschool years, young children's natural networks are largely home- and family-based. However, this is significantly modified by the growing prevalence of day care, family day care homes, and preschool programs in the early years (Cochran & Brassard, 1979; Feiring & Lewis, 1988, 1989; Lewis, Feiring, & Kotsonis, 1984; Parke & Bhavnagri, 1989). This is an important shift in the social ecology of early development because it means that children have access to alternative sources of support outside the home: Caregivers in day care, for example, usually become a young child's attachment figures to whom secure (or insecure) relationships may be formed that supplement the secure or insecure attachments formed to parents (Howes & Hamilton, 1992). Caregivers can also indirectly assist children at risk for maltreatment by providing ongoing monitoring of the child's development and well-being at the center or home where care is provided, outside of parental supervision, and by providing attention to developmental needs that may be unattended at home. They may also provide assistance to parents by informing them of the child's needs and capabilities, answering questions about child rearing, offering informal counseling, and enlisting parents in parenting groups that can provide further assistance and support. They may also, of course, broker contact between parents and community agencies that can provide assistance, or intervene if a child is in danger.

However, it is important to note that these advantages are contingent on the quality of the child care setting and the training and orientation of the child's caregivers. Many child care settings are poor developmental settings, offering limited supervision and inadequate stimulation for healthy socioemotional and cognitive growth, and presenting young children with a barrage of demands (including noise, abrupt transitions between different activities, and the domination of older children) with which they may be unable to cope. The values and child-rearing goals of the caregivers may be similar to those of troubled parents, providing few catalysts to change in parental behavior and little benefit to children, and the high turnover among caregivers in most child care settings also threatens the development of reliable attachments between children and their caregivers. Taken together, the emergence of out-of-home care as a normative feature of early development poses both opportunities and challenges to the social support of young children.

The entry into school in middle childhood further widens natural social networks by acquainting children with a much more extended array of potential peer associates, as well as with adults who, as teachers, coaches, and school counselors, can potentially provide valuable advice, counseling, and other assistance as needed (Asp & Garbarino, 1983; Hirsch & DuBois, 1989). In formal curricula (e.g., abuse prevention programs) as well as during informal conversations, moreover, schools provide a socializing context in which children become acquainted with prevailing community standards concerning appropriate parental behavior and the avenues that are available to them for seeking assistance. Outside of school, after-school programs offer further opportunities for extending social relationships with other children and adults; the same is true of other activities, ranging from youth groups to athletic teams to special-interest clubs to neighborhood gangs (cf. Bryant, 1985; Medrich, Roizen, Rubin, & Buckley, 1982).

In adolescence, social networks become further extended to include more complex peer associations that are largely independent of the family system, especially given the greater mobility and independence that most adolescents enjoy, and these peer networks provide significant benefits as well as risks to teenagers (Berndt, 1989; Blyth, Hill, & Thiel, 1982; Blyth & Traeger, 1988; Garbarino, Burston, Raber, Russell, & Crouter, 1978). Peer associations become more complex for several reasons: They become more extensive (encompassing, for many, workplace and recreational associations as well as school-based friendships), more exclusive (with an emphasis on intimacy and loyalty that emerges in early adolescence), and more multidimensional (including romantic relationships as well as same-sex friendships). In each case, however, they provide added potential avenues of social support through peer associations. In many of these contexts, adolescents are also likely to form new relationships with adults—at work, on athletic teams, and in youth groups—that further extend their social networks.

Taken together, there is an unsurprising, but significant, widening of the natural social networks of children as they mature and become more independent of the family. However, two points should not be missed. The first is that most children have access to extrafamilial social partners from an early age, most commonly in some form of out-of-home care. This means that there are opportunities to provide assistance to children at risk for abuse from outside the family from early in life that is contingent, as earlier noted, on the quality of care.

The second point is that natural social networks widen with development not only because of the opportunities afforded by day care, schooling, and an after-school job, but also owing to children's active efforts to initiate and maintain meaningful social networks of their own. Just like adults, children are creators, sustainers, and inter- preters of their personal social networks. This is revealed in many ways, from a young child's efforts to be friendly to an appealing caregiver in day care to an older child's choices of after-school activi- ties and friends. The importance of children's personal constructions of their social networks is especially revealed in studies that assess children's own reflections on their relationships with others (e.g., Furman & Buhrmester, 1985, 1992; Levitt, Guacci-Franco, & Levitt, 1993; Reid, Landesman, Treder, & Jaccard, 1989). From a remarkably early age, children not only can describe their various network asso- ciates, but offer candid appraisals of the extent of support they expect from each. Teachers, for example, are not generally regarded as sources of supportive assistance, whereas friends are. The importance of extended family members also varies with age. The fact that children are acutely aware not only of the breadth of their personal networks but of the supportiveness of its members suggests that these construc- tions should be taken very seriously in efforts to enlist their natural networks for supportive assistance.

Parents as Mediators
of Children's Natural Networks

One of the noteworthy characteristics of children's social net- works is that they are mediated, directly and indirectly, by their parents (Cochran & Brassard, 1979; Parke & Bhavnagri, 1989). This can occur in many ways. Parents' choices of housing, neighborhoods, and schools directly affect the range of options that children have for forming social relationships with others outside the family. For example, neighborhoods vary in their safety, traffic congestion, availability of parks and other safe play areas, and access to other young families—each of which can affect how much children are likely to encounter others on their own (Bryant, 1985; Medrich et al., 1982). Residential mobility also affects children's natural networks because of the uprooting of friendships and other relationships that it can entail. One study found that the breadth of preschoolers' social networks was inversely associated with the numbers of moves the family had made to a new home (Ladd, Hart, Wadsworth, & Golter, 1988).

Parents also commonly arrange, facilitate, and monitor their children's contacts with others (O'Donnell & Steuve, 1983; Parke & Bhavnagri, 1989). They provide transportation to day care and, quite often, to school. Especially with young children, parents schedule activities, provide transportation, and often remain nearby as offspring encounter others at a neighborhood recreation center or swimming pool, a play group, or a visit to another family. Indeed, parental assistance with transportation remains an enduring feature of children's social activities until offspring can bicycle, use public transportation, and eventually reach the age for a driver's license. Moreover, parents sometimes become enfranchised into the child's extrafamilial social networks more directly by working as a volunteer aide at day care or school, or coaching a sports team, or providing transportation for a class field trip. In these cases, they not only help to organize and provide access to the activities in which children participate, but become intimately acquainted with the other social partners whom their offspring might encounter, and they can monitor these relationships.

It is important to note that as a consequence, the social networks of parents and offspring not only intersect, but the social network of the parent also expands. Indeed, one of the important correlates of the transition to parenthood is an adult's entry into a variety of relationships that are mediated primarily by their offspring, whether with the parents of their child's friends, child care and school personnel, pediatric professionals, recreational directors and coaches, religious mentors, youth group leaders, or others. This child-oriented expansion of an adult's social network has many valuable functions because these social partners can be useful sources of developmental guidance, social comparison, and social support—especially when parents are encountering the many stresses of child rearing. To some extent, this expansion of social contacts is an inevitable consequence of parent-hood. However, the extent to which an adult's social network is broadened by their parenting role depends also on how much they become involved in the extrafamilial interests and activities of off-spring. In a sense, therefore, parental mediation of their children's social networks also broadens the social networks of parents in ways that can expand potential sources of social support.

Of course, parents vary in their willingness and ability to act as mediators of their children's activities, with important consequences for offspring as well as indirectly for themselves. For example, O'Donnell and Steuve (1983) reported that lower-income and middle-class moth-ers differed significantly in the access they provided offspring to community resources and services. Whereas middle-class mothers tended to reliably take their children to regularly scheduled, publicly sponsored community services and to enfranchise themselves into these programs as volunteers and aides, lower-income mothers were more reluctant to commit themselves or their children to scheduled activities, and instead preferred to give their children greater (un-scheduled) freedom for "just being with friends." As a consequence, their children were afforded significantly fewer opportunities to bene-fit from these programs and activities. This may be a double-edged sword, however, when children from advantaged homes are over-scheduled by their parents into organized sports, lessons, and other activities that may provide few opportunities for unscheduled free-dom to "just be with friends." In short, despite their expanded social networks, children remain very dependent on their parents for their extrafamilial social contacts, which can significantly influence how they spend their time, with whom, under what conditions—and with what degree of parental monitoring, supervision, and interference.

Parental mediation of children's social networks also extends to relationships with extended family members. Because parents are at the intersection of children's relationships with their grandparents and other kin, for example, parents help to define the extent of their relationship and the conditions under which it develops (Robertson, 1975; Thompson, Scalora, Castrianno, & Limber, 1992). In some fami-lies, parents promote a close grandparent-grandchild relationship by enlisting their parents as surrogate caregivers, transportation direc-tors, mentors for specific skills, and participants in family activities;

in return, they receive child care relief and other forms of assistance. In other families, a child's relationships with grandparents are more distant because of the infrequency or formality of their contacts. The importance of the role of parents as mediators of kin networks for offspring is seen most clearly when parents divorce, and suddenly many grandparents discover that they have little contact with grandchildren who are being raised by their son's former wife, who is now a single mother (Thompson et al., 1992).

Therefore, it appears that at the same time that the breadth and depth of extrafamilial (and extended family) relationships are expanding markedly, children are only slowly becoming less dependent on parents as mediators of these relationships. In this respect, the social networks of children and their parents intersect, because parents are both supervising and influencing—and being influenced by—the expanding relationships of their children outside the home.

The Intersection of Parent and Child Networks

The reverse is also true: Children are affected by the nature and breadth of their parents' social networks (Cochran, 1990a, 1990b; Cochran & Brassard, 1979). Parental networks are likely to have important consequences for children because they influence parents' sense of well-being, offer opportunities for new experiences and relationships, and directly socialize parenting behavior. In this respect, it is important to consider not only how parents and children are affected by their own natural networks, but also how the family social network has direct and indirect effects on all family members.

For example, social support offered to parents can have beneficial consequences for offspring, and it is striking how early this can occur in a child's development. Cutrona (1984) reported, for example, that an overall index of the support mothers received during pregnancy and a measure of the social integration of their networks together predicted postpartum maternal depression 8 weeks after delivery. Mothers with enhanced support experienced less depressive symptomatology (see Unger & Wandersman, 1985, for similar results). Friends, kin, neighbors, and other network associates have various ways of providing support and reducing stress to new parents: Through sympathetic listening, respite child care, parenting advice and role modeling, material assistance, brokering contact with other helpers, and esteem-enhancing affirmation—as well as monitoring parental and child well-being—they can help ease the transition to parenting (Cochran, 1990a, 1990b; Cochran & Brassard, 1979). Developmental researchers have found that maternal social support enhances many features of children's psychosocial well-being—from the growth of a secure attachment to more positive parent-child interactions to improved peer relations—because of their impact on how mothers perceive their parenting role and act toward their offspring (Jacobson & Frye, 1991; Jennings, Stagg, & Connors, 1991; Melson, Ladd, & Hsu, 1993).

In particular, social support that reduces stress for mothers has beneficial effects on offspring. When Weinraub and Wolfe (1983) observed mothers interacting with their preschoolers, for example, they found that for mothers in two-parent families, more optimal maternal behavior was associated with greater amounts of parenting and emotional support and diminished stress. Similarly, for single mothers, more optimal maternal behavior was associated with diminished stress, greater parenting support from other network associates, and fewer working hours. Crnic and his colleagues have reported similar results for mothers with their infants (see Crnic, Greenberg, Ragozin, Robinson, & Basham, 1983; Crnic, Greenberg, Robinson, & Ragozin, 1984), and others have also noted the links between social support, maternal well-being, diminished stress, and parenting competence (e.g., Cotterell, 1986; Levitt, Weber, & Clark, 1986).

However, these optimistic conclusions must be qualified in important ways. The same natural networks that help to reduce stress by providing support to parents may, in other ways, also heighten stress for them. The workplace is a good illustration of how relations with coworkers can, at times, offer important esteem-enhancing affirmation, opportunities for socializing, and valuable advice and counseling—but their job-related demands can also be time consuming and exhausting. Both are likely to affect parenting. Likewise, parents experience a respite from child care demands when grandparents participate in child-rearing responsibilities (which is especially helpful for single parents), but they also become susceptible to criticism by grandparents of their parenting skills.

Moreover, social support provided to one family member may, on other occasions, have undesirable indirect consequences for other family members. Extended family members may provide much-needed emotional support to parents, for example, but at the same time they may also reinforce harshly punitive or neglectful parenting practices, such as by emphasizing strict corporal punishment of offspring. Conversely, extended kin may be supportive of children but, at the same time, denigrate and undermine their parents through harsh criticism or humiliating insults. In these cases, the benefits to the family system of social support provided to one family member are equivocal.

The potentially deleterious effects of social support on other family members may become especially acute when obtaining support casts other family members in a vulnerable, humiliating, or dependent light, which can occur in troubled families. In an impressive series of investigations, Rand Conger and his colleagues have been studying family patterns of coping with the economic downturn that beset the rural farm economies of Iowa and other midwestern states during the 1980s (Conger et al., 1992; Conger et al., 1990; Robertson, Elder, Skinner, & Conger, 1991; Simons, Lorenz, Conger, & Wu, 1992; Simons, Lorenz, Wu, & Conger, 1993). In general, they have found that when parents could manage their own emotional turmoil in the face of financial distress, their parenting was more effective and constructive, and family well-being was enhanced. For many parents, a strong marital relationship or the assistance of friends, neighbors, or extended kin provided the support that was necessary for competent coping. However, this was not always true. Some husbands who were inconsistently employed during this period became more negative toward their spouses and more punitive in their parenting when their wives sought and obtained emotional support from outside the family. The researchers reasoned that in the context of the values associated with the rural Midwest, a wife's need for counseling and other assistance confirmed her husband's sense of failure and helplessness in the face of economic difficulty. Thus, the availability of social support for one family member may have detriments for others that can, on balance, undermine its net gains to the family system.

Finally, it is important to remember that the direct and indirect consequences of family social networks can be complex. Because these networks are multidimensional, entailing not only the direct assistance offered by friends, kin, neighbors, and other network associates but also broader influences from the workplace, school, and community, parents and offspring are affected in many different ways by the natural networks of other family members.

Two research investigations illustrate this complexity. In a study of Australian families, Homel, Burns, and Goodnow (1987) reported

that the socioemotional adjustment of school-age offspring was predicted by the breadth and reliability of parental support networks, as
indexed by the number of "dependable friends" that parents could
list and the parents' affiliation with voluntary organizations (such as
community groups, religious institutions, and business/professional
organizations). However, the family's "neighborhood risk level" (i.e.,
an index of the neighborhood's socioeconomic status, delinquency
and school truancy rates, and related variables) also influenced child
adjustment, indicating that broader as well as proximate features of
the family's social ecology are relevant to understanding the impact
of social networks. In other words, a family member's well-being is
influenced not only by the availability of immediate supportive partners, but also by the broader quality of the neighborhood and community in which the family lives.

This conclusion is affirmed in the findings of another Australian
study by Cotterell (1986), who found that the child-rearing attitudes
and behavior of parents were strongly predicted by an interaction
of (a) the father's absence from the home (owing to job demands),
(b) the mother's "informational support" from neighbors about raising children, and (c) characteristics of the community (such as the
stability of the population). Support to the mother was the most
significant of these predictors, but all were important. This again
suggests that broader features of the community and the parent's life
circumstances can modify the impact of social support on parenting
and on children's well-being by enhancing (or decreasing) the need
for supportive assistance, increasing (or reducing) the availability and
reliability of potential natural helpers, and exacerbating (or reducing)
life stress for each family member.

Taking Perspective

Taken together, these findings indicate that in no sense do family
members live in independent, autonomous social worlds. Although
it is possible to distinguish the social networks of parents and offspring—and despite the fact that family members often spend their
time in much different social settings, interacting with people who
may be little known to other family members—it is clear that overlapping and intersecting social networks characterize family life. Indeed,
this is almost necessarily true when families have young children who
depend on their parents to arrange, transport, and otherwise facilitate

their encounters with people outside the home, and whose needs and interests compel an expansion of parents' social networks to encompass child-related activities. But even more profoundly do the complex and multidimensional social networks of parents affect their offspring, both directly and indirectly, because of network associates who provide support, impose stress, offer information, give advice, and otherwise influence adults as workers, community members, and parents. Adding further complexity to this ecological tapestry is the fact that the family social network that all family members share is also influenced by the broader neighborhood, including the safety, resources, and opportunities that distinguish local communities as living environments.

The complexity does not end there, for we have not considered how the natural social networks of husbands and wives are different and distinctive, yet complementary and mutually influential. Husbands and wives may differ, for example, in their feelings of loneliness and isolation based on the extent and supportiveness of their workplace associations, personal friendships, and religious and community organizational pursuits. Yet as the research on Iowa farm families reveals, the social ties that a wife may seek to obtain much-needed support can have detriments for her husband's well-being, and the reverse is also likely to be true. Therefore, it is unwise to assume that marital partners have identical social networks, or necessarily complementary social needs.

Nor have we considered yet how formal support networks fit in with, supplement, and (at times) buttress these natural social networks of family members. Individuals rely not only on the natural helpers among their extended families, neighbors, and friends, but also the formal assistance offered by religious leaders, medical personnel, and professional counselors. As we shall see in a later chapter, one of the major challenges of formal helpers (such as social workers and mental health professionals) is to supplement and strengthen, not replace, the assistance afforded by a family's natural helpers.

Finally, we have also not considered the changes that occur in natural social networks over time owing to common transitions (such as residential mobility) or relatively uncommon events (such as parental divorce). Yet we have seen that social networks are inevitably dynamic rather than static, with considerable turnover that occurs in response to naturally occurring changes in life circumstances. At present, however, there is little specific knowledge about how these change processes affect natural social networks and about their broader implications for family functioning.

In sum, social networks are remarkably complex, challenging the efforts of social scientists to portray their organization and influence. But the lesson emerging from this chapter is not only that natural networks are complex, but that families are, too. As students of family policy have discovered, efforts to influence the well-being of one family member can have broader implications for other family members that are often unanticipated or in conflict with intended goals (cf. Thompson et al., 1992). Because families are such complex social institutions, all of their members are likely to be affected by interventions focused primarily on only one. And because social support is a resource from which all members of high-risk families can potentially benefit, programs to enlist supportive agents for one family member should seek to ensure that the effects of the intervention on others are also positive, or at least merely benign. In the context of preventing child maltreatment, a family-oriented approach to social support is thus essential.

This may be hard to do, however, because of the diverse ways that social networks affect family members. Unless care is taken to ensure that supportive assistance to one family member is valued within the broader family, the target of such assistance may not gain at all. For example, children with special needs can potentially benefit from Big Brother or Big Sister programs with activities that occupy after-school time and minimally interfere with family life. But as children are exposed to new values, perspectives, and experiences through such programs, it may arouse the resentment, envy, or anger of parents or siblings. Moreover, the child's participation in such programs may also become the focus of coercive or manipulative efforts by parents who remain, in many ways, crucial mediators of the child's access to such experiences. A parent may threaten to deny access to a supportive adult outside the home, for instance, or discontinue the child's participation in an after-school activity. In general, therefore, social support that is broadly conceived and that takes into consideration its impact on all family members, even when only one is the primary target, is likely to be more successful than more limited or more focused intervention efforts. In the chapter that follows, we consider what social support is, and can do, in such families, and how the structure and functioning of social networks is relevant to the provision of social support.

What Is Social Support?

Unpacking a Well-Known Concept

Like many concepts that are rooted in everyday experience, social support carries considerable intuitive and connotative meaning when it is used by practitioners, researchers, policymakers, and others who are concerned with human welfare. As a consequence, it is easy to assume that discussions of social support are founded on a shared, straightforward definition of the term when, in fact, this may not be true. As we have seen, social support is considerably more complex and multidimensional than is commonly assumed, and different views of the functions of support in human welfare may derive from different underlying conceptions of what social support is and does. The goal of this chapter is to conceptually "unpack" the meaning of social support as a basis for further reflection on its role in combating child maltreatment.

There are many formal definitions of social support used by community psychologists, social workers, family sociologists, developmental psychologists, and others who are concerned about personal well-being. For the purposes of this analysis, I have defined social support in this way:

> Social support consists of social relationships that provide (or can potentially provide) material and interpersonal resources that are of value to the recipient, such as counseling, access to information and services, sharing of tasks and responsibilities, and skill acquisition.

Such a definition begins to help us understand what social support is and can do for individuals and families. But much more is needed to elucidate its diverse potential functions within the relationships in which it occurs. An analysis of what social support entails not only underscores the multifaceted nature of social support but also its many potential roles in preventing and remediating maltreatment, and points to the importance of careful thinking in efforts to design interventions to strengthen supportive ties in the lives of children and families.

In the discussion that follows, we "unpack" the concept of social support in two ways. First, we consider the natural social networks from which social support derives and evaluate both the structural and affiliative features of social networks that provide a basis for the provision of support. Second, we consider the functions that social support assumes in promoting individual well-being, especially with respect to the actors and agencies that can assume these functions in the lives of troubled individuals and families. Throughout, the implications of this analysis for the role of social support in abuse prevention is emphasized.

The Organization of
Social Networks and Social Support

In the preceding chapter, we explored the characteristics of natural social networks from the perspective of the children and families who are at their center. In doing so, the importance of distinguishing between social networks and social support was underscored, together with the value of understanding an individual's subjective construction of his or her network and the support it affords.

Social networks are an important part of social support, of course, because they provide the interpersonal resources—rich and accessible for some individuals, rare and unreliable for others—from which support may be forthcoming. In their efforts to understand these social resources and their links to social support, behavioral scientists have portrayed social networks in various formal ways (cf. Barrera, 1986; Ladd et al., 1988; Mitchell & Trickett, 1980; Vaux, 1988). Some of their descriptions focus on the structural features of networks (such as their size and stability), whereas others emphasize the affiliative features of networks (such as their reciprocity and emotional valence).

In each case, social scientists' more formal and "objective" portrayals of social networks complement the subjective view of natural networks summarized in the preceding chapter and offer potentially valuable insights into how natural social networks are organized, structured, and constituted by the individuals who use them.

Moreover, these descriptive portrayals of social networks can contribute to more thoughtful consideration of how social networks and social support are related, and to the multidimensional potential meaning of the "social isolation" of troubled families. If social networks are multifaceted, varying in their size, emotional tone, and quality of relationships, then social isolation may also be a heterogeneous phenomenon, based on the density, affiliative quality, and/or stability of social network ties. If so, then it is crucial to understand which aspects of insularity, if any, characterize families at risk for child maltreatment. Finally, these ways of portraying social networks can also help us to estimate the likely consequences of interventions designed to enhance the supportiveness of social networks by altering their size, density, or other characteristics. In other words, by considering the relations between social support and the size, density, reciprocity, and homogeneity of social networks, we can begin to understand the extent to which support is likely to be enhanced by interventions designed to alter these features of natural social networks.

Structural Features of Social Networks

What characteristics of social networks best afford social support? Do people benefit most from a large social network? from intimate relationships within the network? from the stability of network associations? or from some combination of these and other factors?

Most portrayals of social networks begin with *network size*, which is the number of persons with whom the individual has contact. By this measure, social isolation can be indexed as a small social network, and interventions to remedy this kind of social isolation would focus on increasing the sheer number of persons included within the target's social network by strengthening involvement with community groups, fostering closer relations with neighbors, enhancing workplace ties, or even by enhancing the target's social skills.

Although a large network of relationships potentially enhances the interpersonal resources on which a person can rely when troubled or distressed, network size is a rather insensitive measure of the supportive features of social networks because many members of the social network may not assume supportive roles. Indeed, large social networks may be "conflicted networks" that contribute stress more than support because of the demands they impose (Barrera, 1981). Moreover, in many instances, only one or a few confidants are sufficient to aid coping, indicating that a large social network is not necessary to social support (Cohen & Wills, 1985; Gottlieb, 1985). Therefore, measures of sheer network size may not sensitively index the features of social networks that are most relevant to social support.

Social embeddedness is a second structural feature of social networks that refers to the frequency of contact with network members. By distinguishing individuals who have regular interaction with others from those who have relatively infrequent contact, even though the size of their social networks may be comparable, it is possible to identify individuals who are socially isolated in terms of their limited social embeddedness. Efforts to enhance social embeddedness might focus on increasing contact with network associates through more frequent participation in formal and informal gatherings, regular phone calls and visits to friends and kin, strengthening social skills pertinent to maintaining relationships with others, and in other ways.

Like network size, embeddedness seems to reveal an important feature of the social resources that networks can provide: Regular contact with others potentially integrates individuals into a supportive community. But like network size, measures of social embeddedness may insensitively index social support: After all, many daily encounters with network associates (such as supervisors at work or teachers at school) can be unsupportive and potentially stress inducing. Social embeddedness does not sensitively index whether frequent contact occurs with the most—or least—supportive individuals within a person's network. Consequently, social embeddedness also may not reliably index the supportiveness of a social network.

A third structural dimension, *dispersion*, refers to the ease with which individuals can obtain contact with social network members. It is, in a sense, an index of accessibility, with social isolation commonly revealed in a widely dispersed social network with few locally available network associates. Dispersion is typically measured in terms of geographical proximity because local network associates are likely to be the most accessible, and thus dispersion commonly distinguishes neighborhood-based from nonneighborhood-based social supports. It is partly because of differences in dispersion, for example, that theorists such as Litwak and Szelenyi (1969) argue that neighbors can best help others with immediate emergencies and everyday assistance because they live nearby, whereas kin—who may live near or far—are most helpful in the context of long-term aid and support. Social isolation that derives from a widely dispersed social network might be remedied by strengthening relationships with local network associates in the workplace and community or, alternatively, providing financial or transportation assistance to enhance contact with long-distance network associates.

Dispersion can thus account for some important functional differences in network relationships. For some socioeconomically impoverished individuals, for example, dispersion may be the most important dimension of their social networks because of the difficulties they encounter in obtaining transportation, telephone service, and other means of access to nonlocal network members. Dispersion is, in short, a network index with important implications for the kinds of relationships shared with network members, although it does so imperfectly: People whom one sees regularly may be among one's most helpful associates, or some of the most demanding and annoying. And, as noted in the previous chapter, the most locally accessible network associates, such as neighbors, may not be those on whom individuals most rely when seeking support. One reason is that, although accessible, local associates may be among the most transient of network members.

Stability, then, refers to the consistency of network associates over time. A stable network is often presumed to be a better resource for social support because network associates share long-term relationships with the target individual and are thus well-acquainted with his or her characteristics and needs. By implication, one feature of social isolation is an unstable, frequently changing social network, and it is difficult to provide immediate interventions to remedy this form of isolation. As we shall see in Chapter 5, this kind of isolation often derives from inadequate social skills or capabilities in the target individuals that cause them to become alienated from neighbors, kin, and workplace associates. Although social skills training provides one potential remedy to this problem, it is a long-term strategy.

As indicated earlier, there is a high degree of turnover in social network membership for most individuals, and different components of the network show different rates of stability over time, with kin constituting the most stable network members, and neighbors among the least stable. The value of stability to social support may be relative, therefore, to the degree of turnover that is common in most social networks, and also to the roles of various network associates. For example, although friends and neighbors seldom achieve the kind of long-term companionship that is typical of kinship, an enduring tie to a friend or neighbor may be especially valued because of its exceptionality. Moreover, stability certainly does not guarantee support: As family relationships reveal all too often, the people one knows the longest can still be very unsupportive.

A fifth, and final, structural feature of social networks is called *extensivity*, which refers to the degree to which social interaction within the network occurs in small groups (including dyads) rather than large groups. Thus, extensivity may have important implications for intimacy and perceived support, at least to the extent that intimacy is more likely to occur in the context of close, one-to-one relationships. However, it is unclear how directly extensivity and support are linked because group size does not necessarily index the emotional tone of the interactions that occur within them. Larger groups certainly can be characterized by close intimacy, and dyadic relationships by animosity.

Taken together, these structural features of social networks are easy to observe and measure and have been, not surprisingly, the focus of most efforts to assess the social networks of various populations, including families who are abusive or neglectful (as we shall see in Chapter 5). Unfortunately, as we have seen, they are not likely to be very sensitive to the social support that is given or received within those networks, and this has been shown empirically. Researchers such as Barrera (1986), for example, have noted that measures of social embeddedness have only a moderate association with the amount of support that individuals report perceiving, or actually receiving, from network members. Similarly, Cohen and Wills (1985) concluded from an extensive literature review that the "stress buffering" aspects of social support (i.e., how support protects individuals from the potentially adverse effects of stressful events) are not well-revealed by structural measures of sheer network size or embeddedness. The implication is not only that the readiest measures of social networks are least informative with respect to social support, but also that indexes of social isolation based on assessments of network size, embeddedness, or other structural features may provide a misleading portrayal of the supportive strengths and weaknesses of natural networks.

Affiliative Features of Social Networks

Clearly, new ways of portraying social networks that emphasize the *meaning* of network associates to the individual are needed. These alternative portrayals focus on the affiliative characteristics of social networks.

Valence refers to the emotional quality of relationships with network members. Recognizing that these relationships may be stressful as well as supportive, this index focuses on the individual's perceptions of the affective quality of network relationships and whether they are experienced as emotionally positive or negative. From the standpoint of this subjective index, individuals may be socially isolated because they perceive few positive features of the relationships they share with others. Efforts to improve the valence of network relationships might focus on shared activities that improve ties with network associates, such as community service projects, recreational activities, and reciprocating material or personal (e.g., child care) assistance. This might be accompanied by counseling that emphasizes the positive as well as stressful features of network relationships, and the social skills inherent in maintaining positive social ties.

Valence is an important but not infallible index of the social support that potentially may exist within a social network because positive relationships obviously provide better conduits of assistance than do negative associations. On the other hand, individuals who are acting helpfully nevertheless may be perceived somewhat negatively by the target individual, such as when they urge the target individual to change inappropriate practices (e.g., smoking, substance abuse, punitive parenting) that put themselves or others at risk.

A second affiliative dimension, *reciprocity,* concerns the extent to which social support in relationships is mutual or unidirectional. Reciprocity thus has broad implications not only for how relationships are defined, but for the interactional processes associated with giving and receiving aid. Reciprocated assistance may consist of the exchange of respite child care; loans of kitchen or lawn equipment, furniture, or other possessions; financial aid; advice about work, children, or other issues; invitations to meals; and other kinds of sharing.

Reciprocal support relationships are usually most satisfying to both partners, and this enhances the basis for long-term mutual aid (this is discussed in depth in Chapter 4). By contrast, relationships characterized by one-way assistance often foster feelings of dependency and/or indebtedness in the recipient. Unrequited assistance may not only be stigmatizing to adults (Fisher, Nadler, & Witcher-Alagna, 1982), it may also be unpleasant for help providers, who may reduce their aid as a consequence. Thus, reciprocity is an important feature not only of the support that is available from natural networks, but also of the maintenance of that support in the future. In the next chapter, we consider in more detail the nature of recipient and provider reactions to aid in the context of understanding the role of reciprocity in help-giving relationships. As we shall see then, remedying the lack of reciprocity in social relationships can be complex because of the diverse reasons that this deficit may arise. A lack of reciprocity in social support may arise from economic or personal inability, from how the relationship is perceived by both help-provider and recipient, or from the recipient's personal reactions to receiving assistance from another, and these have significantly different intervention implications.

Another affiliative dimension, *homogeneity*, refers to the extent to which network members share common attributes, such as their socioeconomic status, occupational goals, religious values, and other features. Because members share common viewpoints, homogeneity may heighten supportiveness within social networks when a congruence of values, norms, and expectations fosters emotional and instrumental aid. However, homogeneity is a double-edged sword from the perspective of enlisting network associates to change a person's behavior, as with perpetrators of child maltreatment. In these situations, the congruence of child-rearing values and norms may cause friends and kin to reinforce potentially abusive caregiving practices rather than challenge them, especially when those values are consistent with neighborhood or subgroup beliefs. Ironically, therefore, homogeneity of social networks may enhance the perceived supportiveness of network associates (i.e., the individual's belief that others are "with me")—but undermine their influence in changing troubling behavior.

Multidimensionality (multiplexity) concerns the number of different functions assumed by individuals within a social network. In some networks, associates are distinguished by specific, unidimensional roles, whether as child care assistants (e.g., baby-sitters, day care workers, etc.), professional mentors (e.g., a more senior workplace associate), job associates (e.g., a coworker), recreational partners (e.g., an exercise partner or recreational league teammate), or in other ways.

Married mothers, for example, tend to enjoy relationships with network members that are characterized by one primary function, whether as close friends who provide emotional support, baby-sitters who provide child care assistance, or other friends who are helpful for recreation. In other networks, however, these associates have multiple, sometimes overlapping, roles. For example, single mothers have multifunctional or multidimensional relationships within their smaller social networks, where close friends simultaneously provide child care help, emotional nurturance, and material assistance (Cochran, Larner, et al., 1990; Gunnarsson & Cochran, 1990).

Multidimensionality thus aids in understanding the roles and relationships of network associates and their significance to the individual, whether social networks are large or small. Understanding these distinctive or overlapping functions of network associates also contributes to understanding how network members can be enlisted to benefit troubled individuals within neighborhoods and communities. Multifunctional relationships may provide stressed individuals with many kinds of assistance, for example, but the capacity of these people to offer additional targeted aid is also affected by their preexisting, complex roles in the person's life and the potential that they might be exhausted or "drained" by providing enhanced assistance. For many single mothers, for example, their network associates who provide emotional nurturance, respite child care assistance, and other forms of support are themselves likely to be single mothers who are also stressed and needy individuals. By contrast, unifunctional social relationships are likely to have a specificity that, for certain individuals, can enhance their socially supportive functions, such as a day care worker who becomes the conduit of much-needed child-rearing advice and support to a troubled parent. Moreover, the unifunctional social relationships shared with formal helpers, such as social workers, counselors, or clergy or other religious leaders, can also contribute to more focused assistance. These issues will be discussed more fully in the following chapter.

A fifth affiliative dimension, *density* (or *complexity*), refers to the extent that network members are themselves associated with each other. Individuals with dense or complex social networks have members who are in mutual contact and can thus share information concerning the target individual. Those with less complex social networks experience relationships with network members who do not know each other.

Although it is easy to assume that greater network density is desirable (especially in the intercoordination of social support to the target individual among different members of a social network), it is important not to underestimate the "strength of weak ties" within less dense networks (Granovetter, 1973) that can contribute diverse opportunities for obtaining information, ideas, and support from many different associates who each have different perspectives on the target individual. In other words, there are special strengths to social networks characterized by little density because of the breadth of perspectives, opportunities, and novelty they afford: One may receive different kinds of child-rearing advice, for instance, from one's parents, a day care worker, other parents whose children are in day care, a coworker, and a neighbor in ways that provide thoughtful catalysts to better parenting. In particular, when a person is engaged in life transitions (e.g., to a new identity or way of behaving), less dense social networks may be most advantageous because the person is not wedded to a dense social network governed by past expectations for behavior among interconnected network members (Mitchell & Trickett, 1980). By contrast, dense social networks may make it hard to break out of well-established and socially reinforced patterns of behavior, whether they are maladaptive or not.

For our purposes, one of the most important affiliative dimensions is *perceived support*, which concerns the extent to which individuals subjectively expect support from their relationships with network members. From this perspective, social isolation is experienced as little expectation of assistance from friends, kin, neighbors, or others they know. This may or may not be an accurate perception, and interventions intended to enhance a person's perception of the supportiveness afforded by their network associates might be accomplished by counseling that emphasizes the social resources that exist among neighbors, kin, friends, coworkers, and other network associates, or involvement in shared activities that have the effect of improving social relationships and of the perceived supportiveness of those ties.

Although it is not the same as actual (or enacted) support, perceived support may be an even more significant predictor of the extent to which contact with network members assumes a stress-buffering function in the lives of stressed people (Barrera, 1986; Cohen & Wills, 1985). In other words, coping with stress may depend more on one's expectations that support is available and accessible than on the past instrumental actions of social network members or the individual's actual utilization of network resources. This is because the feeling that others will provide assistance if needed can contribute to the sense of personal well-being and support that has stress-buffering consequences. Moreover, perceived support is likely to be based (at least in part) on past experiences of actually receiving support from friends, neighbors, coworkers, and kin that confirm expectations that future assistance will be forthcoming.

However, perceived support is not an unequivocal index of social support because an individual's perceptions of the supportiveness of others may not always accord with their associates' efforts or actions. Consider, for example, a person whose friends urge him or her to quit smoking or drinking owing to concern about his or her health. It is likely that the target individual will perceive such actions as unsupportive, even though they are intended to advance that person's well-being. In such cases, perceptions of social support may not be a valuable index of the extent to which network members are acting (or striving to act) in a supportive manner. To be sure, such a conclusion raises the broader issue of whether social support can be provided without the recipient's awareness of it (or, indeed, with the recipient perceiving such actions as nonsupportive). There are good reasons for concluding that this is sometimes the case—and this can be especially true of the actions of supportive network members in the lives of troubled individuals. We will return to this issue in the next chapter.

Finally, *enacted support* refers to the frequency of specific supportive or helpful actions provided by network members. Although it is reasonable to expect congruence between measures of perceived and enacted support, research findings are consistent with the illustration of the preceding paragraph in showing that there is actually a surprisingly low concordance between measures of enacted support and perceived support (Barrera, 1986). The helpful actions of social network members may not always be perceived as supportive by the target, in other words, and one's perceptions of support within the network may not accord with the extent to which members are truly acting helpfully, or have done so in the past. Conversely, a history of enacted support does not necessarily mean that the recipient expects that aid will be forthcoming in the future, especially if there have been changes in the relationship between the recipient and the benefactor. Measures of enacted support and of perceived support are not overlapping, therefore, because they assess different phenomena: a history of past support on one hand, and the recipient's subjective expectations of future assistance on the other. Both are relevant to assessing the social support provided by network members, but in different ways.

Social Networks and Social Support

It is clear that there are many different ways that social networks can be described. In this light, it is unfortunate that so few research studies of abuse-prone parents have included more than one or two of these dimensions in their assessments of social networks, and that most studies have relied largely on structural measures of network size or social embeddedness, as we shall see in Chapter 5. It is also unfortunate that no research has comprehensively evaluated the interrelationships among these multiple dimensions of social networks to evaluate the extent to which they are mutually related and, perhaps, interdependent in troubled and untroubled families. It seems apparent that there is much yet to be learned about these features of social networks and their implications for social support.

However, an awareness of the multiple dimensions of social networks is important not just for descriptive purposes. It is essential for clear thinking about the goals and design of the social support interventions that are intended to benefit families at risk for child maltreatment. The basic question is, What changes should one seek to create in a social network to enhance its supportiveness? The answer obviously depends on the specific characteristics of the natural social network of a high-risk family and the family's specific needs, but this analysis also suggests that alternative goals might be considered in light of the relevance of different network features to the family's well-being.

- Enhancing *perceived support* from network members may be valuable, for example, because it combats feelings of loneliness and isolation, and aids coping because of its effects on a person's appraisal of the interpersonal resources that are available for managing difficult circumstances.
- Reducing (if possible) the *dispersion* of a social network may be pertinent not only to the capacity of network members to provide emergency assistance but also for long-term emotional support and counseling, especially if access to geographically distant network members is problematic because of the family's financial or transportational limitations.

■ Altering network *density* may be an especially important intervention in social networks of sufficient size that the intercoordination of the supportive efforts of network members is valuable, but may be irrelevant to individuals with social networks of smaller size.

■ Enhancing the *homogeneity* of network associates may be important for some support functions (e.g., affirmation and emotional sustenance—the feelings that others are "with me") but not for others (e.g., changing behavior that nevertheless may be normative for the neighborhood or community).

■ Increasing the *reciprocity* inherent in exchanges of assistance among network members may be valuable for strengthening the mutual satisfactions experienced by the providers and targets of assistance, as well as the prospects for long-term support. Similar results may arise by increasing the positive valence of these relationships.

In general, therefore, different dimensions of social networks have varying pertinence to the provision of social support because they affect different functions of the network. House, Umberson, and Landis (1988) have offered a similar observation:

Networks of small size, strong ties, high density, high homogeneity, and low dispersion appear to be helpful in maintaining social identity and, hence, health and well-being outcomes when these are promoted by identity maintenance. However, *change* in social roles and identities, and hence health and well-being during such change, is facilitated by larger networks with weaker ties, lower density, and greater social and cultural heterogeneity. (p. 304, references omitted)

Not only the goals, but the strategies for accomplishing these goals should be guided by a thoughtful analysis of the dimensions of social networks. Quite clearly, interventions that increase network size or enhance social embeddedness will not necessarily accomplish the same goals as interventions that enhance the density of social networks or foster perceptions of support from network members. Given the differences between these dimensions of social networks, moreover, one cannot assume that interventions that target one dimension of a social network will necessarily influence other dimensions in predictable ways. Thus, carefully crafted interventions designed to accomplish thoughtfully considered, specific goals are necessary. This requires consideration of the specific purposes of social support interventions on behalf of troubled families (e.g., to enhance the amount of contact with others? to coordinate support among members of the network? to foster intimacy among a few associates? to heighten perceptions of support from network members? to change behavior?), and then consideration of which features of the social network should be targeted for intervention, and why.

In short, attention to the multiple dimensions of social networks is important because different network dimensions are relevant to different functions of social support in the lives of stressed individuals. Because social networks are multidimensional, so also is social support. Consequently, we turn next to considering the alternative overlapping— and sometimes inconsistent—functions of social support.

The Functions of Social Support

One reason for clear thinking about the intended purposes of social support interventions is that social support can assume diverse functions in family life. Many of the purposes of social support are overlapping, such as the natural link between counseling and emotional sustenance, but some of the functions of social support may be mutually inconsistent, such as when helpers provide emotional affirmation to a recipient but must also challenge and change that person's risky behavior. Thus, a preliminary step to inquiring about the potential role of social support in preventing child maltreatment is defining the intended functions that social support is expected to have. Considering the functions of social support has the added benefit of heightening our recognition that each approach to social support may have weaknesses as well as advantages for preventing child maltreatment.

In broadest terms, social support can have stress-preventive and stress-buffering features (e.g., Barrera, 1986; Cohen & Wills, 1985; House et al., 1988; Vaux, 1988). As stress prevention, social support surrounds its recipient with people who provide emotional and instrumental assistance that contributes to healthy functioning. The company of others enhances self-esteem, a sense of belonging, access to reference figures, models of healthy functioning, and incentives to comply with social norms—each of which can be health enhancing (Vaux, 1988). From this perspective, social support helps to prevent stress and dysfunction. When stress occurs, however, social support can also be enlisted as a stress buffer, undergirding the recipient's effective coping through the kinds of emotional, instrumental, and material assistance provided by network associates. As a buffer of the effects of stress, social support helps to reduce its toll on physical and mental well-being.

Although most of the specific functions of social support described below can have stress-preventive and stress-buffering features depending on the circumstances in which they are enlisted, this distinction is particularly important when considering social support in the context of the primary, secondary, and tertiary prevention of child maltreatment (see Chapter 1). On one hand, in primary prevention (and some secondary prevention) contexts, social support interventions might best serve as stress preventions by enhancing coping skills and reducing some of the difficulties that can enhance the risk of child abuse and neglect. For example, providing emotional assistance, counseling, and developmental guidance to first-time mothers, especially if they are young, impoverished, or socially isolated, might reduce some of their feelings of being overwhelmed by a young infant's needs that can place that child at risk for abuse. Similarly, the availability of inexpensive, on-call, emergency respite child care for single mothers and other parents, coupled with voluntary parent support programs, can also reduce the risk of maltreatment, especially in higher-risk populations.

On the other hand, in the context of many secondary prevention efforts, and almost always in tertiary prevention, social support serves as a stress buffer because of the serious and unavoidable stresses that many high-risk families already experience. In the face of families' financial, legal, relational, and other difficulties, social support can occur via intensive counseling, access to material aid, day care assistance, job training, and other resources to strengthen parents' capacities to manage difficult circumstances and reduce the risk of (further) maltreatment. Thus, some of the specific purposes of social support interventions, and the goals they are intended to accomplish, depend on the preventive context in which they are used and whether stress prevention or stress buffering is the intended result.

Whether as stress prevention or buffering, many of the functions of social support are rooted in everyday experience. Most commonly, for example, social networks are regarded as supportive when their members provide *emotional sustenance,* such as esteem-enhancing affirmation, compassion, and empathy, and a sense that others share one's dilemmas and stresses. Certainly, one of the important benefits of supportive network members is the sense that one is not alone and that others are emotionally "on your side" in coping with stress (what Gottlieb, 1985, has called "milieu reliability"). This enhances one's confidence in the interpersonal resources that are available for coping as well as providing outlets for the release of tension and anxiety that might otherwise find more unfortunate victims.

However, one potential disadvantage to the emotional sustenance entailed in social support is that it may foster dependency in the recipient, increase feelings of indebtedness, and heighten the perceived need to reciprocate the aid that has been received (Fisher et al., 1982). As we shall see in the next chapter, the indebtedness entailed in one-way assistance can ultimately (and somewhat surprisingly) contribute to the breakdown of a helping relationship. Emotional sustenance can also foster conformity pressures in the recipient, especially if emotional support is contingent (explicitly or implicitly) on the recipient's participation in or compliance with group norms (such as in certain closely knit families, religious communities, or adolescent peer groups). This can have negative consequences for the recipient of aid. Finally, when emotional sustenance is the primary function of supportive social exchanges, it may be difficult for supportive agents to critically challenge the recipient's behavior and be perceived as supportive in the view of the recipient. As noted earlier, exhortations to reduce smoking or drinking, end substance abuse, maintain fidelity to well-baby checkups, or eliminate potentially abusive or neglectful behavior toward offspring may be an essential component of social support interventions, but may be regarded by recipients (and perhaps by other network members also) as emotionally unsupportive behavior.

Another function of social support is *counseling, advice, and guidance*. Although such actions also may be emotionally nurturant, their primary purpose is to provide the recipient with guided direction in challenging life events. This may consist of peer counseling that includes instruction in parenting skills or coping with life demands; learning from friends or neighbors about techniques for managing emotional stress; informal guidance about child rearing from members of the extended family; or the kind of guided assistance that can come from a formal helper, such as a professional counselor, religious leader, or social worker (e.g., Cochran & Brassard, 1979).

One important purpose of counseling of this kind is to influence the recipient's "secondary appraisal" of stressful circumstances, that is, to strengthen the individual's awareness of the resources that exist for coping successfully with demanding conditions (Lazarus & Folkman, 1984). This may also buttress the recipient's sense of personal competence and self-efficacy. Another purpose of counseling is the transmission of consensual social values and norms concerning behavior. Counselors often affirm or challenge the recipient's actions when they provide advice concerning the best ways of expressing anger, how to manage strong feelings of sadness or depression, or the treatment of offspring. In this sense, counseling has a socializing as well as a supportive function.

However, it is important to recognize that the values and norms underlying a counselor's advice reflect not just community norms but also personal and, sometimes, subcultural values. In professional counseling, this constellation of values is channeled by professional and ethical standards that are meant to benefit the client. When informal counselors from the extended family, neighborhood, and community are sought, on the other hand, recipients may receive a mixture of helpful and unhelpful advice. If a friend or neighbor interprets domestic problems as primarily a need for greater authority, for example, he or she may inadvertently help to justify physically punitive or abusive behavior in the treatment of marital partners or children (cf. Garbarino & Crouter, 1978). In like fashion, neighbors or extended kin may perceive more benignly certain practices (such as leaving young children unattended for extended periods, or the use of harshly punitive discipline techniques) that are accepted within the neighborhood, but that nevertheless may place children at risk. In such circumstances, counseling may be perceived as emotionally supportive but does not prevent or curb troubling behavior. In effect, the values communicated by a counselor are as important as the emotional support that is offered.

A third function of social support is *access to information, services, and material resources and assistance.* In this respect, support agents act as brokers between the recipient and others who can provide tangible aid. This mode of social support is commonly found in communities where neighbors and friends are consulted for advice about schools or child care settings; provide referrals to community agencies where information or material resources can be obtained; offer advice about how to interact effectively with public assistance, private aid, legal, or other authorities; or lend money or other items that are needed by the recipient. Formal helpers also provide assistance in this manner by referring parents or other family members to valued community resources.

This function of social support can be especially valuable, therefore, when stress derives from inadequate access to needed information or resources (such as in low-income or poverty communities). But this mode of help-giving is valued by individuals throughout the socioeconomic strata as a means of obtaining valuable information and resources. Although this form of social support is potentially important, it can also engender in the recipient feelings of dependency, vulnerability, or stigma, especially if continued access to these material or interpersonal resources is contingent on deference to neighborhood brokers, or if the use of these resources labels family members in denigrating ways.

A fourth, and related, function of social support is *skill acquisition*, such as when social network members assist in training job-related skills; foster nonvocational abilities (whether car repair, lawn maintenance, or athletic skills); or aid in personal skills related to household management, parenting, or financial planning. These functions are commonly assumed informally by workplace colleagues or by friends and neighbors, and are especially valuable for stressed individuals whose coping with life demands is undermined by limited personal or saleable skills, which may be true of certain subpopulations at greatest risk for child abuse and neglect (see Polansky et al., 1981; Seagull, 1987; and Chapter 5). When this kind of assistance can be reciprocated by the recipient, moreover, the exchange of skills can be empowering; when assistance is one way, however, perceptions of vulnerability and dependency may ensue.

Other Functions of Social Support

These four primary functions of social support are those most commonly conceived in research on social support and the design of supportive intervention programs. However, two additional functions of social support must also be considered in efforts to enlist support in the prevention of child maltreatment. The first concerns the social monitoring of another's behavior; the second concerns the developmental remediation of the victims of child maltreatment.

One important function of social support is for *social monitoring and social control.* In other words, social support can be influential in preventing maltreatment because of the regulation provided by social network members, who can uniquely observe the target's behavior in everyday circumstances and can impose unique sanctions on disapproved parental conduct (cf. Garbarino, 1977a). To the extent that friends, neighbors, and extended family members are deliberately enlisted into social networks for preventing maltreatment, in fact, it is hard to deny that social monitoring and control is one important purpose of doing so. Local members of the social network are capable of observing the target's behavior far more effectively than can formal social service or law enforcement agencies, and their sanctions (e.g., public disapproval, ostracism, denial of aid) may be particularly salient in regulating misconduct. Local network members can also be effective in enlisting professional helpers by reporting suspected child maltreatment to local authorities. Social control may be, on the whole, the most important function of natural social networks in the prevention of child maltreatment.

However, the conceptualization of social support as social monitoring/control is much different from the preceding portrayals of social support functions for several reasons. First, whereas conventional portrayals of social support underscore the "provisioning" (of emotional assistance, counseling, skills, material aid, etc.) that results from support, this view emphasizes the control of the recipient's actions by social network members (House et al., 1988). It indicates, in other words, that social support is important for preventing harm, as well as for promoting good. This is a much different purpose that inevitably alters the role of network associates in the eyes of the recipient (especially if the recipient is aware of their efforts to monitor and control his or her behavior) and to network members themselves (who may experience considerable conflict between being emotionally nurturant and their efforts to monitor, control, and possibly report the recipient's troubling actions to authorities).

Second, whereas the initial four functions of social support earlier described can be fairly easily integrated (i.e., the same person can provide emotional nurturance, counseling, and valuable information in the context of a multidimensional relationship), it is not necessarily easy for the same individual who provides emotionally affirming assistance to also monitor and regulate the recipient's behavior, especially as an informal helper. In other words, it takes greater relational dexterity to act in more conventionally defined "supportive" ways while also seeking to change or control the recipient's disturbing actions, especially if reports to authorities are contemplated, because of the coerciveness that is implied by this "helping" relationship. The recipient of such assistance may, in fact, perceive this associate's efforts as distinctly unsupportive. On the other hand, the integration of social control with other forms of social support may be much easier to accomplish in formal helping relationships (such as with a social worker, minister, or professional counselor) because of the more explicit, formal role definition of the helper.

Third, and finally, the conceptualization of social support as social monitoring and control raises questions concerning the agents of social support, and whether the same friends, neighbors, and extended kin who are helpful sources of emotional nurturance and counseling also can be valuable monitors and regulators of misconduct. This is especially true if these natural helpers have different values from formal authorities concerning the parameters of appropriate parental conduct, and thus may apply different standards to their evaluations of parental practices than do the formal authorities who are concerned about high-risk families.

An additional function of social support pertinent to the prevention of maltreatment is the role of supportive agents in the *developmental remediation* of the victims of child abuse and neglect. Consistent with victim-oriented tertiary prevention goals, social support must be conceived also for its potential contributions to remediating the developmental consequences of child maltreatment, especially those contributing to socioemotional dysfunction and psychopathological outcomes in children. As indicated earlier, systematic research on the victims of child maltreatment has revealed many different consequences of abuse and neglect for children's capacities to master the challenges of psychological growth, and these developmental losses should be the targets of social support interventions. Thus, for infants and toddlers, social support might be enlisted to provide alternative attachment figures (perhaps in the context of therapeutic day care programs) with whom children can develop secure emotional bonds. For preschoolers and grade-school children, social support might be oriented toward strengthening peer social skills and integrating children into the positive social networks of age-mates in day care, school, and after-school (e.g., clubs, youth sports) programs. For grade-school children, social support to strengthen academic and intellectual competence should also be considered, as well as using supportive interventions to enhance self-esteem and reduce anxiety and depression through a variety of counseling and peer-oriented interventions. In adolescence, when social deviance is a potentially critical consequence of maltreatment, a broader concern for strengthening extrafamilial peer and adult social support systems is warranted both to provide emotional sustenance and to monitor for self-destructive behavior.

An example of how social support can function in these ways is found in a large study of social networks by Cochran and Riley (1990). By mapping children's social networks and linking them to family structure and children's academic competence, these researchers found that children with more adult relatives who involved them in task-oriented activities (e.g., car washing, shopping, etc.) had higher report card scores and received, from their teachers, more positive reports of the child's cognitive motivation in the classroom. In other words, structured activities with certain network members contributed to stronger academic achievement, and this was particularly true of boys from female-headed, single-parent homes, who benefited especially from activities with their male kin. These findings underscore how social support can enhance children's developmental achievements when viewed within the context of family structure and family processes.

To be sure, the victims of child abuse and neglect are multiproblem children who will benefit from various forms of social support intended to accomplish different purposes: These children not only need assistance to recover developmentally from the effects of child maltreatment, but also the emotional affirmation, counseling and advice, companionship, and instrumental aid that social support can offer them (Peterson, 1990). In the present-day context of social services that systematically address few of these needs, however, providing social support to the victims of child abuse and neglect is a special concern, whether these children remain with their troubled families or are in an out-of-home placement. As indicated above, social support interventions to accomplish these goals can occur through the efforts of child care workers in day care centers, teachers and counselors at school, adult leaders of recreational youth programs, and through specially designed interventions to strengthen social and intellectual skills and enhance self-esteem, which may involve the contributions of mental health experts and enlist both adults and peers from children's natural social networks.

Implications of This Analysis

Taken together, it is clear that there are multiple potential purposes for enlisting social support agents in the networks of maltreating families, and that these functions are not necessarily mutually consistent. Therefore, it is wise to consider carefully the specific stress-preventive and/or stress-buffering goals for social support interventions. Is it to give the recipient the feeling that someone cares? Is it to provide counseling concerning the problems and stresses that may contribute to child maltreatment? Is it to enhance referrals and access to others who might provide material or instrumental assistance? Is it to enhance society's capacity to regulate and control the parental practices of high-risk adults? Is it to provide a forum in which the parent's behavior can be critically self-examined, perhaps with the assistance of close friends or family?

These various purposes are not only diverse, but they entail different risks for the recipient and for the goals of intervention. Social support may, at times, engender feelings of dependency, vulnerability, indebtedness, or stigma; it may be rejected because the recipient is unable to reciprocate; it may reinforce behavior that is undesirable but nevertheless consistent with the norms of the neighborhood or community in which the recipient's social network can be found; it may violate personal privacy; and it may enhance conformity pressures. Moreover, social support may leave recipients feeling affirmed but unchanged, or it may result in a deterioration of the helping relationship because recipients feel unduly criticized or undermined.

In the end, social support interventions are neither a panacea nor a magic solution to the problems of troubled families, and this is why the purposes and avenues of social support interventions must be carefully crafted to ensure that specific, intended goals are advanced while some of the potential disadvantages of the intervention are accommodated. Moreover, characteristics of the recipients must also be considered: It is quite likely that different subpopulations of maltreatment will benefit differently from various social support interventions. Neglectful families who suffer from economic distress, for example, might benefit most from enhancing their access to services and skill acquisition; by contrast, support that offers counseling and monitoring of parenting practices might be more appropriate for different members of sexually abusive families. In short, the functions of social support are not unitary but diverse, and require consideration of their mutual compatibility, the agents who provide them, and trade-offs between the costs and benefits of social support from formal sources and from neighborhood and community helpers.

These considerations underscore how complex the familiar concept of social support can be when it is conceptually unpacked. Adding further complexity to this analysis are the findings of studies that examine the predictors of the success of social support in the lives of stressed individuals. Such studies seek to answer how—once we understand what social support is and does—we can best predict the *impact* of social support interventions. Thus, we turn to a consideration of this literature in the next chapter.

4

Understanding the
Effects of Social Support

Because it is such a universal human resource, social support can be offered, sought, and received by almost anybody. Yet predicting its effects can be tricky, especially because recipients differ in a variety of ways that affect the impact of supportive efforts. People differ, as we have seen, in the characteristics of their natural networks from which support is obtained. They vary in the stresses, or potential stressors, that may cause them to seek support, or others to offer it. Troubled individuals vary in the personal resources they bring to the relationships they share with network associates, including their social skills, emotional stability, developmental status, and their receptivity to support (which is itself complexly affected by their feelings of vulnerability, trust, and willingness to allow others into their personal lives). Support providers themselves vary in their formal or informal roles in relation to the recipient of aid, the values and other resources they bring to a helping relationship, the other demands on their time and energy, and their vulnerability to becoming exhausted by providing social support or being undermined by the support recipient. Neighborhoods also differ in the sense of shared interests and concerns that characterize community life, as well as the perceptions of danger and out-mobility that can cause neighbors to either strive to improve their shared circumstances (and exhibit concern for one another) or plan to take flight as soon as possible (and make no commitment to those left behind). Taken together, these considerations suggest a complex calculus in understanding the effects of specific social support efforts on behalf of individuals in need.

This complexity has also daunted researchers, who have discovered that the effects of social support interventions are often population specific, depending on the particular characteristics, circumstances, and needs of the recipient population, as well as the ecology in which they live. In other words, interventions that benefit older adults in nursing homes are not necessarily the same interventions that will assist families with a developmentally delayed child or aid an adolescent mother because of differences in their resources, needs for support, and the formal and informal networks on which they rely. Although this makes the generalization of conclusions concerning the effects of social support more problematic for our purposes, it is nevertheless possible to distill several general factors that may underlie the likely success of social support—especially naturally occurring social support—in the lives of maltreating and high-risk families. This chapter discusses these factors, with special attention to their relevance to enlisting neighborhood- and community-based social supports in the prevention of child abuse and neglect. The relevance of more formal helping agents is also considered.

When Does Social Support Change Behavior?

The first question to be pondered is, How much can social support effectively curb child maltreatment? Although many reasons exist to expect that individuals who perceive that they are surrounded by supportive neighbors, kin, and friends will function more successfully, the preceding chapter revealed many reasons to doubt that this support will necessarily diminish the risk of child abuse and neglect. For example, if members of a natural network mutually tolerate behavior that puts children at risk, a parent is less likely to regard his or her actions as aberrant, and abusive behavior is less likely to be recognized, sanctioned, and reported as such. A similar outcome will occur if network associates are afraid of retaliation, rejection, or criticism for challenging a parent's abusive actions toward offspring, or if, perhaps more commonly, they perceive "supportiveness" as essentially noncritical emotional affirmation. In each case, a supportive social network not only fails to curb child maltreatment, but may actually enhance it by providing esteem-supportive affirmation to the abusive parent and reassurances to others concerning parental conduct, without anything else to curb inappropriate behavior.

The question of how much social support can effectively prevent child maltreatment is dramatically posed in a series of in-depth, ethnographic interviews by Korbin (1989, 1991, in press) of nine mothers who were convicted of fatal child abuse. By examining the circumstances surrounding the history of abuse and its culmination in a child's death, Korbin showed that these mothers were far from socially isolated. Indeed, they were surrounded by social networks that they often perceived as being emotionally supportive of them. The reason the maltreatment continued, however, is that these friends, neighbors, and family members not only failed to challenge and report the abusive or neglectful actions they observed, but sought instead to minimize the seriousness of abuse, offer reassurance about the difficulties of raising children, and preserve the mothers' self-esteem by affirming that they remained "good mothers" despite the bruises and welts they inflicted on their offspring. In effect, these network associates—in their efforts to be emotionally "supportive" in an affirmative, noncritical manner—failed to respond appropriately to the seriousness of the risks that these mothers posed to their offspring. This allowed the mothers to rationalize and at times justify their behavior as nonserious and nonabusive, but which eventually resulted in the death of a child.

The reasons for network members' inattention to the seriousness of the problems they observed are revealed in several of Korbin's (1989, 1991) case studies of these mothers. In one instance, for example, friends of one mother had long noticed that her child was limping, dirty, and bruised while scavenging for garbage on the street to eat, but none stepped forward to notify authorities despite the fact that some of them were aware of the mother's prior incarcerations for drug-related offenses. It is hardly surprising that this mother felt betrayed by these associates, who subsequently testified at her murder trial. In another case, a mother who physically beat her infant in the presence of her sister threatened her sister with physical assault if she tried to intervene. As Korbin reports, because all of the mother's siblings also hit their children, the sister's failure to intervene may have been due to the family's acceptance of such behavior and the fear of detection of her own abuse if she should report the mother's maltreatment to child protection authorities. In a third case, a woman who beat her preschool daughter telephoned her mother to report this incident, only to be reassured that she was indeed a "good mother" and that child rearing is a difficult task. Her mother's offer to provide respite care the next weekend was too late to avert the child's death before the weekend arrived.

A fourth case reveals the dissonance between mothers' perceptions of support from their network associates and their reactions to genuine efforts to challenge their maltreating behavior. A mother, "Jane," showed her husband the bruises on her infant son, but was reassured that he "understood how these things can happen but knew that it would not happen again." The baby-sitter was similarly reassuring but, concerned about the bruises, suggested that the mother get professional help and gave her a book on child care. Jane read the book and found that it described abusive parents as "sick," and this led her not only to put it aside but also to perceive the baby-sitter as nonsupportive and critical. She never talked about the incident again with the baby-sitter, who never pursued the problem. A few weeks later, this mother suffocated her son. Korbin (1991) noted:

> A high level of perceived support sustained, probably unintentionally, these women in their pattern of abusive behavior. A low level of perceived support, in contrast, that did not bolster the woman's self-concept as a good mother, but that might have acted against the continuing abuse would have not been perceived as supportive. For example, I suggested to Jane that if I had been her baby-sitter, I would have reported her to child protective services. She responded that she would have fought hard to prove that she was doing just fine and probably would have "won," convincing child protective services that she was doing just fine. She quietly added that if someone had reported her, her child might still be alive. Her perceived social support from me, then, would have been low while her perceived social support from her husband would have been high. (p. 23)

In the end, it took more than an emotionally nurturant social network to curb abusive behavior by these mothers. It required a particular kind of supportive network with (a) consensual values that were inconsistent with parental maltreatment; (b) courageous associates who would risk being perceived as emotionally nonnurturant in the interest of protecting the mother's offspring; and (c) a willingness to immediately challenge parental behavior even in the face of threats of recrimination, rejection, or even physical assault. (The fear of recrimination is not just associated with the mother's reactions; it also concerns the reactions of other bystanders, who are as likely to criticize someone who intervenes publicly to aid an at-risk child as they are to criticize the parent's abusive behavior [Davis, 1991; Korbin, in press].) By contrast, the social networks of these women were emotionally nurturant but problematic in other ways, consisting of people who were themselves often abusive and inclined to deny and minimize the seriousness of the abuse they observed in their efforts to be "supportive" and avoid risking threat to themselves. There seemed to be little consensus within these networks as to how to define the parameters of appropriate parental conduct (and instead, undue deference to parental authority) or how to respond when clearly abusive behavior was witnessed (and instead, undue deference to family privacy). This is partly attributable to the abusive behavior of network associates themselves toward their offspring. In some cases, moreover, the fact that network associates saw only a fraction of the abusive behavior that actually occurred (sometimes in the company of other network members) probably also reduced their incentives to act more assertively to protect the child.

These considerations suggest that perceived social support does not necessarily change behavior—at least from the standpoint of curbing abusive behavior—and that it is therefore important to understand the factors predicting the effects of social support on troubled individuals in designing effective supportive interventions on their behalf. Korbin's provocative research findings also challenge the conventional view of abusive parents as socially isolated and thus lacking social support, which will be examined in more detail in the following chapter.

Effects of Stress on the
Availability of Social Support

Although it is easy to perceive social support as a stress prevention or a stress buffer, it is sometimes more difficult to appreciate the reciprocal relationship that exists between stress and social support.

Support may reduce the incidence or impact of stressful events, but stress may also alter the availability of social support. Serious stressors, such as job loss, divorce, and hospitalization, have a significant impact on the nature of the support networks on which one can rely, and they may also affect one's accessibility to those networks (Shinn et al., 1984; Vaux, 1988).

Stressful events can, in fact, either enhance access to social support or diminish it. On one hand, stressors may enhance social support as support agents become mobilized to provide assistance and as the recipient more actively seeks aid and becomes more receptive to the assistance that is offered (Vaux, 1988). Moreover, formal support agents may become involved with a family experiencing stress and turmoil. On the other hand, stressors may diminish social support because they decrease network size or the recipient's access to support agents (Shinn et al., 1984). Loss of a job or divorce, for example, can eliminate access to support agents on whom one has typically relied at the workplace or as part of a marital social network. Children who have been abused may lose access to supportive social partners for several reasons, including parents' active efforts to isolate them, their withdrawal from social activities, or the deterioration of social relationships resulting from the emotional impact of maltreatment on children's social skills and predispositions (cf. Salzinger et al., 1993). As a consequence, support agents may be least available and/or accessible on precisely those occasions when they are most needed, and social isolation derives, in part, from the stressor itself.

The impact of stress on the availability of social support is apparent not only with respect to episodic, severe stressful events, such as job loss or divorce. Under chronic stressful conditions—especially when those stresses are widely shared among members of the social network—social support may be less accessible because potential support providers are themselves undermined by the same difficulties. For example, economic stress and poverty are commonly shared within low-income neighborhoods and by members of an extended family, reducing the social resources on which individuals can rely (Cochran, Gunnarsson, et al., 1990; Fischer, 1982; Vaux, 1988). Likewise, single mothers must often cope with difficult economic and domestic demands, and the support they experience is unreliable because their networks are smaller, have higher rates of turnover (compared with married mothers), and include a high proportion of other single mothers experiencing similar problems (Belle, 1982;

Gunnarsson & Cochran, 1990; Larner, 1990a; Leslie & Grady, 1985;
Weinraub & Wolf, 1983). In each case, support providers are often also
needy individuals.

Efforts to enlist informal helpers in the natural networks of higher-
risk families (especially from their neighborhoods) to prevent child
maltreatment thus requires considering not only the potential agents
of support, but how the stressors experienced by these families may
alter potential support networks. The impact of socioeconomic stress
is just one example of a more general concern. When a substance abuse
problem partly accounts for abuse or neglect, for instance, this may
also limit the range of potential support agents in the parent's environment and alter the quality of support they can provide, especially
if close friends also have problems with drug dependency. When
parents have been found guilty of sexual abuse, the social stigma
attached to this finding may itself alter the nature and number of
support agents who can be found to assist in preventing reabuse,
especially if neighbors and community members react with outrage
or anger to sexual abuse reports. The same is likely to be true with
respect to other forms of maltreatment. In short, it is important to
consider not only the unique circumstances of the distressed individuals who are targets of social support interventions, but how those
stressful circumstances affect the sources of support that are available
to them.

One implication of this analysis is that efforts to assist troubled
families in difficult communities should emphasize enlisting formal
support agents who, because of their background and training, are
less prone to sharing many of the problems afflicting troubled parents.
Alternatively, a partnership can be created between formal and informal helpers such that the capacity of a willing neighbor, friend, or
extended family member to offer help is assisted by a social worker,
family counselor, clergyman, or other formal helper who can provide
counseling, advice, and other guidance to them.

Effects of the Recipient's Personal
Characteristics on Social Support

Social support is usually not received passively. Especially when
natural social networks are concerned, support must be sought, accessed, and maintained by the recipient. Viewed in this light, one

predictor of the extent to which social support can reduce stress is not just the availability of supportive agents, but the recipient's capacity to gain help from these agents. Therefore, the recipient's personal characteristics may be an important mediating variable in the relation between social networks, social support, and well-being (Heller & Swindle, 1983; Shinn et al., 1984). This is especially true of informal helping relationships, but even in the context of formal assistance from a trained professional, the recipient's personal characteristics are influential.

At a minimum, these personal characteristics include the social skills needed to establish and maintain positive relationships with network members. Deficits in this capacity may derive from many sources, including the effects of stress itself (e.g., when stress results in depression or generalized anxiety), or limits in the intellectual competencies, mental health, or emotional stability needed to engage in satisfying sociability with others. Personal characteristics needed to use social support also include the motivation for help-seeking, such as an awareness of the relevance of support to one's coping capacities and the perception that support is worth seeking. These personal characteristics also include the time and energy necessary to enlist assistance from others, which may be significantly reduced by stress or other factors. Beyond these minima, other personal characteristics of the recipient may affect the extent to which social support is obtained from network members. These characteristics include the recipient's extroversion, self-disclosure, defensiveness, comfort in intimate relations with others, and other social dispositions.

The personal characteristics needed to acquire and maintain social support from network associates can be affected by many factors, including, as noted earlier, the effects of stress itself on emotional well-being. Psychological difficulties or a substance abuse problem can also undermine the skills needed to benefit from the resources of a social network. Troubled individuals who are overwhelmed by life stresses may lack the time, energy, or hopefulness needed to seek and maintain supportive relationships with others. Neighborhoods can themselves be a detriment to accessing social support, especially because they enhance perceptions of danger or risk that reduce a person's willingness to establish relationships in the community, or they contribute to depression, anxiety, or other detriments to emotional stability.

The recipient's developmental status is also an important personal characteristic relevant to accessing and maintaining social support for the victims of child maltreatment. Most adults do not expect young children to assume much responsibility for obtaining assistance because young children have fewer effective competencies for establishing and maintaining their own supportive social networks, and children have little control over their network membership. As a result, the social support they receive is usually not contingent on their personal skills and abilities, but on the beneficence of adults. But even during the preschool years—and certainly by grade school—certain forms of social support become contingent on the recipient's personal characteristics. Peers and adults increasingly establish and maintain relationships with attractive children, and during the late preschool and early grade school years, the social skills and social competence of children become important predictors of their peer status (Hartup, 1983).

This is important because maltreated children develop deficiencies in social skills that can impair peer relationships, and this can make it harder to enlist peers in interventions to provide support and remediate the effects of abuse. The aggressive and impulsive behavior of children who have been abused or neglected is likely to undermine the very peer relationships that can potentially aid them. This becomes especially significant as, with increasing age, children rely more on self-constructed peer social networks and as the nature and quality of their social experiences depend more on the personal competencies that are needed to create and maintain satisfying peer relationships, such as during late childhood and adolescence. Thus, the importance of the recipient's personal characteristics for enlisting social support are developmentally graded, but become important from a surprisingly early age.

To be sure, not all forms of social support are so contingent on the recipient's personal characteristics. It does not require significant skill, for example, to receive the kinds of material or financial assistance that others can provide, or to receive unsolicited advice from others (some of which may be unwanted). However, the qualities of social support that are most valued—such as emotional affirmation or counseling—are indeed mediated by the personal characteristics of the recipient. This means that support resources may exist in an individual's natural network without the potential recipient benefiting from them, or that a formal helping relationship may become undermined by the recipient's inability, or unwillingness, to accept counseling, keep appointments, or otherwise maintain an assisting relationship.

These considerations have provoked a lively debate among students of social support about whether the apparent positive effects of social support on stress result primarily from the social competence of the recipient. In other words, are those who receive social support benefited by doing so, or are their psychological strengths the cause, not the result, of their capacity to maintain supportive relationships with others? As stated by Heller (1979):

> The often repeated finding in naturalistic studies that persons with established support networks are in better mental and physical health than are the unsupported may be due to variables other than social support. . . . It is possible that competent persons, who are more immune to the adverse effects of stress, are also more likely to have well developed social networks as a direct result of their more general social competence. (p. 361)

Whereas most other commentators have not adopted such a strong position, especially in light of prospective research suggesting a strong causal role for social support per se (see House et al., 1988), the argument that social competence is the basis for the apparent stress-buffering effects of social support underscores its important mediating role. At a minimum, a certain amount of social competence is necessary to access the support that is potentially available from natural and formal support networks.

This is directly relevant to an understanding of the social isolation of maltreating families. Seagull (1987) has argued that studies of maltreating families provide very little evidence for social isolation, but when they do, isolation derives more from their limited social skills than from deficits in the social support provided by their neighbors, friends, and kin. Consistent with the research of Polansky and his colleagues (Gaudin & Polansky, 1986; Gaudin & Pollane, 1983; Polansky et al., 1981; Polansky, Gaudin, Ammons, & David, 1985) reviewed in the next chapter, Seagull argues that this is especially apparent in neglectful families, whose characterological deficits in social skills and competence constrain their capacities to access and maintain supportive networks. In this view, therefore, social skills training may be an important component of intervention efforts to strengthen social support for some neglectful parents because improved social competence is a prerequisite to obtaining support from network associates. These considerations will be discussed more fully in the next chapter, when the social isolation of maltreating families is examined in depth, but the clear implication of this analysis is that because the recipient's personal characteristics mediate access to social support, interventions to assist them may require enhancing their capacities to receive and benefit from this support as well as strengthening the efforts of network associates.

Recipient Reactions to Aid

Social support carries, as we have seen, many potential benefits for its recipients. But for most people, the experience of receiving assistance from others engenders both positive and negative reactions that color the experience of being aided and affect one's future willingness to receive assistance. Understanding these recipient reactions to aid is especially important when considering the potential role of social support in the prevention of child maltreatment because social support is often regarded as a continuing resource for troubled individuals. Recipient reactions to aid may be unimportant, in other words, if assistance occurs on only one occasion (e.g., a financial donation), but social support is typically conceived as an ongoing benefit that adds up over time. Because we have noted that the recipient's efforts are necessary (at least in part) for the maintenance of social support, recipient reactions to aid may significantly mediate the efficacy of continuing, long-term social support interventions.

Assistance from others can evoke diverse reactions in recipients (Fisher et al., 1982; Shumaker & Brownell, 1984). Along with the positive feelings of affirmation and gratitude that accompany aid, recipients may also experience feelings of failure, indebtedness, vulnerability, inferiority, and dependency. These may occur for several reasons. First, norms of equity in most societies motivate individuals to try to reciprocate the assistance they receive from others and, failing to do so (because they cannot or are prevented from doing so), they experience discomfort and anxiety (Greenberg, 1980; Greenberg & Westcott, 1983; Hatfield & Sprecher, 1983). Discomfort may occur because of the humiliation arising from an inability to repay assistance, and potential fears of exploitation because of the unreciprocated receipt of assistance, especially if the provider of aid is a nonprofessional and is of equal status to the recipient. These feelings are especially acute when support is costly to the one providing aid, the benefactor's motives are voluntary and altruistic, and/or the recipient receives large benefits, which in each case heighten the reciprocity obligation and, consequently, perceptions of inequity and indebtedness.

Second, help-giving often involves implicit assessments not only of the benefactor's motives but also of the reasons the recipient requires help. If help is needed because of external conditions afflicting the recipient (e.g., socioeconomic stress, sudden financial or legal difficulties, etc.), help-giving involves little stigma as long as those circumstances are not specifically attributable to the recipient. However, if help is needed because of the recipient's personal attributes (e.g., poor skills at personal or family management, inadequate impulse control, poor child-rearing skills, etc.), then help-giving reflects the recipient's failure and inadequacy, and receiving help in these circumstances may be stigmatizing. Moreover, receiving assistance in the context of perceptions of personal inadequacy may paradoxically increase the recipient's helplessness and dependency, insofar as it conveys clear messages about the recipient's inability to succeed on his or her own. In this respect, a helping relationship may foster further need for assistance.

Third, receiving assistance may also directly challenge self-esteem because of its threats to autonomy, privacy, and self-reliance (Fisher et al., 1982). Self-disclosure in a socially supportive relationship (whether formal or informal) is often accompanied by the uncomfortable awareness that another knows things about oneself that could be embarrassing or threatening if they were publicly disclosed. Privacy violations in the context of helping may be especially threatening to self-esteem because they attack the integrity of possessional and informational self-control. Nevertheless, it may be difficult for recipients to resist privacy violations, if they so wish, because of the indebtedness entailed in helping relationships.

To be sure, help-giving typically involves a mingling of positive and negative perceptions of the benefactor, the assistance, the recipient, and the circumstances in which help is offered and received—and perceptions may vary depending on whether it is the recipient, the benefactor, or others who are making these judgments; the conditions in which assistance is offered; who initiated the relationship; and other factors. In some circumstances, these factors can contribute to markedly varying assessments of deservedness and need, expectations of gratitude, and perceptions of the conditions warranting further assistance that can significantly complicate helping relationships. Indeed, it is easy to see how both professional and nonprofessional helping relationships can founder on these differing assessments of their relationship.

It is important to recognize, however, that although unrequited altruism often inspires mixed feelings in those who benefit, gratitude is also almost inevitable (Hatfield & Sprecher, 1983). The importance of attending to potentially negative recipient reactions to aid is not just because of how they affect the experience of receiving help, but primarily because of their effects on future access to assistance. When recipients cannot restore equity in help-giving relationships, or they experience assistance as stigmatizing or humiliating, they are less likely to seek help in the future and are more likely to terminate a help-giving relationship if they are able to do so (Fisher et al., 1982; Shumaker & Brownell, 1984). In these circumstances, moreover, recipients are more likely to reinterpret the situation to restore their self-esteem, such as by derogating the benefactor, minimizing the extent of the assistance or its costs to the benefactor, and/or perceiving the benefactor as less altruistic and more manipulative than he or she really is. They may, in other words, somewhat paradoxically resent the assistance they receive and the person providing it. This is especially likely when assistance is received from strangers (with whom one does not share an ongoing relationship of mutual aid), nonprofessionals (for whom reciprocity and equity norms are more salient than with professional help-givers because the assistance is altruistic), and when the benefactor and the recipient come from similar social circumstances, such as sharing neighborhood and community ties, in which the inequity of the helping relationship is especially salient (Fisher et al., 1982; Greenberg & Westcott, 1983; Shumaker & Brownell, 1984). Needless to say, these conditions make the maintenance and continuity of assistance especially difficult in informal, neighborhood-based helping relationships and pose special challenges for social support interventions that require, at least in part, the recipient's tacit participation.

The research literature on recipient reactions to aid suggests, therefore, that several factors can contribute to recipient perceptions of assistance that support, rather than undermine, the maintenance of help-giving relationships. Recipients are most likely to regard assistance positively when they:

■ Have opportunities to reciprocate (or are required to repay) the aid they receive—with repayment going either to the benefactor or to others who require help, especially in the context of a relationship of reciprocal aid. One of the reasons why assistance from kin is so easily given and received, for example, is that it often occurs in a context of ongoing mutual aid.

■ Accept assistance because they perceive the need for help, rather than because of external judgments of inadequacy or incompetency. Help is more likely to be accepted based on a joint assessment of need that is shared by the recipient and the helper.

■ Perceive the benefactor's intentions as a combination of self-interest and altruism. In other words, help providers are regarded as receiving some benefit from their assistance and are thus not wholly altruistic, perhaps because they are paid, or are provided other benefits for their help-giving. In this regard, one advantage of formal helpers over informal helpers from the neighborhood or community is that providing assistance is not necessarily an altruistic activity, but part of the helper's job.

■ Estimate that assistance comes at little direct cost to the benefactor, with costs borne primarily, perhaps, by impersonal social institutions and agencies, or from other large organizations or collectives. Formal helpers who are affiliated with social institutions or agencies are unlikely to be perceived as paying a personal price for providing assistance.

■ Regard their own need for assistance as externally instigated (e.g., arising from difficult life demands at work or neighborhood) rather than deriving from personal inadequacies or incompetence.

■ Perceive assistance as a human right or entitlement deriving from mutual respect, rather than a gift of aid resulting from judgments of failure.

■ Receive assistance in settings and circumstances that reduce stigma, perhaps as a component of normative formal or informal benefits. Assistance can easily and comfortably occur in the context of everyday encounters with friends and neighbors, for example, or during routine transactions with institutional agents, such as public assistance caseworkers, or deriving from participation in programs whose benefits are widely shared by community members. In this regard, programs to provide assistance are most likely to succeed when they provide universal benefits so that recipient populations are not stigmatized by their identification with the program. If this is impossible, assistance can be incorporated into programs that target a broad and heterogeneous population.

■ Obtain aid in a manner that does not unduly invade privacy or limit autonomy (Pettigrew, 1983). Efforts to incorporate the beliefs and opinions of recipients into the design and functioning of assistance interventions help to preserve the dignity of recipients.

When young children are the recipients of assistance, it is less clear that these considerations entirely apply. One reason is that social norms of equity and reciprocity are less rigidly applied to children who are, almost by definition, regular recipients of unrequited benefits from adults. Moreover, young children are likely to be less cognizant of the attributions of neediness and dependency involved in receiving support in conditions that may be stigmatizing or contribute to perceptions of personal inadequacy for adults. Although preschoolers often reciprocate the benefits they receive from others (especially peers), it is not clear that this reflects their awareness of social norms of equity rather than simply acting in a manner that maintains good relations with others (Eisenberg, 1983).

However, it is important to recognize that expectations of reciprocity begin to be influential during the early school years and are especially important in late school-age and adolescence, when more mature appraisals of social norms, inferences concerning motives, and attributions concerning the recipient are normative (Eisenberg, 1983). Thus, from middle childhood, children become vulnerable to the feelings of indebtedness, inferiority, and dependency that commonly mark adults' reactions to aid, and considerations pertinent to the nature of the assistance and the contexts in which it is obtained should also apply to the social support they receive.

Support Agents and
Their Social Network Membership

Another important consideration in predicting the effects of social support on stress concerns the nature of the support agents and their place in the recipient's social network. In essence, knowing who is offering assistance and what other roles they have in the life of the recipient can help to predict the efficacy of social support efforts. It is important not only to distinguish the roles and functions of formal and informal support agents—the differences, for example, between a social worker, counselor, or a paraprofessional home visitor on one hand and a neighbor, parent, or coworker on the other—but to appreciate how each kind of support agent has other commitments and responsibilities that can alter his or her support role. Encompassed within this broad concern are a number of more specific issues.

First, because informal support agents—such as a relative, neighbor, coworker, classmate, clergy, doctor, barber, or hairdresser—often have additional roles and responsibilities in relation to the recipient, there exists potential conflict between providing support and the provider's institutional commitments, professional responsibilities, and personal values and interests. Neighbors may be more concerned about finding a quick exit from a dangerous or impoverished community than with providing support to troubled individuals who live nearby. They may also be as concerned with establishing distance from a difficult, unsociable family as they are with monitoring child abuse. The assistance of a relative may be colored by a legacy of family conflict, or by the kin's greater concern for preserving the self-esteem of an abusive brother or sister than the well-being of the niece or nephew who is being maltreated, or by the fear that broader patterns of family dysfunction will be revealed by an abuse investigation (cf. Korbin, 1989, 1991). Community caregivers may be more concerned about maintaining a professional partnership, pleasing a customer (or employer), or advancing a favorite program as they are with combating child maltreatment in the most effective manner possible. Coworkers may be divided between their allegiance to a troubled fellow employee and their fidelity to the employer, especially when stress affects an employee's competence or productivity, or abuse allegations would reflect unfavorably on the workplace. Other natural helpers who encounter troubled family members as their customers may be unwilling to threaten a proprietary relationship with comments about child rearing or other personal concerns. Members of a religious community may perceive their role as one of offering uncritical acceptance to troubled family members, and will certainly feel more comfortable in this role than the alternative of providing incisive counseling or referrals to professional helpers or child protection agents.

Likewise, doctors, school personnel, counselors, clergy, or other professionals who could be considered formal helpers may respond cautiously to a suspected abusive incident in light of mandatory child abuse reporting laws that color their professional interactions with parents or children from high-risk families. They may limit contact, for example, with family members who demand more attention and concern than the formal helpers can comfortably provide and who additionally pose difficult problems for the helpers' professional roles, because reporting suspected abuse threatens their relationship with the family, invokes their professional authority as mandated reporters, and embroils them in child protection investigations. This is one reason for concern, that formal helpers like these are aware of many more child abuse cases than they formally report (Zellman, 1990; Zellman & Anter, 1990). Moreover, there is always risk that their suspicions of abuse are wrong, which tends to introduce caution and, at times, avoidance of further inquiry.

In short, support agents have multiple interests and commitments that may influence the support they can offer distressed individuals. This may be especially true when the recipient is a maltreating parent or is at high risk for child abuse or neglect, when the social stigma attached to the adult's behavior is considerable in our society, and when the implications of a false allegation of abuse are significant.

Second, because support agents occupy unique niches in the recipient's life, they can offer unique forms of social support. A neighbor can provide respite child care, emergency assistance, and sometimes material aid; a coworker can assist in managing workplace stress and, at times, offer emotional relief from family-based demands; kin can offer understanding based on long-term personal intimacy; a schoolteacher can be someone apart from the natural network who knows the child and parent and can provide dispassionate advice; a doctor or minister can provide a likewise dispassionate perspective and, at times, professional guidance or a referral. This kind of "situation specificity" of support agents (Unger & Powell, 1980) suggests that network members are specialized for specific kinds of social support. It suggests also that because of "situation specificity," some network associates may be less capable than others of providing certain kinds of support to troubled families.

Third, efforts to prevent child maltreatment need not rely exclusively on informal support systems. Along with the efforts of informal network members are the activities of formal support agents, which include social service personnel in the community, welfare workers, therapists, law enforcement agents, and people associated with a variety of public-private initiatives, such as food pantries, soup kitchens, and other programs. Like informal support agents, they can offer unique assistance because of their unique roles in the life of the recipient; moreover, their recognized experience and authority can confer weight on the advice, information, guidance, or instruction they offer. Because these personnel often provide social support along with other services, the integration and coordination of formal and informal support efforts should be a key ingredient of any prevention effort (cf. Collins & Pancoast, 1976; Froland, Pancoast, Chapman, & Kimboko, 1981; Lewis & Fraser, 1987; Miller & Whittaker, 1988; Tracy & Whittaker, 1987; Whittaker, Schinke, & Gilchrist, 1986).

The coordination of formal and informal helpers is important because each kind of helping agent can offer unique contributions to high-risk families. Whereas professional helpers have expertise, enhanced personnel and material resources, the benefits of a clear role definition in relation to recipients, and professional accountability, informal support agents can provide more ongoing and multifaceted forms of assistance in the context of mutual helpgiving, using styles and strategies that are consistent with the values of the community in which recipients live (Collins & Pancoast, 1976; Froland et al., 1981). Gottlieb (1983) argues that a natural support network differs from professional services in other ways as well, including

(a) its natural accessibility; (b) its congruence with local norms about when and how support ought to be expressed; (c) its rootedness in long-standing peer relationships; (d) its variability, ranging from the provision of tangible goods and services to simple companionship; and (e) its freedom from financial and psychological (stigmatizing) costs incurred when professional resources are used. (p. 27)

The importance of the distinction between formal and informal helpers is that, just as informal, neighborhood-based support agents should not try to emulate the functions and skills of professionals, it may be impossible for professional helpers to assume many of the unique roles identified by Gottlieb that social network members assume in the lives of recipients of social support. Both forms of helping are unique, and each benefits by mutual intercoordination.

But coordinating the efforts of formal and informal helpers is difficult. Informal helpers may define problems differently from how professional helpers do, their values and goals may be different, and they may seek different kinds of solutions that are not as oriented toward professional norms and responsibilities (Froland et al., 1981). Defining the nature and limits of their roles vis-à-vis those of professional helpers can sometimes create mutual conflict, and formalization of the roles of natural helpers is likely to undermine their efficacy. In short, the coordination of formal and informal assistance is attractive in the abstract, but hard to accomplish effectively.

Coordination efforts should occur, however, especially to avoid two potential dangers. One is that informal support agents in the neighborhood, workplace, or extended family will be undermined by the involvement of formal agents, which can occur when formal agents (a) contribute to labeling or stigmatizing recipient families and their communities, (b) disrupt informal support networks by assuming their functions or diminishing their perceived importance or influence to the recipient, or (c) undermine informal support agents by criticizing or increasing demands on them (Froland et al., 1981). In a sense, a successful abuse prevention strategy requires that agents of formal support systems respect and assist the informal social networks that often provide tangible and meaningful aid to targeted individuals (Collins & Pancoast, 1976).

A second danger is the reverse: that informal network members will undermine the recipient's access to formal agents, such as when extended family members conceal abuse or seek to limit access to the perpetrator or victim, or neighbors reinforce the recipient's skepticism of the benefits of contacting formal help agents. In general, the coordination of formal and informal support systems in child protection can reduce the likelihood that agents of each system will act in a mutually antagonistic fashion or with conflicting goals.

Finally, it is worthwhile questioning whether social support must always come from individuals who have personal relationships with the recipient. Sometimes support can be obtained from anonymous sources, such as in conversations with strangers on airplanes or buses, or with casual acquaintances at work or school, or through hotline telephone counseling services. These kinds of casual or anonymous providers have several important advantages to the recipient. Shumaker and Brownell (1984) have pointed out that self-disclosure and helpful advice may occur more easily in fairly anonymous social encounters: The lack of personal intimacy contributes to candid communication because the personal risks of self-disclosure are low. In a similar manner, crisis hotlines or warm-lines (from which even children can benefit; see Peterson, 1990) permit the candid discussion of personal conflicts or stressful circumstances with strangers, and helpful counseling can occur in these nonthreatening circumstances because anonymity can foster self-disclosure and honest advice-giving.

In short, social support may be obtained from individuals who are not part of one's social network at all—indeed, people who are completely anonymous—because some forms of social support avail when the risks of self-disclosure are low. In these cases, the disadvantages of receiving support from individuals who do not know you well, and who usually cannot provide ongoing assistance, may be compensated by the opportunity for candid conversation with someone who will not carry this information into future encounters with the recipient.

Taken together, these considerations suggest that identifying potential support agents in the social networks of stressed individuals requires considering their broader roles in the individuals' lives. The possibility of conflicts with institutional commitments and personal values, the "situation specificity" of the kind of help they can offer, and the need for the integration of formal and informal support services together suggest that careful network mapping is an essential ingredient to the design of effective social support programs oriented to the prevention of child maltreatment.

Provider Reactions to Assistance

As these considerations imply, help-giving can be demanding and stressful to providers of assistance. Social support, in particular, requires emotional as well as material resources that can be quickly consumed by needy recipients in the context of an ongoing, long-term relationship. One additional consideration in predicting the effects of social support is determining the capacity of help providers to offer the kind of demanding, long-term assistance that might be required to effectively reduce the risk of child maltreatment.

This is especially true when support relationships are enlisted for abuse prevention purposes. In these circumstances, providers experience additional stresses for several reasons. First, parents and offspring who are at high risk for maltreatment often experience multiple needs (economic, personal, residential, legal) that can overwhelm potential providers, especially those found in informal support networks. Second, parents and children from high-risk families are often unable or unwilling to reciprocate the support they receive, either because of their negative reactions to the experience of receiving help or because of personal characteristics or external stresses that make it difficult for them to devote attention to others' needs and concerns. They may be disinterested or actively resistant to the assistance they are offered (being absent for scheduled appointments, for example, or failing to return phone calls), manifestly ignore the advice they are provided, and make unreasonable demands on the helper. They may also experience depression, substance abuse problems, mental illness, or have very limited social skills that can undermine the helping relationship. As a consequence, providers are likely to experience their relationships with recipients as frustrating conduits of one-way (rather than mutual) aid (Polansky, Ammons, & Gaudin, 1985).

Third, the goals for help-giving are likely to be differently conceived by the providers and recipients of social support when the prevention of maltreatment is concerned (Shumaker & Brownell, 1984). Especially when social support is enlisted for secondary or tertiary prevention, providers are (at best) likely to be most concerned with strengthening positive parenting practices and monitoring the family to ensure that children are not maltreated. Recipients, by contrast, may be most interested in obtaining emotional nurturance, as Korbin's study of fatally abusive mothers seems to indicate, and/or access to material resources. The conflict between these goals may cause both providers and recipients of assistance to feel frustrated by the relationship or disappointed in the partner, to experience their relationship as being "out of sync," or to engage in open conflict.

For these reasons, well-conceived social support programs that focus on informal neighborhood assistance will devote as much attention to "supporting the supporters" as to targeting the recipients of assistance. The same is also important when formal support programs are used, even though staff are paid and professionally trained. In each case, far more might be accomplished by addressing the needs of support agents than by focusing on recipients alone. Because of the unique features of helping relationships with needy, troubled families—which are different, by definition, from other social relationships—and the potential for the exhaustion (or "drain," in the parlance of social scientists) of support providers, assistance to potential benefactors is an important ingredient to the success of social support programs. As suggested above, this might occur as formal and informal support agents coordinate and integrate their efforts, or it might require directly targeting resources to the informal support agents who are identified in the neighborhoods and families of troubled individuals. These resources can include formal or informal training or supervision, counseling, material aid, and other kinds of assistance.

Social Networks as
Sources of Social Stress

As many aspects of the foregoing discussion have implied, relationships with social network members can mean different things to different individuals. Friends, neighbors, relatives, coworkers, and other social agents can be potent sources of social support, but may also instigate conflict, create frustration or humiliation, and impose undesired demands on the target individual (cf. Garbarino, 1977a). In short, social networks provide benefits but also impose costs, and any effort to enlist informal support systems for preventing child maltreatment must take into account the fact that relationships with social network members can be stressful, demanding, and evaluative. Indeed, the conflict experienced with network members may influence one's level of stress more potently than the amount of support they provide (Shinn et al., 1984). In efforts to prevent child maltreatment, therefore, it is important to ensure that the network associates who are supposed to offer social support do not become sources of stress instead.

This is an especially important consideration with respect to the populations that are at highest risk for child maltreatment and who are likely to experience multiple stressors of various kinds. As Belle (1982) has evocatively noted with respect to socioeconomically distressed single mothers, "One cannot receive support without also risking the costs of rejection, betrayal, burdensome dependence, and vicarious pain. This is probably especially true among the poor, whose relatives, friends, and neighbors are likely to be stressed and needy themselves" (p. 143). Such a conclusion was aptly demonstrated in her interviews with women who experienced their extended kin as demanding and burdensome, husbands and boyfriends as unreliable (and frequently abusive), and their neighborhoods as dangerous or entrapping. Contrary to conventional intuitions about social networks and social support, Belle (1982) found that women with larger social networks, who lived in closer proximity to network members or who interacted more frequently with them, were no less depressed and anxious or more psychologically healthy when compared with women who had less contact with their network associates. Similarly, women who were extensively involved with their neighbors were not those who reported experiencing the greatest social support. The reason, she concluded, is that these network associates were sources of stress as well as support, partly because they experienced the same needs and stresses.

In short, in communities where residents experience the greatest need for social support from their natural networks, and for whom social support might be most helpful in reducing the potential of child abuse, informal networks are most limited because potential helpers are sometimes also demanding, difficult, and unreliable, or may themselves be stressed and needy. In either case, they are not optimal helpers because of the weight of their own agendas on their capacities to provide assistance. This is perhaps one of the greatest challenges in enlisting informal social support systems that rely on natural helpers in communities where families are at high risk for child maltreatment.

Conclusions and Implications

In all, it is clear that predicting the effects of social support is a very complex calculus of considerations related to characteristics of the recipient of help, the provider of assistance, their social networks, and the physicosocial ecology in which this occurs. These are important, however, because they indicate why support providers become burned out by their roles, why recipients sometimes reject the assistance they are provided, why certain informal support agents are ineffective, why support can exist in communities without being used, why troubled parents can feel supported but still abuse their children, and why social network members are sometimes the best, and worst, sources of informal support. In short, these considerations indicate mistakes to be avoided, avenues to be pursued, and complexities to be encompassed in the design of social support interventions.

These considerations also have important implications for understanding the strengths and liabilities of the natural networks of troubled individuals and families. As the provocative research of Korbin (1989, 1991, in press), summarized at the beginning of this chapter, aptly illustrates, abuse-prone parents can be surrounded by network associates whom they perceive to be supportive without these individuals effectively helping to protect their offspring. Conversely, troubled families may be isolated, but this may have a different meaning for social support in the context of neighborhood and kin networks that are reliable sources of stress, or of neighborhoods that are threatening or dangerous. In this context, it is hard to say whether infrequent contact with network associates is a liability or a buffer. Finally, the needy potential recipients of social support and the potential providers of this assistance may be separated by a psychological gulf of differing perceptions, expectations, attributions, and inferences about need that cause them to be mutually distrustful, even resentful, of their relationship—and doom that relationship not only to be unhelpful, but to be short-lived.

In all, it is clear that there is no straightforward association between social networks, social support, and psychological well-being, not to mention the links between these processes and the prevention of child maltreatment. Creating meaningful associations between social network members with specific characteristics and attributes, helping them to provide support that is likely to be accepted, and incorporating this support into a concerted abuse-prevention strategy requires careful thought, assessment, and planning. With this in mind, the next chapter presents a detailed examination of the social networks of abuse-prone families that such interventions are meant to influence.

5

The Social Context
of Child Maltreatment

Current interest in neighborhood social networks as abuse prevention avenues derives from a growing recognition that child maltreatment must be viewed within its broader social ecology (cf. Belsky, 1980; Belsky, Robins, & Gamble, 1984; Belsky & Vondra, 1989; Gelles, 1973, 1992). Although traditional views linking abuse to parental psychopathology remain tenable for many families, most researchers, clinicians, and social workers have recognized that an ecological view meaningfully widens the scope of understanding the origins, correlates, and sequelae of child maltreatment by encompassing the poverty, substance abuse problems, and life stresses that also assume a role in abuse and neglect. In addition, an ecological view has intervention applications: Proposals for enhancing social support from formal or informal providers have their genesis, as we have seen, in the view that such an ecological intervention will combat abuse by enhancing a parent's psychological well-being, incorporating positive influences into the family's life, reducing social isolation, and benefiting family members in other ways.

But all of these ecological approaches are predicated on a thoughtful, systematic understanding of the social ecologies of families that are prone to abuse or neglect their offspring. In other words, without a thorough appreciation of the social networks that characterize high-risk families, it makes little sense either to speculate about how ecological processes contribute to abuse potential, or how supportive interventions can reduce this potential. With the considerations of the preceding chapters in mind, it is now appropriate to examine the social context of child maltreatment and, in particular, to consider how an understanding of the nature and functions of social networks, and of the various factors contributing to support and stress within those networks, can inform our understanding of the social ecology of child abuse and neglect. Among the questions meriting consideration are the following:

■ How does the social context of high-risk families differ from the ecology of lower-risk families? In what ways do ecological factors contribute to their propensity for maltreatment?

■ What are the potential social resources on which these families can rely for obtaining assistance and support?

■ What is the meaning of the commonly noted "social isolation" of maltreating families? In what ways are these families socially isolated, and what are the reasons?

■ What potential avenues exist for strengthening informal social supports within their neighborhoods and communities, among extended family members, and from other sources? What roles can formal helpers assume?

As we shall see, these provocative questions have received only partial answers in existing research studies, yielding a considerable number of issues for future research. The task of this chapter is to examine the answers that exist and identify the questions that remain.

This ambitious agenda begins with a summary of research knowledge of the broader socioeconomic conditions associated with child maltreatment. We then turn to a detailed review of studies documenting the social isolation of maltreating families to understand (a) the criteria by which these families are often deemed to be isolated, (b) the dimensions of their social networks that appear to be different from as well as similar to those of untroubled families, and (c) the potential resources for support that may exist within their social ecologies. Finally, we turn to a reconsideration of why these families may experience social isolation in their neighborhoods and communities.

The Socioeconomic Context of Child Maltreatment

Throughout this book, the association between child maltreatment and socioeconomic stress has been underscored. This is not to deny that children are abused or neglected in homes that range throughout the spectrum of family income and education, or that certain forms of maltreatment are more distally linked to socioeconomic stress. However, a variety of researchers have noted that family income and education (together with unemployment and underemployment, poor and/or public housing, welfare reliance, single parenting, and more dangerous neighborhoods) are strong correlates of child maltreatment (Coohey, 1993, 1994; Daro, 1988, 1994; Deccio, Horner, & Wilson, 1991; Garbarino, 1976; Garbarino & Crouter, 1978; Garbarino & Sherman, 1980a, 1980b; Gaudin & Pollane, 1983; Gaudin, Wodarski, Arkinson, & Avery, 1990-1991; Gelles, 1992; Gelles & Cornell, 1990; Gil, 1970; Giovannoni & Billingsley, 1970; Lovell & Hawkins, 1988; Newberger, Reed, Daniel, Hyde, & Kotelchuck, 1977; Pelton, 1978, 1994; Polansky, Ammons, & Gaudin, 1985; Polansky et al., 1981; Polansky, Gaudin, et al., 1985; Salzinger, Kaplan, & Artemyeff, 1983; Smith, 1975; Smith, Hanson, & Noble, 1974; Starr, 1982; Steinberg, Catalano, & Dooley, 1981; Straus, 1980; Straus et al., 1980; Wolock & Horowitz, 1979; Young, 1964; Zuravin, 1986, 1989). In short, although child maltreatment is not limited by the boundaries of socioeconomic status, it is wise to conceive this problem in the context of poverty and financial stress.

This means that proposed programs emphasizing neighborhood-based social support must build on the resources of economically stressed communities that are typically characterized by higher levels of crime and perceptions of danger by their residents, high residential mobility, limited local business initiatives, higher unemployment and reliance on welfare benefits, heightened use of public housing, limited local community activism, and neighbors who are themselves buffeted, victimized, and often frightened by these social conditions. Moreover, programs striving to enlist extended kin into supportive networks for abuse-prone families must take into consideration the probability that socioeconomic stress also characterizes extended kin networks, with the enhanced stress and more limited resources that these family members bring to their relations with troubled families. In addition, other potential sources of social support also may be constrained by the socioeconomic conditions of child maltreatment. Workplace networks are likely to be less supportive when family members are working inconsistently or not at all, and the low-wage jobs that employ parents may provide few opportunities for establishing social ties and are likely to be sources of greater stress than of affirmation. Schools also may be inadequate sources of support for children and/or their parents, insofar as they are also characterized by limited economic resources; community danger; and stressed teachers, administrators, and other personnel.

There are other indications that high-risk families are multiproblem families. Daro (1988) noted in her extensive compendium of demonstration programs that maltreating families are characterized by other forms of domestic violence, including interspousal fighting (especially apparent in physically abusive families) and physical violence between siblings (especially apparent in emotionally maltreating families). She noted that maltreatment is more likely in families with a parent who has a substance abuse problem (which was primarily associated with emotional maltreatment in her samples) or mental illness. Other researchers have reported similar results (see Coohey, 1994; Gelles & Cornell, 1990; Starr, 1982; Straus et al., 1980; Wolock & Horowitz, 1979; Young, 1964). Families with maltreated children are less likely to be intact compared to nonmaltreating families, but likely to have more children, underscoring that these families have enhanced child-rearing demands and child care needs (Gaudin & Pollane, 1983; Gil, 1970; Giovannoni & Billingsley, 1970; Polansky, Gaudin, et al., 1985; Smith et al., 1974; Wolock & Horowitz, 1979; Young, 1964; but see Ory & Earp, 1980). These families are also characterized by heightened residential mobility, which may undermine the strength and stability of relationships with neighbors and other community members (Deccio et al., 1991; Elmer, 1967, 1977; Gaudin & Pollane, 1983; Gil, 1970; Newberger et al., 1977; Polansky, Gaudin, et al., 1985; Starr, 1982; Straus et al., 1980; Zuravin, 1989).

Generalizing from this empirical picture, it is not surprising that most researchers studying maltreating families describe them as highly stressed by their living conditions as well as by their personal problems. Their capacities to cope are additionally constrained by the limited resources of their neighborhoods and communities. Supportive ties within the family as well as with extended kin are likely to be affected by economic stress as well as interfamilial conflict. Workplace supports are undermined by the association of maltreatment with underemployment and with the kinds of low-paying jobs that do not foster strong, supportive relationships among employees. Child care needs and child-rearing demands are heightened in abuse-prone families in ways that are likely to make children the focus of many of the difficulties and frustrations that parents must face. Neighbors, like the families themselves, are often struggling to cope with these circumstances and are thus likely to have few resources to devote to the needs of others. Communities may have few organized recreational, social, or educational activities (outside of the school system) that can foster neighborhood cohesion and a sense of community among its residents. Schools, like the neighborhoods themselves, may be perceived by children as dangerous and unpredictable settings, with its personnel already preoccupied with other demands. In short, the normative conditions experienced by families at high risk for child maltreatment appear to offer few meaningful resources for coping with life stress and enhancing informal supportive networks.

Dimensions of Social Isolation

In addition to the other correlates of child maltreatment, numerous investigators have also commented on their social isolation. Daro (1988), for example, found that social isolation cut across the different maltreatment subpopulations that were the focus of her intensive demonstration programs, suggesting that isolation is a pervasive rather than subpopulation-specific correlate of child abuse or neglect. Other researchers (e.g., Giovannoni & Billingsley, 1970; Polansky et al., 1981) perceive social isolation as particularly characteristic of neglectful families. However, many researchers regard the lack of connection to supportive figures as one of the most consistent features of maltreating families.

What do researchers mean when they refer to the "social isolation" of maltreating families? Are they referring to personal or familial social networks of limited size or scope? Are they concerned with the infrequency with which family members are in contact with friends, relatives, and neighbors? Are they primarily describing the loneliness and lack of perceived support from others as it appears to family members themselves? Are they referring to the extent to which interactions with others are experienced as stressful rather than supportive? Are they describing their social networks as lacking density and interconnectedness among its members? Are they implying limitations in the functional roles assumed by social network members: diminished emotional sustenance, for example, or an inability to obtain counseling, advice, or access to information or services from social network members?

The analysis of social networks and social support in Chapters 3 and 4 invites such queries in an effort to obtain a systematic analysis of the social ecology of child maltreatment. But more important is that answers to such questions provide avenues to understanding the nature of the links that exist (or do not exist) between maltreating family members and others in the neighborhood, surrounding community, and elsewhere, and what can be done to improve these linkages.

Unfortunately, it is often very difficult to understand what researchers have meant by the social isolation of maltreating families. Many studies surveyed in this literature did not include appropriate comparison or control groups, so it is impossible to determine whether the social network characteristics of maltreating families are unique to families who abuse or neglect their offspring, or instead derive from other characteristics of these families and their social ecologies (e.g., poverty and low socioeconomic status) that do not specifically denote abuse potential (cf. Coohey, 1993). Many studies relied on global impressionistic or summary measures of social isolation that do not enable us to understand more precisely the features of their social networks that are lacking. Studies using global ratings of the social isolation of families do not distinguish whether social isolation is based on small network size or instead on limited social embeddedness, perceived lack of support, or other reasons. In many cases, researchers relied on highly imprecise, second-hand, and/or potentially biased reporting sources (such as social service caseworkers) in assessing the social networks of maltreating families. Moreover, the majority of studies are based on the reports of mothers that, although offering some insights into the family system as a whole, may not fully represent the social networks of other family members. Perhaps most distressing, the widespread perception that these families are socially isolated in their neighborhoods led most researchers to focus largely, if not exclusively, on the deficits in their social networks, with much less interest in the potential strengths and resources that their networks might possess, despite the obvious relevance of the latter to enhancing support within their natural networks.

Network Size and Social Embeddedness

Despite these limitations, however, some conclusions can be drawn about the social network characteristics of high-risk families that have led researchers to regard them as socially isolated. In most studies, judgments of social isolation derive from the fact that mothers in these families have a smaller network size compared to other families (Corse, Schmid, & Trickett, 1990; Elmer, 1967; Kotelchuck, 1982; Salzinger et al., 1983; Smith et al., 1974; Young, 1964), or that they exhibit limited social embeddedness; that is, they see network members less frequently than do others (Bryant et al., 1963; Crittenden, 1985; Elmer, 1967; Gaudin et al., 1990-1991; Giovannoni & Billingsley, 1970; Hunter & Kilstrom, 1979; Jensen, Prandoni, Hagenau, Wisdom, & Riley, 1977; Kotelchuck, 1982; Nurse, 1964; Oates, Davis, Ryan, & Stewart, 1979; Polansky et al., 1981; Polansky, Gaudin, et al., 1985; Salzinger et al., 1983; Smith et al., 1974; Starr, 1982; Straus et al., 1980; Wolock & Horowitz, 1979; Young, 1964).

In an evocative but impressionistic study based on the social service case records of 300 maltreating families, for example, Young (1964) reported that neglectful families lacked steady contact with friends and relatives, and 85% belonged to no organized group. However, this was also characteristic of other maltreating families: 95% of families deemed "severely abusive," for example, had no continuing relationship with others outside the family. In a more systematic comparison of physically abusive and control families who were matched on important socioeconomic, ethnic, and other variables, Starr (1982) reported that abusive mothers visited fewer people on a regular basis, made fewer total visits, met with relatives less often, and were less likely to feel that they met with relatives frequently enough (although maltreatment and control groups did not differ on 24 other measures of social isolation, some of which will be discussed further below). Salzinger et al. (1983) reported similar findings and noted that frequency of contact with extended kin was a more important predictor of maltreatment than was the regularity of peer interactions for the mothers in their sample. Giovannoni and Billingsley (1970) compared socioeconomically distressed neglectful mothers with nonmaltreating mothers from similar backgrounds and found that although the two groups did not differ significantly on measures of contact with friends, the neglectful mothers were significantly less likely to see extended family on a regular basis (especially if they were White). On the other hand, in a study of physically abusive mothers, Corse et al. (1990) reported that only contact and support from peers differentiated these mothers from a matched control group; in relations with other network associates, the two groups were similar. In a British study, Smith et al. (1974) compared matched samples of physically abusive and nonabusive mothers and found that when social class differences were controlled, the groups differed in their frequency of contact with extended family members (but not with neighbors and friends), and a higher proportion of abusive mothers reported having no social activities and few opportunities to have a break from the child. Wolock and Horowitz (1979) compared the social service case records of welfare recipients who either maltreated their offspring (primarily through neglect) or did not, and reported that maltreating families had significantly fewer contacts with friends, relatives, and organized groups outside their households.

It is important to note that these conclusions concerning the limited network size and social embeddedness of maltreating families are not entirely uniform. As we have seen, researchers have reported inconsistent findings, sometimes based on other measures from the same study. Starr (1982), for example, found no differences between abusive and nonabusive mothers on measures of the number of personal phone conversations, personal letters written, the number of good friends in the neighborhood, the number of neighbors known by name, help with child care, and organizational membership. Giovannoni and Billingsley (1970) found no differences between neglectful and nonneglectful mothers in organizational ties (which included involvement in various service systems), use of recreational facilities, and related services. Only church involvement distinguished these groups, with neglectful mothers less committed to religious activities (see also Polansky, Gaudin, et al., 1985, for similar results). Corse et al. (1990) found no differences between abusive and non-abusive mothers in the size and support of nuclear family members, extended family members, and professional network members. Crittenden (1985) found that although neglectful mothers had less contact with friends than did nonneglectful mothers, they had more regular interaction with relatives. Lovell and Hawkins (1988) reported that mothers referred to a therapeutic program because of child maltreatment contacted more than 46% of their network members on either a daily basis or several times weekly, with another 28% seen once a week. And although Smith et al. (1974) reported that physically abusive mothers felt socially isolated compared to nonabusive mothers, they found no differences in the husbands' reports of their social activities compared to the husbands in nonabusive families!

Thus, even the studies providing the most significant evidence for the social isolation of maltreating families suggest that these families might not be so isolated after all, even when simple measures of network size and social embeddedness are considered. The diversity of these findings probably derives from several factors. First, the studies surveyed here varied significantly in the nature of the reporting sources and in the detail and specificity of the information concerning social network features, with some studies obtaining a richly detailed portrayal of the strengths and weaknesses of the networks of maltreating families and other researchers obtaining a much more impoverished picture. When different aspects of social networks were measured (e.g., contact with extended family, friends, neighbors, etc.), the measures often varied in their sensitivity to social connectedness. This may have helped to account for inconsistent results.

Second, researchers studied samples of maltreating families that varied, sometimes strikingly, in the severity of family dysfunction. By comparison with the sample studied by Young (1964), in which severe child maltreatment was accompanied by high rates of alcoholism, mental illness, and criminality, other researchers (e.g., Giovannoni & Billingsley, 1970; Ory & Earp, 1980) studied samples in which child maltreatment and accompanying family dysfunction were much less severe. These differences in study samples—together with the fact that many samples were very small, and thus might yield unreliable results—can help account for different results from one study to the next.

Third, and finally, the samples also varied in the extent to which the families studied were primarily abusive or neglectful. Insofar as abusive and neglectful families have different kinds of social networks and different reasons for seeking, or restricting, contact with network associates, this may affect the patterns of results yielded by these researchers (although the overlap in subpopulations of abusive and neglectful families must also be kept in mind).

Despite this variability, some conclusions seem warranted from this review of network size and social embeddedness. First, when group differences were noted, they usually portrayed maltreating mothers as having less regular contact with social network members. Limited contact with members of the extended family was particularly distinctive in several studies, although the evidence is inconsistent across the entire literature (cf. Corse et al., 1990; Crittenden, 1985). As noted in Chapter 3, relations with extended kin may be crucial in view of their importance to reliable, long-term support, although the potential for relatives to induce stress as well as provide support complicates any clear prediction about whether frequent contact with extended family members buffers abuse potential. Reflecting this complexity, Straus and Kantor (1987) found that child abuse was more likely to occur when extended family lived within an hour's drive, which may indicate the demands as well as assistance afforded by extended family members (see also Cazenave & Straus, 1979; Korbin, 1989, in press; Straus et al., 1980). In the end, it may not be the frequency of contact with extended family members alone but rather frequency in the context of perceived support that is important: Kin assume a stress-buffering role when parents regard them as helpful and can see them frequently. Taken together, therefore, there is evidence for the limited social embeddedness of high-risk families, and the extent of contact with extended kin may be an especially crucial, albeit complex, predictor of proneness to abuse.

Second, limited embeddedness appears to be specific to particular associations: It was rarely a comprehensive feature of the mother's entire network of social connections. These studies portray some mothers who had limited contact with extended kin but frequent interaction with neighbors, for example, and others who rarely saw their kin but were involved with friends or community groups. The fact that mothers in these high-risk families maintained some social connections while lacking others is a very different portrayal of social isolation than the conventional view that maltreating families become isolated from virtually every potential source of support. Moreover, the picture of poor social embeddedness yielded by these studies may also be a limited one because there are various ways that family members can establish and maintain contact with others outside the home, including using the telephone and writing letters. These diverse modes of social connection were sometimes missed by investigators who focused primarily on face-to-face interactions with social network members, but they constitute important alternative ways of maintaining sociability. This is especially relevant to studies of socioeconomically distressed families, whose opportunities for direct contact with extended kin or friends who live far away may be restricted by limited access to transportation, but who may compensate with phone calls if they can afford phone service (but some cannot; see Gaudin et al., 1990-1991; Parke & Collmer, 1975; Wolock & Horowitz, 1979). In sum, the limited social embeddedness of abuse-prone families is not a comprehensive feature of their network associations, but is rather specific to particular kinds of associates (e.g., extended family), and this conclusion may fail to take into consideration the indirect ways that mothers and other family members can keep in contact with these associates.

Third, the findings of Smith et al. (1974) are unique in suggesting that spouses within a high-risk family may differ in their social embeddedness and that this may be associated with proneness to abuse. Unfortunately, theirs is the only study to independently assess the social networks of mothers and fathers within the same families: Most studies assessed only the network characteristics of mothers. It is important to broaden assessments in future research because social isolation may not be uniformly shared by all family members, especially when one parent has regular outside employment and the other does not. By focusing primarily on maternal networks rather than those of both parents, researchers may miss the stresses and insularity that put fathers at high risk for child maltreatment, but which mothers do not share. Moreover, given the frequent reports of the child care needs of high-risk families, a mother who reports limited opportunities for social contact, especially with a husband who has a broad social network, may be revealing stresses related to isolation and child-rearing demands that also merit special attention.

Density and Reciprocity

The conclusion emerging from this research review is a tentative and limited one: High-risk family members, especially mothers, may have somewhat less contact with some of their network associates than do nonabusive families. But as noted in Chapter 3, measures of network size and social embeddedness are among the least sensitive indexes of the social support derived from network members: Large social networks are not necessarily supportive networks, and frequent contact with network members may be stressful as well as helpful. Unfortunately, few studies of the social isolation of maltreating families have moved beyond these rather global, and convenient, social network measures.

In one impressive exception, however, Salzinger et al. (1983) compared the social network characteristics of maltreating mothers referred to a hospital-based family crisis program with nonmaltreating mothers seeking routine pediatric care. Based on maternal reports, they found that maltreating mothers not only had smaller networks and were more insulated from contact with network members, but their social networks also exhibited less density; that is, network members were infrequently in contact with each other. Salzinger et al. pointed out that circumscribed contacts with a small number of social network members may undermine efforts to change parenting practices. Maltreating mothers receive fewer consistent social supports for maintaining revised patterns of child rearing because network members are in little contact with each other (see also Wahler, 1980, and Wahler & Hann, 1984, for supportive evidence of this view).

Crittenden (1985) calculated a measure of reciprocity based on mothers' reports about the amount of help that was given and received from significant network members and reported that maltreating mothers experienced less reciprocity in their relationships with network members than did nonmaltreating mothers. The assistance they received from their network associates, in other words, tended to be experienced as one-way aid by the providers. Similar results have been reported in a study of neglectful mothers by Polansky, Gaudin, et al. (1985), which is reported in detail later in this chapter. These findings are important in light of the evidence, reviewed in the preceding chapter, that reciprocity is an important facet of natural helping and is especially pertinent to cultural norms of equity in mutual assistance.

Finally, Lovell and Hawkins (1988) also reported that maltreating mothers experienced a lack of reciprocity in relationships with social network members, and further concluded that their social networks were characterized by high density; that is, network members knew each other quite often. This is, of course, contrary to the findings of Salzinger et al. noted above, and underscores how little can be concluded about whether differences in density characterize comparisons between high-risk and lower-risk families.

Perceived Support
and Enacted Support

The network dimensions that are probably of greatest relevance to understanding their supportive functions to maltreating families, of course, are *perceived support* and *enacted support*. Based on measures of these dimensions, in other words, we can learn the extent to which (a) social network members are regarded as accessible sources of social support and are expected to provide assistance when needed and (b) social network members have actually provided instrumental assistance in the past.

Unfortunately, information concerning these dimensions of the social networks of maltreating families is impoverished. There are very few studies concerned with enacted support from extended kin, friends, or neighbors, and most are concerned with support in child care. According to Lovell and Hawkins (1988), for example, maltreating mothers reported that very few of their network associates provided help with child care or parenting responsibilities, even though the same mothers reported considerable satisfaction with their relationships with these people. For instance, mothers reported enjoying seeing nearly 80% of network members very much and said they could "share their thoughts and feelings frequently" with nearly 50% of these associates. The incongruity between these perceptions is explained, the authors argue, by the fact that most maltreating mothers indicated that they regarded their network members as supportive in general, but lacking useful or helpful advice on parenting and child care issues.

Somewhat similar findings are described by Corse et al. (1990), who reported that physically abusive mothers experienced significantly less satisfaction with the support they received in parenting than did mothers in a matched control group, primarily because of their impoverished support from peers. On other measures of perceived support, however, researchers have found surprisingly few reliable differences between maltreating families and nonmaltreating families. As noted at the beginning of Chapter 4, for example, the mothers studied by Korbin (1989, 1991, in press) perceived considerable support among their social network members, even though this did not prevent fatal child abuse. Starr (1982) likewise discerned no group differences on self-report measures of relatives or friends who could be counted on when needed (similar findings have also been reported by Smith & Adler, 1991), even though maltreating mothers saw their extended families less often. Elmer (1977) noted that a sample of hospital-referred mothers of maltreated infants differed from mothers of infants hospitalized for other reasons on a global measure of social support, but although they reported lower "satisfaction with a male partner" compared with nonmaltreating mothers, there were no group differences on measures of "availability of help from friends or neighbors" or "availability of another person to confide in." Egeland and Brunquell (1979) similarly found that maltreating mothers reported less support from the "alleged father" of their child and from their families, but equal amounts of perceived support from friends, when compared with a nonmaltreating control group. And when Smith et al. (1974) compared the responses of identified abusive mothers with the rest of their sample, the former group had a significantly lower proportion reporting loneliness.

But, again, the evidence is inconsistent. Polansky and his colleagues (Polansky, Ammons, et al., 1985; Polansky et al., 1981; Polansky, Gaudin, et al., 1985) have consistently found in several studies that neglectful mothers reported greater loneliness and lack of neighborhood support compared with socioeconomically comparable nonneglectful mothers, and this series of studies will be discussed later in greater detail. Similar results have been obtained by Jensen et al. (1977) and by Gaudin et al. (1990-1991) concerning physically abusive and physically neglectful families, respectively, and by Turner and Avison (1985). Moreover, Coohey (1994) has reported that "emotional disconnectedness" and perceived lack of support was one of the most important discriminators of maltreating from nonmaltreating mothers.

It appears, therefore, that considerable inconsistency characterizes the limited findings concerning enacted support and perceptions of social support among abusive and neglectful mothers. As with the research on social network size and embeddedness, this inconsistency is attributable in part to differences in characteristics of the samples studied by researchers, the measures they used, and the manner in which inquiries concerning perceived and enacted support were posed. Contrary to the research on network size and embeddedness, however, the weight of the evidence does not indicate that differences in perceived support reliably distinguish high-risk families from similar families who are nonabusive. Consistent with Korbin (1989, 1991), who found that abusive mothers were surrounded by an emotionally supportive but ineffective social network, it appears that many abuse-prone parents perceive their friends, kin, neighbors, and other network associates as being affirming and helpful—at least in some ways. Although it may be important that network associates are sometimes regarded as least helpful in child care and parenting responsibilities, on the whole it appears that it is not a lack of access to supportive individuals that distinguishes abuse-prone from low-risk families.

What We Know—And What We Don't Know

Taken together, therefore, much of the basis for the perceived social isolation of maltreating families is the limited amount of contact (i.e., limited embeddedness) with social network members that mothers report experiencing. This significantly constrains conventional portrayals of the isolation of abuse-prone families because it suggests that mothers may experience limited embeddedness without feeling that they are lacking access to support from among friends, neighbors, and/or extended family, and some studies directly confirm that this is true (e.g., Korbin, 1989, 1991; Starr, 1982). Moreover, although enhancing social embeddedness may be a useful goal for social support interventions, based on this evidence it is unclear whether high-risk mothers would experience or perceive greater support from their network associates as a consequence, or whether this would reduce their proneness to abuse.

However, even if limited social embeddedness is the only reliably distinctive characteristic of abuse-prone families, it might nevertheless have important implications for maltreating parents, and also for their offspring. Parents who avoid, escape, or simply do not establish regular contact with others outside the home (especially extended kin) not only fail to benefit from the kind of informal assistance that these people can provide, but their parenting behavior remains unmonitored by outside agents who might provide alternative role modeling, counseling, criticism, or information to professional agents. Although it seems apparent that their limited embeddedness is only partial rather than comprehensive—that is, abuse-prone mothers are in fairly regular contact with some network associates and see others infrequently—it is unclear whether this guarantees the counseling, modeling, and monitoring functions of natural networks for abuse prevention. It is possible, of course, to maintain regular contact with those network associates who are most emotionally affirming and least critical while reducing or limiting contact with those who challenge one's parenting practices, although more evidence on this issue is clearly needed.

For offspring, insularity not only limits their own opportunities for contact with people outside the home (given the manner in which the social networks of parents and children typically overlap), but more limited contact with outsiders may also bias their perceptions of appropriate social behavior and contribute to their impoverished social skills. This is of special concern given Young's (1964) report that abusive parents actively sought to insulate their offspring against outside contact, preventing their children's involvement in neighborhood recreational, educational, and other social activities, forbidding attendance at sports and parties, and in other ways limiting contact with outsiders. As Parke and Collmer (1975) have noted, this is not only likely to inhibit the child's development of social skills and contribute to peer rejection, but also keeps the child at home and thus increases the child's association with the range of other domestic stresses that can heighten the risk of abuse. Insofar as being out of the home may be a protective factor for the offspring of stressed, abuse-prone parents, parental efforts to keep offspring close to home heightens the risk of an abusive encounter. Needless to say, such parental insularity also restricts the opportunities for children to benefit from informal support in the neighborhood and elsewhere.

But although social isolation-qua-limited social embeddedness provides a potentially informative picture of the social ecology of child maltreatment, it is important to note that researchers have failed to elucidate whether maltreating families differ from nonmaltreating families on other, potentially more informative, dimensions of their social networks. We know much less than we should, for example, about how maltreating family members perceive the valence of the relationships they share with different social network members—that is, whether they experience their encounters with extended family, neighbors, friends, and other associates as primarily pleasant, ambivalent, stressful, unpredictable, meaningless, or in other ways (see, however, Corse et al., 1990, and Lovell & Hawkins, 1988). Does their lack of social embeddedness derive, in other words, from uncertainty about their status in the eyes of certain network associates, conflict and stress within these relationships, limited interest and/or motivation to strengthen particular social ties, and/or fears of criticism or rejection? These are important and different reasons for a lack of social embeddedness that existing research has failed to distinguish and examine.

We also require far greater insight into other structural and affiliational features of the natural networks of maltreating families that might help us to understand whether, for example, networks of smaller size are nevertheless characterized by greater multidimensionality (as suggested by Belle's, 1982, analysis of the social networks of lower-income single mothers) or homogeneity. High homogeneity suggests that network associates are likely to share the same stresses, perspectives, and values of high-risk families themselves, which can reduce the likelihood that their support will reduce abuse potential. As Wahler and Hann (1984) have noted, encounters with these network associates may actually exacerbate family stress as mothers share complaints and "war stories" about the unrelenting demands of child rearing rather than fostering constructive problem solving or other forms of tangible assistance.

We also know far less than is needed about how maltreating family members perceive the different support functions that are assumed by their network associates, and how these functions relate to the quality and supportiveness of their relationships with friends, relatives, neighbors, and others they see regularly. Is there a small but reliable group of network members who provide unequivocal emotional sustenance, for example, or are the same friends and relations who provide support also the sources of greatest stress? In the former case, a small network may nevertheless be the source of considerable assistance; in the latter case, the opposite is true. We also know relatively little about how maltreating families regard the neighborhood contexts in which many of these functions are enacted (Polansky, Gaudin, et al., 1985; Starr, 1982; Wolock & Horowitz, 1979).

Researchers must also explore further the possibility (suggested by Smith et al., 1974) that characteristics of the social networks of maltreating mothers (who have been the focus of most research) may differ from those of their spouses, and explore its implications for understanding the ecology of child maltreatment as well as potential avenues for intervention. What does it mean for a socially isolated woman to perceive her spouse as socially embedded in a network that is meaningful and supportive of him, and to what extent do workplace contacts (or the lack of them, for a mother who is rearing offspring at home full-time) account for this difference? We also know very little about how maltreated children and their siblings construct perceptions of *their* social networks and where they regard potential sources of interpersonal support in the social ecologies in which they live.

In short, our research knowledge of the social isolation of maltreating families is breathtakingly shallow given the extent to which social isolation has been assumed to be true of family members who abuse or neglect their offspring.

The emphasis of many of these inquiries for future research is on family members' subjective *perceptions* of their social networks because understanding how they conceive the social resources available to them provides the greatest potential for insight into whether, and how, they experience social isolation and what avenues for changing their social insularity might exist. Indeed, as Polansky and his colleagues have suggested, studying abuse-prone family members' subjective perceptions of social support may be particularly informative because their perceptions of neighborhood support resources might differ from how the same resources are regarded by nonmaltreating parents in the same community (Polansky, Gaudin, et al., 1985). Indeed, studies of recipient reactions to aid, summarized in Chapter 4, would predict this to be true. The existing research literature, summarized above, offers a tantalizing mixture of inconsistent findings concerning how maltreating parents perceive the supportiveness of their network associates, suggesting that further analysis might be fruitfully devoted to revealing the sources of this variability among high-risk parents.

Moreover, such an analysis might reveal resources as well as deficits in the social networks of maltreating families. Exemplary of a balanced approach to network assessment is a study by Tracy (1990) that sought to provide a comprehensive view of the self-perceived social networks of families with children at risk for out-of-home placement, often because of child maltreatment. Tracy reported that, in accord with other research, most network associates consisted of either family or friends, with neighbors and workplace associates each constituting an additional 10% of social network membership. More significantly, respondents were in contact with 42% of their network members either daily or several times a week (by phone or in face-to-face encounters), and reported feeling close to nearly half their network members, who could be relied on to provide concrete support, emotional sustenance, or informational assistance. Most of this help was provided by friends, with whom respondents also reported the greatest reciprocity in their relationships (cf. Fisher et al., 1982). Tracy (1990), however, reported no significant association between total network size and perceived support, suggesting that an extensive social network was not necessarily a supportive one. In comprehensively mapping the social networks of high-risk families in this manner, researchers in the future might achieve a better understanding of the resources on which social support interventions can be built, as well as the deficits to be addressed in assisting maltreating families.

Explanations for Social Isolation

If limited social embeddedness is the crucial constituent of their social isolation, why do maltreating families avoid contact with certain network associates? The pertinent data to address this question are scarce and, in the absence of information concerning other social network dimensions, explanations are necessarily speculative. But several potential reasons can be outlined.

1. Maltreating families may isolate themselves from certain community and kin contacts because they recognize that their behavior is nonnormative and they seek to escape detection. Young (1964) proposed this portrayal of abusive (but not neglectful) families in characterizing 59% of the abusive families she studied as "secretive and suspicious" in avoiding contact with outsiders. Powell (1979) has similarly noted that when families detect significant discrepancies between their child-rearing approaches and community norms, one solution is to avoid contact with neighbors who are likely to recognize and criticize the discrepancy. Relationships with extended kin may also be limited to avoid detection of inappropriate parenting practices—except, of course, when family standards for appropriate parenting are either amorphous or tolerant of assaultive and neglectful behavior (cf. Korbin, 1989, 1991).

2. Maltreated families instead may be isolated by certain community residents and family members for several reasons. Many of their characteristics, including poverty, domestic violence, substance abuse, mental illness, and welfare dependency, are likely to inspire rejection from neighbors and kin quite apart from child abuse or neglect. Moreover, to the extent that some of their problems are associated with poor social skills, maltreating parents present very unattractive prospects for new friendships or strengthened family ties. In addition, their children are likely to be rejected by peers for their atypical behavior, and they may be regarded by adults in the community as asocial, unkempt, delinquent, or simply "strange." Furthermore, encounters with maltreating families may engender salient but ill-defined anxiety in others owing to a perception that "something is very wrong" that may cause certain community and extended family members to avoid contact with them, even (perhaps especially) in the context of suspicions of child abuse. To be sure,

neighbors and kin may share many of the characteristics of these families, such as low socioeconomic status. It is, rather, the combination of several of these characteristics that may distinguish abuse-prone families in their communities and contribute to their being rejected and stigmatized by others.

3. Maltreating families may be unmotivated to strengthen and maintain contact with certain extended family and community residents because they regard them as having little to offer. This perception may occur for several reasons. First, if these families are, indeed, rejected and stigmatized by their kin and neighbors, it may confirm their sense that social support is unavailable within their natural networks. Second, if these families experience aid from certain neighbors, friends, and relatives as humiliating, denigrating, or demeaning, they may make a rational calculus that assistance is too costly when it comes at such a high price to self-esteem and privacy. Consequently, they may not seek enhanced sociability, and may actually reject offers of assistance. Third, the diverse socioeconomic, personal, and child-related stresses experienced by high-risk families may make it very difficult for them to expend the time and energy required to establish and strengthen local social ties. Indeed, they may perceive it as too costly to do so, with few benefits in return, especially for adults whose depression, distress, or other personal problems cause them to underestimate the potential benefits of supportive social relationships. The same calculus may apply to their ties with kin, which do not require establishing new relationships but, instead, strengthening or renewing long-standing family associations. Fourth, maltreating families, like other families in our culture, embrace values of family privacy and noninterference in domestic affairs that may cause them not only to avoid involvement in others' families, but to resent others' interest in their own family situation.

For all these reasons, the motivational underpinnings to strengthening relationships with network members are undermined. This is especially likely if these parents are basically satisfied with their existing social relationships, even in the context of limited contact. As we have seen, this seems to be true for a significant proportion of the high-risk families who have been studied.

4. Finally, maltreating families may be marginal or peripheral community members who are largely ignored by neighbors and other community members. Rather than regarding these families as being

actively rejected by others in the neighborhood, or who purposely avoid contact with outsiders, their limited social embeddedness may derive simply from the fact that there are few natural challenges to a status quo of community marginality brought about by their socio-economic and personal conditions. To some extent, the same may be true of extended kin, who may have little interest in and concern about troubled family members who live far away, or whose personal conditions put them at the periphery of family affairs.

Each of these possible explanations is consistent with the research literature on maltreating families, but choosing among them requires far greater insight into their social ecologies, and their perceptions of those ecologies, than researchers presently possess. This defines an essential research agenda for future progress in our understanding of the social ecology of child maltreatment. However, there are two ambitious programs of research that have helped to elucidate the social conditions of abuse-prone families and that provide a basis for comparing and evaluating the foregoing explanations of social isolation. The first is the research by Norman Polansky and his associates on neglectful families and their neighborhoods; the second is research on the community context of child maltreatment by James Garbarino and his colleagues.

Polansky's Studies of Child Neglect

In a series of studies of neglectful families conducted in Appalachia, Philadelphia, and urban and rural settings in Georgia, Polansky and his colleagues (e.g., Polansky, Ammons, et al., 1985; Polansky et al., 1981; Polansky, Gaudin, et al., 1985) have sought to describe the personal and ecological characteristics that contribute to neglect in lower-income families. More unique among investigators in this field, Polansky has adopted the view of a personality theorist in arguing that enduring character disorders assume a major role in the loneliness and social isolation experienced by neglectful families (Polansky et al., 1981). He does not deny the importance of the socioeconomic stresses and neighborhood dysfunction that other investigators (especially Garbarino) have emphasized in their accounts of child maltreatment. However, Polansky has argued that what distinguishes neglectful from nonneglectful families in these settings—and what biases their perceptions of their social networks, impairs their capacity to enlist others in supportive ways, and alters the responses of network members to them—are long-standing personality problems of early origin.

In particular, Polansky argues that a high proportion of neglectful mothers use psychological defenses involving detachment to cope with the demands and stresses of their life circumstances, and this defensive style originates in the mothers' own early histories of inadequate parental care. Polansky has identified an "apathy-futility syndrome" that can account for the passive, withdrawn demeanor of these mothers and that is characterized by (a) "a pervasive conviction that nothing is worth doing," (b) emotional "numbness" that is sometimes mistaken for depression, (c) limited competence in many areas of living, (d) lack of commitment to positive standards, and (e) verbal "inaccessibility" to others, as well as other maladaptive features. Other neglectful mothers are instead characterized by an "impulse-ridden character" that limits self-monitoring and self-control in many aspects of their behavior. Polansky's neglectful mothers (like Elmer's, 1967, maltreating families, but contrary to those studied by Wolock and Horowitz's, 1979, neglectful sample) were also characterized by anomie, that is, distrust of and retreat from society. Character disorders are very difficult to treat in even the best of therapeutic regimes, but Polansky argues that the social worker's role is necessarily a quasi-therapeutic one while also trying to limit the effects of the parent's psychopathology on children (Polansky et al., 1981).

In more recent research, Polansky and his colleagues have closely examined how neglectful mothers perceive their neighborhoods, and have compared their perceptions with those of their nonneglectful neighbors with somewhat startling results (Polansky, Ammons, et al., 1985; Polansky, Gaudin, et al., 1985). Polansky found that neglectful mothers perceived themselves as being significantly more lonely than did a comparison group of mothers, matched for socioeconomic status and other variables, who lived in the same communities. In contrast to the comparison mothers, neglectful mothers also perceived their neighborhoods as less friendly (contrary to what Starr, 1982, and Wolock and Horowitz, 1979, have reported) and their neighbors as less helpful, and they reported that there was less instrumental assistance and emotional support available to them. When the neighbors of these two groups of mothers were interviewed, however, much different perceptions of the same communities were revealed: There were no differences between neighbors of neglectful mothers and neighbors of comparison mothers in their perceptions of the friendliness of the neighborhood, the helpfulness of neighbors, or the availability of emotional and instrumental support. The difference was not in the neighborhood, in other words, but in how neighborhood stresses and resources were perceived by abuse-prone mothers. In short, neglectful mothers' views that neighbors were unsupportive and unfriendly were unique, and were not confirmed in the judgments of others who lived nearby. Rather than reflecting objective features of "neighborhoods at risk," these perceptions were significantly colored by neglectful mothers' own backgrounds, needs, and experiences.

Furthermore, when neighbors were asked about their own social networks, informal analyses of their responses indicated that neglectful mothers were less likely than comparison mothers to be regarded as someone to whom neighbors could turn for assistance, and instead were more likely to be viewed as someone who "need[s] help in raising their children" and "it would not pay to call on." Indeed, neglectful mothers reported that they helped others who lived nearby less often than did comparison mothers. There was also evidence in these responses that the offspring of neglectful mothers were being ostracized in their neighborhoods. Polansky concluded that neglectful families had become identified in their communities as families requiring assistance but not offering it, and their failure to reciprocate led to the stigmatizing of parents and offspring alike.

These findings are fairly complex and require replication not only because of the rather informal manner in which they are reported, but also because some of these findings differ from other research on neglectful families described above. But Polansky's research contributes to a portrayal of neglectful families as neighborhood members who experience a cascading series of difficulties that result in their progressive isolation within the community. The origins of their social difficulties may derive from long-standing character disorders, as Polansky argues, or instead from lack of social skills or competence (cf. Seagull, 1987), overwhelming life stress, limited coping capacities, or for other reasons. In any case, the adults in these families are needy individuals who are quickly recognized as such by neighbors. But they become distinguished from others within the community also by their inability or unwillingness to reciprocate the assistance offered them within the neighborhood. Consequently, parents and their offspring become stigmatized and excluded from the local network of supportive relations, and this probably contributes to their discordant perceptions of neighborhood friendliness and helpfulness compared to the views of others who live nearby. It is easy to see how this would diminish their incentives to develop relationships with neighbors. Moreover, their motivation to enhance and strengthen social ties within the neighborhood is likely to be further diminished by the humiliation that grudging assistance from neighbors in these contexts may involve. Whether or not Polansky is correct that it is not neighborhood structure per se that distinguishes the social ecologies of neglectful families from nonneglectful families (see Garbarino's research below), it is certainly true that their perceptions of their communities are markedly more negative than those of nonmaltreating families living in the same area.

The important and evocative features of Polansky's account of child neglect consist largely of his portrayal of an escalating series of characterological, situational, socioeconomic, and relational problems experienced by these families that leads, together with the "social distancing" of neighbors (cf. Gaudin & Polansky, 1986; Polansky & Gaudin, 1983), to their progressive isolation within the community. It is important to note, however, that Polansky's research does not assess other features of social network ties—particularly relationships with coworkers, friends outside of the immediate neighborhood, and extended kin—that may be important alternative sources of social support for these families. This remains an important limitation to this work, especially in light of studies reviewed earlier that the social networks of lower-income families are smaller and are more kin focused—and less neighborhood based—than for other kinds of families (cf. Cochran, Gunnarsson, et al., 1990; Fischer, 1982; Vaux, 1988). Lovell and Hawkins (1988), for example, in another study of maltreating mothers, indicated that mothers reported that neighbors constituted only about 10% of their network associates. As a consequence, important sources of nonneighborhood-based social support may exist for maltreating families that Polansky has not included in his description of their social isolation. Nevertheless, this research provides one of the most richly elaborated characterizations of the social isolation of maltreating families that exists in the literature, and thus should provide the basis for follow-up research inquiry.

Garbarino's Studies of the
Social Ecology of Child Maltreatment

By contrast, the work of Garbarino and his colleagues has focused on the social ecology of the neighborhoods of maltreating families, particularly abusive ones. In a series of conceptual analyses, Garbarino (1977a, 1977b, 1980; Garbarino & Gilliam, 1980) has argued that child abuse requires at least three ecological conditions: (a) a cultural context that condones domestic violence in general and violence toward children in particular, (b) families that experience stress in their life circumstances combined with isolation from important support systems that might buffer or protect them, and (c) consensual values concerning family autonomy and parental "ownership" of children. Although each is a critical component of the conditions leading to abuse, Garbarino has focused on the second in creative research efforts examining the neighborhood ecology of child maltreatment.

In a series of pioneering studies, Garbarino and his colleagues (Garbarino, 1976; Garbarino & Crouter, 1978; Garbarino & Sherman, 1980a) used social indicators data for specific counties in New York, neighborhoods in Omaha, Nebraska, and communities in Chicago to examine the associations between reports of child maltreatment and information concerning income, education, residential patterns and housing, neighborhood development, community attitudes, and sources of social support, especially as they affected mothers in these communities. Not surprisingly, socioeconomic indexes were very strong predictors of reports of child maltreatment in New York, but beyond these, other important predictors were the proportion of women in the labor force with children under age 18, the median income of households headed by females, and various measures of educational attainment (Garbarino, 1976). In Omaha, socioeconomic factors together with variables reflecting maternal stress'and high geographic mobility were potent predictors of child maltreatment (Garbarino & Crouter, 1978). In both studies, between 36% and 81% of the variance in child maltreatment rates between neighborhoods (i.e., not necessarily between families or individuals) was explained by these measures. These relationships have been substantively replicated by several other investigators (Coulton, Korbin, Su, & Chow, in press; Deccio et al., 1991; Young & Gately, 1988; see Zuravin, 1989, for a review). Taken together, they indicate that a series of demographic indicators—including socioeconomic indexes, but also including measures of maternal stress related to child care and family well-being—could predict very strongly the abuse proneness of neighborhoods where high-risk families resided. The quality of neighborhoods is a predictor of their proneness to abuse.

In follow-up research, Garbarino and Sherman (1980a) used the results of this research to identify socioeconomically comparable high-risk and low-risk neighborhoods in the Omaha area (see Garbarino & Sherman, 1980b). A high-risk neighborhood was one in which the actual rate of maltreatment was higher than expected, based on the socioeconomic indexes revealed in the previous studies; a low-risk neighborhood had a lower-than-expected rate of maltreatment. "Expert informants" in these neighborhoods (e.g., public health nurses, elementary school principals, mail carriers, Girl Scout leaders, police, clergy, staff of the city planning department) as well as randomly selected local residents were interviewed in detail to discover differences in the supportive and stressful features of daily life in each neighborhood. In addition, nonabusive mothers from each type of community were also interviewed to assess their perceptions of the neighborhoods in which they lived.

In a partial report of these data, Garbarino and Sherman (1980a) noted that mothers in high-risk and low-risk neighborhoods differed significantly in their perceptions of neighborhood "exchanges": Mothers in high-risk neighborhoods were more likely not to ask for assistance from neighbors. Garbarino and Sherman interpreted this difference to reflect the limited reciprocity of assistance in high-risk neighborhoods that has been noted also by other researchers. Mothers in high-risk and low-risk neighborhoods differed also in their reports of the social networks of offspring: Larger networks were reported for children in low-risk neighborhoods. What is interesting, however, is that there were no significant differences in maternal perceptions of sources of help for meeting life demands, which included assessments of the helpers on whom they could draw (e.g., family, coworkers, friends, and neighbors), the helpful responsiveness of these people, and mothers' overall satisfaction with the help provided.

Finally, on a measure of family stresses and supports, mothers from high-risk and low-risk neighborhoods differed significantly in their perceptions of child care availability (i.e., more options in low-risk neighborhoods) and the suitability of the neighborhood as a place for raising children (i.e., viewed less positively in high-risk neighborhoods), but they did not differ in perceptions of the quality of child care, the friendliness of neighbors, recreational opportunities, and assistance in child rearing provided by family, friends, and neighbors. In short, although mothers in high-risk neighborhoods differed in their perceptions of important social resources from mothers in low-risk neighborhoods, each group had comparable assessments of sources of potential social support. In a replication of this investigation in Spokane, Washington, Deccio et al. (1991) likewise found that parents in high-risk and low-risk neighborhoods differed in basic resources such as their access to a telephone and residential stability, but they did not differ significantly in either the personal support or the parenting support that they reported receiving from local network associates.

Taken together, this series of studies provides a vivid portrayal of the kind of "social impoverishment" (Garbarino & Kostelny, 1991) that may contribute to heightened rates of child abuse in high-risk neighborhoods. It is apparent that when seeking to explain why certain neighborhoods (rather than individuals) are more abuse prone than others, very powerful predictive models can be created based on several socioeconomic indicators. These underscore the links between socioeconomic status and child maltreatment, but further this understanding by identifying some of the unique attributes of especially risky lower-income neighborhoods. In particular, poverty combined with maternal stressors seems to be especially salient in predicting maltreatment.

The work of Garbarino, as well as others (e.g., Coulton et al., in press; Furstenberg, 1993; Zuravin, 1989), is consistent with emerging models of community social disorganization that have been used to explain neighborhood criminality, juvenile delinquency, and other local problems (cf. Sampson, 1992). From this perspective, high-risk neighborhoods lack the "social capital"—that is, the integrated, structured, mutually supportive relations between individuals within a community—necessary for productive activity and growth. In communities denoted by economic impoverishment, distrust between neighbors, a high proportion of single mothers, little awareness or use of local services, and concerns about the neighborhood as a child-rearing environment, limited social capital exists for the community to function supportively or effectively.

These processes are evocatively depicted in research by Furstenberg (1993) and his colleagues, who have described, in a series of in-depth case studies, the strategies of parents raising children in communities that vary in their resources, support, and challenges. As they have summarized their initial conclusions:

> We see in transitional neighborhoods a shift from collective to individualistic strategies of family management. Fewer parents are willing to delegate authority to formal institutions that have lost their credibility and command of external resources. Informal networks become attenuated as kin and close friends move out and are replaced by new residents who are regarded as outsiders. The perception of normative consensus in the community diminishes accordingly. As parents come to believe that their standards for child rearing are not shared by others, they begin to distrust other families nearby.
>
> These changes at the community level help to bring about the disengagement of the family from the community. The family becomes less and less embedded in formal and informal structures that reinforce parental standards. Other adults in the community are no longer relied on to supervise and sponsor children. And systems of formal and informal control are attenuated. As the family becomes separated from the community, parents resort to more individualistic strategies of managing the external world. They are disinclined to delegate authority to other parents or, reciprocally, to assume responsibility for other children. (Furstenberg, 1993, p. 253)

In this respect, at-risk communities that are characterized by limited social capital, diminished resources, and heightened perceptions of danger breed at-risk parents who experience social insularity, distrust, and confinement within these neighborhoods.

These neighborhood depictions provide an insightful portrayal of the community stresses and lack of resources that can undermine effective parenting. They are only partially helpful, however, in identifying why certain *families* are more abuse prone than others within these neighborhoods, especially because most parents within high-risk and low-risk communities do not abuse their offspring. Distinguishing the predictors of maltreatment for families within communities that vary in the social capital they offer is especially important in view of the rather mixed perceptions of high-risk and low-risk neighborhood residents of the stressful and supportive features of their communities. It is important also because there may be different

predictors of abuse potential within high-risk and low-risk neighborhoods. For families in neighborhoods that are drained of their social
capital, it may be the very limited social embeddedness of parents
who are essentially confined to their homes because of their fear and
distrust of neighborhood residents that contributes most to the risk of
maltreatment, along with socioeconomic and other enduring stresses,
as Garbarino and his colleagues have suggested. For families in other
neighborhoods that offer greater resources, different factors—such as
the lack of consensus about the appropriate treatment of children—
may be most predictive of child maltreatment. Further exploration of
these issues awaits future research.

Furthermore, like the research of Polansky, this series of studies
emphasizes social support networks that are neighborhood based,
and thus provides much less insight into extended support systems
organized around coworkers, nonneighborhood friendships, and family members. In the Omaha research, Garbarino gathered data concerning citywide support services and discovered that families in
high-risk neighborhoods had less awareness and made less use of these
services than did families in low-risk neighborhoods (Garbarino, personal communication, 1992). This suggests that the intersection of
local neighborhoods and broader community support structures requires further exploration. So also does the intersection of neighborhood and kin networks. As Garbarino himself has noted, neighborhoods do not create abuse, but this research provides a provocative
picture of their contributions.

Conclusions

What, then, have we learned from these studies about the origins
of the social isolation of maltreating families? Given our impoverished understanding of the nature of their insularity itself—that is,
uncertainty about which features of their social networks beyond
social embeddedness distinguish maltreating families from others—it
is difficult to draw more than provocative hypotheses from these
interesting studies. In other words, a variety of processes could account for the lack of social embeddedness experienced by maltreating
families, including their own efforts to escape detection and criticism
from certain members of their communities and their families, their
rejection and stigmatization by certain network members, their un-

dermined motivation to establish and maintain supportive relationships owing to social stigma, reactions to receiving aid, stress and/or privacy concerns, their marginality in the community and among extended kin, their social pathology and limited social skills, the sheer danger of the housing projects and other neighborhoods within which they may live, or other reasons. Existing research does not yet provide a basis for establishing which of these alternative explanations are preeminently or insignificantly influential in the insularity of maltreating families.

However, these studies do permit a few tentative conclusions. First, it seems likely that single-factor accounts—such as attributing their social isolation to the character disorders of maltreating families, the social impoverishment of their neighborhoods, economic stresses, or other factors—will prove inadequate, both because social insularity is likely to have multiple origins in the life experience of any high-risk family, and because different, overlapping causes run across the diverse population of abuse-prone families. In this respect, Seagull's (1987) conclusions are basically correct but are too limited: Social isolation characterizes some, but not all, maltreating families; for some, but not all, it derives from character disorders. In the end, diversity, rather than uniformity, probably characterizes the necessary portrayal of the social isolation of abuse-prone families, recognizing the multiple personal and ecological influences that are pertinent to child abuse and neglect. Multicausal longitudinal process models are a conceptual as well as an empirical necessity in future research designed to elucidate these diverse, interacting influences on social insularity.

Second, it is possible that different processes account for (a) the initial behaviors and characteristics that distinguish early on these families as different within their families and neighborhoods, and (b) the perpetuation of their social stigma and their progressive insularity from certain kinds of family and community support. In other words, a somewhat different web of personal and ecological forces may be influential in creating and subsequently maintaining a family's proneness to child maltreatment. Therefore, in this temporal aspect, it is again unwise to assume that the social insularity of maltreating families is unicausal, especially when their multiple problems and history of neighborhood residence is considered. Moreover, different risk factors may become preeminent at different stages of the family life course, such that the difficulties most pertinent to a young mother giving birth to her first child may be much different from those that apply when her child has become a preadolescent, siblings have been born, and a broader network of personal and ecological factors affect her and her offspring. It will again take detailed longitudinal studies, probably initially in the form of case study accounts, for researchers to begin to unravel these changing influences over the course of family history.

Third, and finally, there is suggestive evidence that the origins of the social isolation of physically neglectful and physically abusive families may have reliably different causes. As Young (1964) suggested more than 30 years ago, neglectful families may become isolated largely because of their limited social competence, overwhelming stresses, and diminished motivation to find rewards in contact with outsiders, which are combined with substance abuse problems and mental disorders for a major proportion of neglectful families. Abusive families, by contrast, may be more actively (rather than passively) socially insulated, with their isolation deriving from avoidance and suspicion of others, combined with conflict with potentially supportive agents in the neighborhood and extended family. This hypothesis must remain conjectural, however, in view of the very limited data addressing these differences.

Beyond this, there are few reliable conclusions that can be drawn concerning the origins of the social isolation of maltreating families. Far too much important research remains to be done.

6

Strategies for Intervention

It would be an ideal—but highly unusual—set of circumstances if all the necessary information was available before program planners needed to design intervention strategies. In the case of preventing child maltreatment, unfortunately, it appears that enough has been learned about social support as a preventive strategy only to reveal how much more must be known, and thoughtfully considered, in designing effective interventions.

We have seen, for example, that efforts to enlist formal or natural helpers into the lives of high-risk families to provide support must take into account the complexities of natural social networks, the multidimensionality of social support, and the various predictors of whether social networks will actually be supportive, and whether such support will actually reduce the risk of maltreatment. Moreover, the preceding chapter showed that the conventional portrayal of abuse-prone families as socially isolated is both nonspecific and incomplete: nonspecific because it implies a comprehensive lack of natural network ties that does not appear to be well-supported by pertinent research, and incomplete because it fails to address the potential strengths and resources of their network associations on which well-designed social support interventions might rely. The conclusion of the preceding chapter was that abuse-prone families are probably quite diverse in the support they experience, with some fitting conventional portrayals of social insularity (but doing so for many different reasons), others experiencing considerable support from their natural networks (that is nevertheless often ineffective in reducing their abuse potential), and others falling somewhere in between. Understanding the heterogeneity of the population of parents who abuse or neglect their offspring—matched by the diversity of the neighborhood and kin networks on which they rely—is perhaps one of the most important challenges to future researchers.

A national problem of the scope and significance of child abuse cannot await the final conclusions of follow-up research, however, before programs must be designed to protect children by reducing their risk within their families. Whether to accomplish primary, secondary, or tertiary prevention goals, efforts to assist children and their troubled families must include the best available research evidence, however incomplete, into the design of intervention programs. And despite the numerous caveats on the conclusions of the preceding chapter, it does appear that an appreciable proportion of abuse-prone families experience some form of social insularity. Although the reasons for their limited social embeddedness may vary, and its association with their proneness to maltreatment is not consistently clear, the lack of social support, monitoring, and regulation of parenting behavior provided by regular interaction with a broad range of network associates presents one potentially valuable target for intervention efforts to prevent child abuse.

Moreover, whether social isolation characterizes family life or whether it is directly associated with child maltreatment, it seems likely that high-risk parents and their offspring would benefit from thoughtfully crafted programs that are designed to increase the amount of social support they receive, either from formal agents or from informal helpers in their natural networks. Although enhancing social support is clearly not a panacea for the multiple problems experienced by many abuse-prone families, broadly defined and carefully crafted efforts to enhance support seem likely to address some of their most important needs related to family functioning and parental competence. It can enhance parents' access to counseling and parenting information, monitor children's well-being, provide modeling and reinforcement of appropriate parenting practices, and aid in integrating family members into broader community networks that may offer long-term assistance. Well-crafted social support programs can also enhance family members' access to resources in the neighborhood that address some of their other needs, such as welfare assistance, child care, job training, and educational assistance. Therefore, as long as expectations for success are appropriately constrained by limitations in knowledge and an awareness of the multiple problems facing abuse-prone families, it seems worthwhile to seek to enhance supportive efforts on behalf of abuse-prone families at the same time that researchers seek a better understanding of the social ecology of child maltreatment.

This chapter makes the leap between research and practice by reviewing two strategies for enhancing social support, each designed to address the complex problems of high-risk families who are the typical focus of abuse prevention efforts. The approaches are home visitation strategies that strive to accomplish secondary (and sometimes primary) prevention goals by providing support to young mothers, and intensive family preservation strategies that indirectly seek to accomplish tertiary prevention goals by providing a range of supportive services to families that are at risk of having a child removed from the home because of abuse, delinquency, or other signs of family dysfunction. By looking closely at research that evaluates the strengths and weaknesses of each strategy, it may be possible to identify important constituents of effective social support interventions across the range of prevention efforts.

To be sure, home visitation and intensive family preservation approaches are only two of many possible alternative strategies of social support for preventing abuse that have been tried. There are many alternatives (see Bryant, 1993, and Garbarino & Kostelny, 1994, for further details), including:

- School-based programs (such as the Family Resource Centers established by the state of Kentucky, or Minnesota's Early Childhood and Family Education programs) that provide a community clearinghouse for family assistance that may include preschool education, child development education for expectant and young mothers, parent support activities, home visits, training for child care providers, health screening for children, and health and social service referrals for client families.
- Teen-oriented support programs (such as California's Adolescent and Family Life Program) that offer parent education and counseling, peer support, home visits, and social service referrals to pregnant and parenting adolescents. Many of these programs are based in schools where child care can be provided and adolescents encouraged to continue their education.
- Substance abuse programs that are designed for mothers who screen positive for illicit drugs after delivery and their drug-exposed offspring (such as Maryland's Reaching Families Early program), and

that provide drug treatment and parent education, together with referrals to community agencies, immunizations and well-child care, home
visits, and regular follow-up assessments of client families.

- Preschool programs for lower-income families that, modeled on the
  federal Head Start program, offer preschool education that involves
  parents, together with parent education programs, home visits, and
  health and developmental screening for children.

- Big Brother and Big Sister programs that provide at-risk children
  with the support and assistance of adults outside the home (but
  within the community).

- Community-based day care programs (such as California's Parent
  Services Project) that support parents with available and affordable
  high-quality respite and regular child care services while offering
  peer counseling and parent education to adults.

- Long-term parental support groups (such as Minnesota's Early
  Learning Demonstration program, or the Avance program in Texas)
  that use a guided peer self-help strategy to provide parent education, child development information, family management, and
  other kinds of support. Specialized programs have been created for
  adolescent mothers, fathers, minority families, and the parents of
  special needs children.

Each of these strategies has considerable merit and is worth
further development and examination. However, there are several
reasons for focusing in detail on home visitation and intensive family
preservation programs as models of social support interventions.
First, home visitation is a primary prevention strategy for abuse
prevention that has been extensively evaluated in several demonstration projects entailing different target populations, program designs,
and personnel. As a consequence, the factors predicting the success of
this strategy for preventing child maltreatment can be more sensitively appraised than other primary prevention strategies, whose
success in actually preventing abuse is seldom systematically evaluated (Thompson & Wilcox, in press). Second, although intensive
family preservation programs are primarily concerned with preventing foster care placements, rather than abuse, they offer a thoughtful
model of how tertiary prevention approaches involving social support might be designed with abuse prevention goals. Moreover, like
home visitation programs, intensive family preservation programs
also have been comprehensively evaluated in different sites and with
different client populations, so the strengths and weaknesses of different program features can be appraised. Third, each approach incor-
porates social support, broadly defined, into a range of other forms of

assistance to abuse-prone families to strengthen their collective benefits to recipients. As such, they exemplify the conclusion of preceding chapters that social support must be incorporated into other interventions designed to address other family needs, and they show how this might be accomplished.

Home Visitation

In many respects, recent enthusiasm for home visitation approaches to preventing child maltreatment reflects the ideal of instituting, in a formal support program, the kind of everyday assistance by natural helpers that is believed to be lacking in the lives of abuse-prone parents. By going to the recipient's home and offering many kinds of supportive assistance, home visitors hope to compensate for the absence of this aid from neighbors, friends, and extended kin. Although home visitation is a fairly new idea in the United States, it is extensively integrated into the fabric of social services in many European countries to aid in child health screening and perinatal care (General Accounting Office [GAO], 1990; Kamerman & Kahn, 1993; Wasik, Bryant, & Lyons, 1990).

What Is Home Visitation?

At a minimum, a well-conceived home visitation program entails regular contact between a home visitor and the family, during which the visitor talks with the parent(s), listens to their problems, offers advice about child development and child-rearing issues, connects the family to other resources in the community, monitors the child (or children) for signs of maltreatment that may be occurring, and tailors other interventions to the specific constellation of needs and challenges of that particular family. Such assistance may be offered by a paid professional or a lay volunteer; it may include health screening, parent education, social networking, and/or referrals to other community agencies; it may begin before the birth of the child or later; and it may last for a few months or for several years. Central to this strategy, however, is that home visitation programs seek to assist families in their home environments rather than requiring travel to a medical clinic or community center, and they try to provide a variety of forms of assistance that are tailored to the family's unique needs.

One of the special advantages of the home visitation strategy is that it reduces some of the natural obstacles to families otherwise receiving these services: By providing assistance in the home, a home visitor can surmount the difficulties with transportation, lack of health insurance, distrust of formal service providers, and lack of motivation that often undermine the access of high-risk families to these services elsewhere.

There is considerable diversity in the orientation and scope of home visitation programs (Wasik et al., 1990). For example, home visitation may involve one or more orientations to the assistance offered by the visitor, based on different program models.

Some home visitation programs employ a *social support* model, in which the visitor's efforts are focused on providing counseling, emotional reassurance, friendly advice, parenting guidance, concrete aid (e.g., help with transportation, shopping, etc.), and other kinds of assistance to enhance the emotional well-being and coping skills of the parent (cf. Olds & Kitzman, 1990). In addition to these services, home visitors seek to monitor the child's well-being and guide the development of parenting behaviors in ways that will support the child's healthy growth. Home visitors within a social support model often draw on their personal experiences of parenting to provide helpful advice, as well as seeking to enlist the assistance of others in the family's natural networks. The overall goal of this approach to home visitation, therefore, is to provide the family with many kinds of supportive assistance that will ease the transition to parenting (for first-time parents), strengthen parental competencies and/or coping, and otherwise contribute to family well-being by reducing the family's limited social embeddedness.

Other home visitation programs employ a *health maintenance* model in which the home visitor's focus is on fostering healthy practices in parents and conducting health and developmental screenings of offspring. Home visitors may also directly provide routine health care for children at home (such as immunizations), ensure that parents obtain regular physical exams and medical care for offspring at local clinics, help parents monitor and treat routine child illnesses, and enable parents to more effectively care for their offspring through instruction in breast-feeding, nutrition, bathing, taking temperatures, treating minor ailments, and accident prevention, and also take better care of themselves by reducing drinking, smoking, and substance abuse, improving diet, and in other ways.

The focus on health maintenance in home visitation to prevent abuse has three bases. The first is a recognition that child maltreatment is often undetected until its effects have become severe, owing partly to the parent's social insularity and failure to obtain regular medical examinations for offspring. Second, some parents experience problems in child care owing to their own ignorance, inexperience, or confusion about children's nutritional, medical, and other developmental needs. Finally, children who are abused or neglected are often medically or psychologically compromised: low-birthweight and/or premature infants, colicky or temperamentally difficult babies, and children with medical problems are overrepresented among maltreatment populations because these children are difficult to care for and contribute significant additional stress to parents who may already experience many other life difficulties (Parke & Collmer, 1975). Home visitation with a health maintenance orientation addresses all of these issues by monitoring the child's physical and psychological well-being, providing instruction to parents about the child's needs, and assisting with the special needs or challenges of offspring.

A third model guiding home visitation is the *parent education* model, in which the focus of intervention is not just the child's physical well-being but also the child's cognitive and socioemotional growth. By instructing parents about the child's developmental needs, the home visitor seeks to shape parents' expectations for child behavior to accord with the child's age and other characteristics (such as temperament). The primary goal of these efforts, like that of the health maintenance model, is to combat the ignorance or misunderstanding that can sometimes underlie maltreatment, strengthen parental knowledge and sympathetic understanding of children's needs, and enhance parental pride and self-confidence in the growth and achievements of offspring. It differs from the health maintenance model primarily in the broader scope of developmental concerns that are the focus of the visitor's attention and, consequently, the varying strategies that are used to influence parental behavior and enhance the child's well-being. The visitor may observe informally how the parent and child interact together and use these observations as the basis for constructive suggestions and guidance. The visitor may model, and help parents to emulate, interactions that foster the child's healthy cognitive and socioemotional development. Depending on the child's age, this might involve teaching simple infant games, demonstrating modes of feeding that ensure that the baby eats adequately, modeling alternative strategies of child management and discipline, reinforcing teaching methods that parents can use, and/or highlighting signs of the child's growing skill and well-being.

Finally, some home visitation approaches employ an *ecological* model (cf. Olds & Kitzman, 1990) that, although incorporating aspects of the social support, health maintenance, and parent education approaches, additionally emphasizes strengthening the family's ties to the neighborhood and community. The primary purpose of doing so is to enhance parents' access to the variety of medical, educational, vocational, recreational, and other resources that are beyond the scope of even the most ambitious home visitor to provide. To enhance community ties, the home visitor acts as a mediator by informing the parent of public and private services for which they are eligible; contacting administrators of these agencies on behalf of the family concerning eligibility requirements, program access, and related matters; seeking sources of financial assistance for the family; and assisting in transportation to clinics, community centers, and other locations. In a well-designed, ecologically based program, moreover, the home visitor seeks not only to ensure the family's knowledge of these neighborhood resources, but to strengthen ties between parents and community personnel to heighten the likelihood that they will be a long-term resource to the family.

Although these approaches to home visitation differ somewhat in their focus and orientation, it should be clear that they share much in common, and are complementary rather than incompatible in their overall philosophy and strategy. This provides considerable flexibility in tailoring home visitation approaches to the unique needs of the recipient population, and the specific resources of the community, to offer the most effective assistance. Moreover, because abuse-prone families are often multiproblem families, a combination of program features is most likely to address their diverse needs. Thus, many home visitation programs incorporate elements of several different program designs into a comprehensive intervention.

Two Exemplary Programs

One reflection of the diversity of program design, but with the consistency of goals and strategy of home visitation efforts, are two programs that have been most carefully evaluated for their success in preventing abuse and neglect. The Elmira Prenatal/Early Infancy

Project and the Hawaii Healthy Start Program each have inspired the greatest hope that a thoughtfully conceived, carefully instituted home visitation program can succeed in accomplishing abuse-prevention goals. For this reason, and also because they offer program models that apply some of the conclusions of the social support research reviewed in earlier chapters, each program is described in detail.

The Elmira Prenatal/Early Infancy Project

The Elmira project was an experimental home visitation demonstration and evaluation project inaugurated by Dr. David Olds of the University of Rochester and his colleagues, with funding support from federal and private agencies (see Olds, 1988; Olds & Henderson, 1989; Olds, Henderson, Chamberlin, & Tatelbaum, 1986; Olds, Henderson, Tatelbaum, & Chamberlin, 1986; Olds & Kitzman, 1993; see also General Accounting Office [GAO], 1992). Based primarily on an ecological model of home visitation, together with important social support, parent education, and health maintenance components, the project consisted of an intensive program of home visits conducted by highly trained nurses who offered a variety of services to high-risk mothers and their offspring beginning prenatally and lasting for 2 years after the child's birth. The home visits centered on providing parent education, enhancing the social support offered by friends and extended family members, and connecting the family with community service providers. A rigorous evaluation of the results of the intervention followed, based on a randomized trial design comparing the outcomes of high-risk families who had been randomly assigned to different experimental groups, including one receiving intensive home visitation services. Outcome measures included assessments of the frequency of emergency room visits, measures of parent-child interaction, the health practices of mothers, and maternal employment and subsequent pregnancies, as well as substantiated child abuse or neglect reports. Olds and his colleagues reported not only a meaningful reduction in the rate of child maltreatment among the high-risk sample receiving intensive home visitation services, but also improvements in parent-child interaction, reductions in emergency room visits, and improvements in mothers' own health care and employment. These benefits were especially apparent in subgroups most at risk for child maltreatment.

This study was conducted in a small, semirural community in the Appalachian area of New York State, which was chosen because it had one of the highest rates of child abuse and neglect in the state. The target population consisted of first-time mothers who were less than 19 years old, a single parent, or of low socioeconomic status because of the relation between these risk factors and child maltreatment. However, any woman in the area who was a first-time parent was invited to participate in the program to avoid the stigma for project participants of being perceived as needing special assistance, and consequently, the study included some women (about 15% of the total sample) who were not necessarily at serious risk of abusing or neglecting offspring. Olds and his colleagues have argued that by avoiding the stigmatizing consequences of more restrictive eligibility requirements, high-risk mothers who might otherwise have avoided participating in the project were recruited, and their attrition rate was kept reasonably low. Women were recruited through the public health department clinic, private obstetric offices, Planned Parenthood, the public schools, and various other health and human service agencies. All of those who participated were enrolled in the project before their 30th week of pregnancy.

Once enrolled in the project, the women were randomly assigned to one of four treatment conditions (with approximately 90 or more women in each group) for the duration of the study, which lasted from pregnancy through the child's second birthday.

- Women in Group 1 constituted a control group that received no services through the research project; however, as part of their participation in the study, their infants received sensory and developmental screening on their first and second birthdays.
- Women in Group 2 received, in addition to the developmental screening, free transportation to and from their regular prenatal and well-child clinic visits throughout the period of the research, but no other services. Thus, health maintenance was fostered, but without home visitation.
- For women in Group 3, in addition to screening and transportation, a nurse provided home visitation during pregnancy but not after the baby's birth. Nurses visited the home approximately once every 2 weeks, for a period of slightly more than an hour each occasion, and focused on concerns related to fetal and infant development, as well as fostering the involvement of family members and friends in the pregnancy and enlisting outside community resources.

■ Women in Group 4 received, in addition to screening, transportation, and prenatal nurse visits, regular visits from the same nurse throughout the first 2 years of the baby's life. These visits occurred weekly for the first 6 weeks following delivery, then every 2 weeks to age 4 months, and eventually tapered off to visits every 6 weeks by the end of the child's second year. Visits lasted slightly more than an hour each time and, for some families, more frequent visits were arranged when family needs and circumstances warranted.

The prenatal and postnatal home visits had three primary goals. The first was parent education: The nurse sought to answer questions and provide information concerning the child's growth and developmental needs and about parental practices that could affect maternal and/or child well-being. The nurse encouraged mothers to improve their diets, for example, and to eliminate cigarette, alcohol, and drug use; helped mothers understand the infant's temperament and especially the meaning of the baby's crying; provided information concerning the baby's socioemotional and cognitive needs, including the importance of responsive caregiving; demonstrated physical health care for the baby, such as feeding and bathing, taking the child's temperature and monitoring common health problems, and ensuring the child's safety, immunizations, and regular health examinations; and encouraged mothers to consider their own future development (e.g., completing their education, finding work, securing appropriate child care, and/or reducing future pregnancies through effective contraception). Most of the nurses' time during home visits was devoted to parent education.

A second goal was social support, primarily by enhancing informal support provided by extended family members, neighbors, or friends. Nurses encouraged the mother's close friends and relatives (including the husband or boyfriend, and/or her parents) to attend the home visits, assist with household responsibilities, help with delivery and the subsequent care of the baby, and constructively reinforce the advice and guidance provided by the nurse herself.

The third goal was to enhance the mother's ties to formal service providers. Nurses facilitated the mother's regular prenatal and well-child clinic visits, encouraged mothers to contact the obstetrician or pediatrician when health concerns arose, and provided referrals to other health and human services, such as legal aid, mental health counseling, Planned Parenthood, and WIC programs. In advancing each of these three primary goals, nurses were also guided by their own objectives, specific to each family, as well as by a detailed curriculum developed by Olds and his colleagues.

The nurses who conducted home visitation had backgrounds in maternal and child health, and all had children of their own. Nurses received a 3-month training program that included detailed instruction as well as practicum training. They were required to keep detailed notes concerning each of their home visits, had day-to-day supervision, and participated in weekly case reviews to ensure that the program's home visitation goals were advanced consistently and that nurses could discuss problems or challenges with another expert. Nurses worked in teams of two, with each nurse serving as a backup for the other's cases to provide mutual support.

The success of this experimental home visitation program was evaluated by comparing the maternal and offspring outcomes for each of the four treatment groups at the end of the intervention (Groups 1 and 2 were combined because there were no significant differences in their outcome measures, and together they are called the comparison group). With respect to child maltreatment during the first 2 years of the child's life, when families at greatest risk were compared (i.e., mothers who were poor, unmarried teenagers), 19% of the children in the comparison group had been the victims of substantiated abuse or neglect (comparable to national figures for high-risk groups), whereas only 4% of the children in Group 4 had been maltreated. The maltreatment rate of Group 3 was similar to that of the comparison group. The reduction in abuse resulting from intensive home visiting was not apparent for nonrisk families, however: There were much smaller group differences when older, non-poor, or married mothers were also considered, although group comparisons almost always favored Group 4. Thus, home visitation was most helpful in reducing the risk of maltreatment for mothers at greatest risk of abuse.

There were other group differences as well. The high-risk mothers in Group 4 interacted more positively with their offspring during home observations at 10 months and 22 months than did comparison group mothers: They punished less, for example, scolded less, and provided more appropriate play materials. Their infants, in turn, showed greater cognitive gains during their first 2 years than did the offspring of comparison group mothers, and made fewer emergency room visits during the first year. Their mothers also modified their lives in other ways. The high-risk mothers in Group 4 showed an 82% increase in the number of months they were employed and had 43% fewer subsequent pregnancies during the 4 years after their first child was born when compared with comparison group mothers. Although these differences were apparent only when comparing the mothers in each group who were at greatest risk for child maltreatment, other group differences were broader in their impact. For example, all nurse-visited mothers (Groups 3 and 4) showed an average improvement in their diets during pregnancy, reduced their smoking, became more aware of the community services available to them, attended childbirth education classes more frequently, received more WIC program vouchers, and received greater social support than did comparison group mothers. In short, home visitation had rather broad consequences for the recipient mothers.

This was, not surprisingly, an expensive as well as intensive intervention program, employing highly trained nursing personnel as home visitors for a sustained period after the baby's birth. Were the costs of these services warranted by the benefits that families—and society in general—obtained? Although any answer to this question is complicated by putting a value on the human benefits obtained from home visitation, Olds and his research team have reported that, when the costs per family of nurse visitation services and the broader benefits of the program, including averted social services, were compared, nearly all of the costs of the Elmira Project were recovered within 2 years after the family's involvement in the program had ended (GAO, 1992; see also Olds & Kitzman, 1993).

Although longer term effects were not studied intensively, these are, nevertheless, impressive results. In interpreting them, however, Olds and his colleagues have included several cautionary caveats. First, the sample they studied consisted exclusively of first-time mothers. Although the stresses of the initial transition to parenthood, especially when mothers are young, single, and poor, warrant concern about the potential for abuse, intensive home visitation may not have the same benefits for more experienced high-risk parents. Second, the benefits of home visitation for families with additional problems (such as those with a serious substance abuse problem, mental illness, or other serious difficulties) or in more challenging ecologies (such as dangerous inner-city neighborhoods) also remain to be demonstrated. Third, home visitation sometimes contributed to family conflict, such as when nurse visitors advocated child-rearing or health practices that directly contradicted those taught by other family members. Although this did not significantly undermine the benefits of the services they could offer, it provides a reminder of how social stresses can accompany social support, especially when support comes from providers outside a family's natural social networks.

Nevertheless, the Elmira Prenatal/Early Infancy Project provides some of the most comprehensive and best-documented evidence that intensive home visitation can have significant effects on the incidence of child abuse or neglect in high-risk families. According to Olds and his colleagues, several factors are especially relevant to understanding the program's success. First, home visitation began during pregnancy. This is a time when parents-to-be are in psychological transition, have many questions, are planning for the future, and are therefore most receptive to outside assistance from someone with counseling, information, and expertise to offer. Second, home visitors were highly trained nurses with expertise in maternal and child health and personal experience as parents. Consequently, they could offer a broader range of helpful information than could lay visitors or nonparents. Olds has emphasized, in particular, the special benefits with which nursing training equips a home visitor because of how health care and medical issues concern parents during pregnancy and the first 2 years of a child's life, as well as the enhanced ease with which nurses can mediate the family's contacts with other health care practitioners.

Third, the Elmira project's success is also partly attributable to the broadly based intervention strategy that encompassed social support, health maintenance, parent education, and ecological concern for the family's living conditions and contact with community resources. As Olds and Kitzman (1990) have argued, more limited abuse prevention programs, even if built around a home visitation strategy, have generally not shown the kinds of successful outcomes that the Elmira project did because of their inability to address, in an integrated manner, the variety of needs that high-risk families have. By adopting an ecological model, the Elmira program sought to connect families to community resources that could augment and reinforce the in-home services provided by the nurse visitor, and that could maintain these services long after home visitation had been completed. Finally, the home visitation program was intensive and long lasting, beginning during pregnancy and continuing through the first 2 years of the child's life.

Taken together, the Elmira project, although small in scale and experimental, offers one basis for optimism that a similarly designed program of intensive home visitation services can meaningfully advance abuse prevention goals.

The Hawaii Healthy Start Program

This optimism is further enhanced by the results of a second, more comprehensive home visitation program that also shows some promise for reducing the incidence of child maltreatment in a broader sample. Hawaii's Healthy Start Program was the first statewide home visitation program with abuse prevention goals in the United States, and has provided part of the inspiration for similar efforts in many other states (Breakey & Pratt, 1991; Bryant, 1993; Fuddy, 1994; GAO, 1992; Hawaii Department of Health, 1992). Healthy Start began in 1985 as a 3-year demonstration project for a small geographical region on the island of Oahu distinguished by high abuse rates, with funding provided by a state grant of about $200,000. Three years later, after the project reported evidence of no child abuse among the treatment group, Healthy Start was approved for expansion to 11 sites, and the project currently serves a majority of the civilian population in at least 13 sites with annual legislative appropriations of several million dollars. The program is administered through contracts with private agencies supervised by the Maternal and Child Health Branch of the Hawaii State Department of Health.

Like the Elmira project, Healthy Start emphasizes early and long-term contact between high-risk families and a well-trained paraprofessional home visitor. The program identifies potential participants through the screening of hospital birth records and interviews with new mothers. Participation is voluntary, and home visitation can continue until children reach age 5. Home visits may occur weekly or less often, and services are tailored to a family's constellation of unique needs, but typically include parent counseling, education about child development needs, and assistance in obtaining necessary resources for the family (such as medical aid, respite care, employment, and transportation). Referrals are also provided to other social service agencies as well as to physicians. Home visitors are paid paraprofessionals with specialized training.

A family's contact with Healthy Start typically begins at the hospital at the time of the child's birth (although prenatal identification of eligible families can also occur through referrals from physicians and public health agencies). Specially trained early identification (EID) workers scan hospital childbirth admissions records using a checklist of abuse risk indicators developed by independent researchers. The risk indicators consist of 15 factors in the life experience of the mother and family and include socioeconomic data, social isolation, lack of prenatal care, history of substance abuse, previous abortions, psychiatric care, past or current depression, and marital or family problems. Based on the number of risk indicators present from admissions data, EID workers may subsequently interview the mother using a standard question format and offer Healthy Start services. Fewer than 20% of screened families are eventually asked to participate in Healthy Start. Although participation is voluntary, more than 80% of mothers offered these services participate in the program. Needless to say, the cooperation of local hospitals is crucial to the success of these screening procedures, and sometimes hospital personnel or social workers conduct the screening rather than EID workers.

After mothers have consented to participate in Healthy Start, the home visitor usually meets the mother in the hospital before discharge or shortly afterward. Visits initially occur weekly, during which home visitors focus on providing emotional support to parents, assisting in coping with the demands of family life and obtaining needed resources for the mother and child, and modeling positive modes of parent-infant interaction to promote parent-infant bonding. Home visitors may arrive with gifts (e.g., diapers or toys) donated by corporate supporters of Healthy Start. Standard assessments of child development and of parent-infant interaction are conducted periodically to identify problems and devise intervention strategies, and written curriculum materials are used to help visitors support the development of positive parent-child relationships. The home visitor also encourages the mother to find a "medical home"—that is, a primary care provider who can be regularly consulted for preventive health care. In addition to in-home services, some home visitors offer parent education and social activities outside the home, respite day care, access to toy-lending libraries, coordination of health and social services to the family, and referrals to physicians and social service agencies, as well as assistance in making and keeping appointments for regular health care and well-baby checkups.

Home visitors write a family case plan after about 2 months of home visitation that articulates goals and intervention strategies; this plan is updated regularly to note progress and update goals. Based on the severity of family problems and the family's progress in achieving case goals, the frequency of home visits may be reduced to twice monthly, or to monthly or quarterly visits in many cases, which can continue until the child is 5 years old. Home visitor caseloads are, in turn, determined partly by the severity of a family's circumstances and challenges. One home visitor may have fewer families but with more serious challenges compared to other visitors, who may have a greater number of families to visit (but never more than 15 families total) with fewer serious problems. At times, the access of high-risk families to home visitors is limited because of full caseloads, at which time EID workers refer families to other community agencies.

The recruitment of home visitors usually involves efforts to enlist individuals from both formal and informal community networks. Most home visitors have high school diplomas and parenting experience, and all participate in a standard 5-week training curriculum that includes instruction about child abuse, EID screening, crisis intervention, parent-child interaction, and problem-solving and communication skills. Home visitors are also trained in the standardized assessment tools used periodically to assess child development and parent-child interaction. The initial home visitor training is supplemented by in-service and advanced training courses that provide additional information about child development, medical concerns, domestic violence, counseling, cultural sensitivity, and related matters. Home visitors are supervised regularly by professionals with advanced training and experience who are also employed by Healthy Start. Managers and supervisors from each site meet regularly with personnel from other sites to coordinate and compare program developments. Program sites vary in the salary and benefit packages they can offer.

The success of this home visitation intervention in curbing child maltreatment has been evaluated less systematically thus far than the Elmira project (Fuddy, 1994). The Maternal and Child Health Branch of the Hawaii State Department of Health has matched the names and dates of Healthy Start program participants served during 1987-1991 with concurrent Child Protective Service case data. For the 2,254 families served during this period, there were only 16 cases of abuse (less than 1%) substantiated from CPS files, and 32 (1.4%) substantiated cases of neglect. When additional cases of "imminent harm" were included, the total proportion of children remaining at risk was about 3.3% in a high-risk population that typically averages 18% to 20% of children who are abused or neglected by national and state norms. However, the high-risk families who were not served by Healthy Start, but who were subsequently tracked by the program, had a substantiated rate of abuse/neglect/imminent harm of only 5%, a figure that is not much different from the 3.3% rate of the Healthy Start population, but that may underestimate the actual maltreatment rate in this group. Further assessments of the program's success in preventing maltreatment are currently under way. There is currently no information concerning longer term consequences of the program.

Advocates for Healthy Start attribute its success to its community connections (with home visitors recruited, in many cases, from the same neighborhoods where client families are located); referrals to local physicians, clinics, and social service agencies; the duration of contact with high-risk families; and the high visibility and public approval of the program and its goals. Nevertheless, a lack of funds to offer comprehensive or complete services to all eligible families, together with inconsistent cooperation from hospitals and medical personnel, are also cited as problems that continue to hamper the success of the Healthy Start initiative.

A cost-benefit analysis of this program was presented in a GAO (1992) report on child abuse prevention:

> Program projections indicate that in 1993 the cost to provide the full 5 years of service to a family would be about $7,800. However, the total cost of preventing one case of abuse through the program is about $38,800 (*i.e., based on a 20% abuse rate in high risk populations, services @ $7,800 each would have to be offered to 5 families in order to ensure the prevention of one case of abuse* [italics added]). It is possible that this cost may be justified in cost-benefit terms because child abuse can be an expensive outcome. The cost of child abuse includes, but may not be limited to, the costs of the immediate consequences of child abuse, such as hospitalization and foster care. A hospital official in Hawaii said that the cost of hospitalizing an abused child for 1 week would range from $3,000 to $15,000. A Hawaii social services official said that providing foster care for 1 year would cost more than $6,000. Adding the costs of the potential long-term consequences of abuse could raise this amount substantially. For example, the Hawaii program estimates the cost of incarcerating a juvenile for 1 year at

about $30,000, the cost of providing foster care to an abused child to age 18 at $123,000, and the cost of institutionalizing a brain-damaged child for life at $720,000. However, not all abused children will incur costs at this level. (p. 24)

Added to this cost-benefit ledger are the additional benefits derived from Healthy Start: 90% of the 2-year-olds whose families participated in the program were fully immunized, 95% of the children had a primary health care provider, and 90% of the mothers had received family planning information (Fuddy, 1994). Thus, the potential benefits of home visitation might be appropriately conceived in broader terms than merely abuse prevention to include enhanced family functioning and child development outcomes—and thus might possibly reduce the expenses of welfare assistance, domestic violence treatment programs, and special education, as well as added tax contributions from parents' employment. On the other hand, additional costs that might be incurred in a comprehensive home visitation program include funds for parent counseling or job training, or supplementary developmental guidance for offspring.

Cautions

Considerably more research is needed, however, to replicate and substantiate these findings. This is important for at least three reasons. First, in light of some uncertainty concerning the extent to which participation in Healthy Start substantially reduces maltreatment rates indicated above, it is important to conduct systematic, long-term studies that evaluate both the immediate and enduring effects of program participation. This is especially important because the Healthy Start model is being implemented in many different states with different economic and cultural characteristics, different risk factors related to child maltreatment, and different target populations. This kind of long-term follow-up research is currently in progress by the National Committee to Prevent Child Abuse.

Second, replicating and substantiating the outcomes of home visitation are important also for identifying which program elements are most central to its success in abuse prevention. Note, for example, that although the Hawaii initiative is similar to the Elmira project in the provision of long-term, regular home visitation that includes a broad constellation of services and efforts to connect high-risk families to community resources and personnel, these two home visitation programs differ in other important ways. Although both programs enlisted client families early, for example, the Elmira project recruited mothers during their pregnancies, whereas the Hawaii program relies primarily on postpartum hospital recruitment. The programs also differ in the background and training of home visitors: Olds and his colleagues have emphasized the importance of the specialized training of nurse home visitors for the success of the Elmira project, whereas the Healthy Start project instead employs well-trained paraprofessionals, many without college degrees but better resembling the families they serve. These comparisons between the two most successful home visitation initiatives raise inevitable questions concerning which program elements are most predictive of success in abuse prevention. Further research to replicate and substantiate the effects of well-designed home visitation programs will contribute greater insight on this issue.

Third, and relatedly, further research on the consequences of home visitation for abuse prevention is important also because there are several other home visitation programs that have failed to affect child maltreatment rates in client families. Thus, it is especially important to understand which features of the Healthy Start initiative and the Elmira project accounted for their somewhat greater success. Siegel, Bauman, Schaefer, Saunders, and Ingram (1980), for example, randomly assigned 321 low-income women to one of three treatment groups that included a group receiving nine home visits during the infant's first 3 months from highly-trained paraprofessional visitors. The home visits emphasized parent-infant bonding, social support, and connections to community resources. Neither home visitation nor any of the other treatments resulted in significant differences between the groups in child maltreatment reports during the child's first year, nor were there differences in the number of emergency room visits, hospitalizations, or other health-related variables. Similarly, Gray, Cutler, Dean, and Kempe (1979) provided 50 high-risk mothers with enhanced pediatric care supplemented by weekly home visits from a public health nurse or "lay health visitor" who monitored the health status of the child, provided emotional support to the family, and was a liaison to the professional health system from the newborn period through 17 months of age. Compared to a control sample of 50 high-risk mothers who did not receive these services, the home visitation group did not differ in child maltreatment reports nor on measures of child accidents or "abnormal parenting practices" at the conclusion of the study, although the home visitation group children experienced fewer hospitalizations for serious injury. Barth (1991) enlisted 97 high-risk mothers in a Child Parent Enrichment Project that included 6 months of home visiting by a paraprofessional and focused on tasks related to good parenting. Compared to a similar high-risk control group, mothers who received home visiting did not differ in reported child maltreatment during a follow-up survey obtained 2 to 5 years after they completed the program. By contrast with these results, however, a home visitation program in which a community-based visitor provided parenting and child care information to high-risk, inner-city mothers at 7 and 10 days after birth, and at 2- or 3-month intervals during the child's first year, yielded small but meaningful differences in the rates of suspected child abuse and neglect, together with other indicators of improved parental functioning (Hardy & Streett, 1989). Thus, the findings from various home visitation interventions are very mixed, not uniformly positive.

A number of reasons can be hypothesized to account for the failure of these home visitation programs, some of them associated with the factors predicting the efficacy of social support interventions described in Chapter 4. In most cases, for example, the duration of visitation services was much briefer than in the Elmira and Hawaii projects, and this may have blunted the beneficial impact that home visits could have had on maternal and child outcomes. This is especially important when the effects of a relatively short period of visitation were evaluated in a long-term follow-up assessment that occurred several months or years after the program was completed (cf. Barth, 1991; Siegel et al., 1980), because it may not be realistic to expect brief interventions to have such an enduring impact. The one project with the longest duration of visiting yielded, in fact, the strongest results (cf. Hardy & Streett, 1989).

In addition, in some studies, the home visitors appear to have been inadequately trained or prepared for the multiproblem families they would encounter, they experienced limited or poor supervision, and their activities were not clearly guided by a well-developed curriculum for parent education and assistance, leaving home visitors to rely on their own ideas for providing assistance. These factors, too, could have reduced program impact by leaving home visitors ill-prepared for their task, isolated in coping with the demands presented by client families, and at risk themselves of becoming exhausted and dispirited. By contrast, the Elmira and Hawaii home visitors were well-supported: They had extensive training and supervision, limited caseloads, and (in the Elmira project) worked in mutually supportive teams.

Finally, these programs varied also in their ecological orientation—that is, in their efforts to connect troubled families to community programs, resources, and personnel—that derived partly from differences in program philosophy and partly from the inadequacy of community resources (cf. Barth, 1991). This difference could also help to account for the limited success of some visitation programs because there was little basis for enabling families to obtain long-term assistance that the home visitor could not directly provide. In addition, both the Elmira and Hawaii home visitors emphasized enlisting other members of the natural networks of recipient families—inviting friends and kin to participate in home visits, for example—that foster the integration of formal and informal helping networks and, hopefully, strengthen the efficacy of each. Moreover, the Hawaii project explicitly seeks to recruit home visitors from the same communities in which recipient families live.

These hypotheses are speculative, of course, and underscore the need for further research that will help to identify the program elements that are most crucial to the success of home visitation projects with abuse prevention goals. However, these studies also underscore that home visitation per se is not a panacea for the problems of preventing child maltreatment. Home visitation may succeed or fail with multiproblem families owing to the care with which the intervention is designed and the resources available to support this work (cf. Halpern, 1984). Which factors in program design, therefore, are most predictive of success? Consider those factors that might be tentatively identified as such, based on the comparison of efficacious and ineffective programs described above, as well as other pertinent research.

Predicting the Success of Home Visitation Efforts

As noted above, several factors may be relevant to the success of home visitation efforts when comparing programs that vary in their impact on high-risk families. First is the duration of visitation, with the greatest probability of long-term impact occurring when home visitors have early and extensive contact with recipient families. Second is the nature of the training, supervision, and support afforded home visitors because, as noted in Chapter 4, it is important to support the providers of social support to reduce their own proneness to exhaustion (GAO, 1990; Wasik, 1993; Wasik et al., 1990). In the case of home visitation, extensive training (combined, perhaps, with a professional background), regular supervision, a well-defined and applicable curriculum, caseloads of limited size, and teamwork among home visitors each can help to reduce the exhaustion that home visitors are naturally likely to experience in the course of their efforts. Third, the importance of an ecological orientation to program success suggests that if home visitors can help to integrate formal and informal helping networks by mediating between recipient families and community agencies, sharing the same neighborhoods as the families they serve, enlisting members of the family's natural social networks into their home visits, or in other ways, they provide a basis for the kinds of extended, long-term assistance that can come only from outside a formal home visitation arrangement.

There are other factors that are likely to predict the success of home visitation. They include the following:

1. A paid staff rather than volunteers. Although paid staff significantly increase program costs, the Elmira and Hawaii program models, as well as other research, suggest three reasons that paid staff are advantageous over a volunteer staff. First, home visitors who are paid enhance recruitment efforts by appealing to a broader applicant pool, and this may be especially useful if visitors with substantial professional and/or technical skill are required. Most often, visitors who are capable of performing reliable developmental screening or other assessments of offspring, providing systematic health guidance or parent education, or who must address the needs of complex, multiproblem families in dangerous neighborhoods must be recruited from professional or paraprofessional groups who will require a salary. Even when specialized skills are not required, a salary can strengthen recruitment efforts because only a limited pool of potential visitors exists who can contribute substantial volunteer services to a demanding, time-consuming visitation role.

Second, paid staff enhance retention and streamline training and supervision. Although volunteer home visitors approach their roles with sensitivity and enthusiasm, home visitation programs that rely on volunteers are often beset with high attrition and turnover of staff, rapid burnout, and the need to severely limit caseloads to avoid overtaxing volunteers. A very large volunteer staff is therefore required to aid targeted families, and high turnover means that training and supervisory efforts must be continuous and intensive. For these reasons, the training and supervisory demands required for volunteer visitors can significantly erode the cost savings of using volunteers rather than paid staff.

Third, paid staff may help to reduce some recipients' negative reactions to aid that can pose important obstacles to accepting services, as noted in Chapter 4. When home visitors are perceived as being motivated, at least in part, by the fact that this is a salaried job, recipient families may be more willing to benefit from their assistance and less likely to feel indebted and obligated to reciprocate than if a volunteer, motivated primarily by altruism, is the visitor. It is also possible that recipients will value these services more if they come from a paid rather than unpaid visitor because of the presumed authority and expertise that underlie their advice.

2. Services that are broadly accessed rather than specifically targeted. Although the efficient use of funds for a home visitation program suggests that focusing intervention efforts on the highest-risk families is most economical, Olds and his colleagues recognized that doing so would enhance the stigma associated with participation in the Elmira program. As a consequence, they opened the project to any first-time mother while striving to recruit high-risk mothers into their study. Likewise, the Hawaii program employs screening procedures to enlist the most needy families, but the recruited sample is so large that recipients are unlikely to become readily identified by the community as troubled, dysfunctional, or abuse prone. Reducing stigma, which is another factor in recipient reactions to assistance (see Chapter 4), is an important incentive to the broad, rather than narrow, targeting of home visitation services. Although targeting services in this manner must be necessarily constrained by program funds and staff time, creative strategies can be employed to broaden the recipient population and thus reduce the likelihood that recipient families are perceived negatively by the community. For instance, program participation can be an option for any family who wishes services, or a sliding fee scale can be implemented for families who can afford to pay, or alternative "packages" of home- and clinic-based services can be created, depending on the family's needs and risk status.

3. Services that are obtained in a voluntary, rather than compulsory, manner. Both the Elmira and Hawaii projects invited families to participate while ensuring their right of refusal, and voluntary participation is another factor that can enhance the likelihood of targeted families enlisting into a home visitation program. To be sure, a variety of incentives may accompany any invitation to participate, but safeguarding the families' right to decline, regardless of their risk status, helps to ensure that their participation, acceptance of services, and response to the program are not colored by perceived coercion to join.

4. Reliable funding. One of the most important ingredients to a successful home visitation program is stable and reliable funding for the long term (GAO, 1990, 1992). There are several reasons why this is so. First, the continuous search for funding renewal and institutional commitments of support can undermine the achievement of program goals by redirecting the time and energies of program directors, as well as by altering the nature of the intervention itself. Indeed, the Elmira project does not currently exist in the form in which it was originally developed by Olds and his colleagues, partly because of the different goals and orientations adopted by the local health department when it absorbed the program into its administration (GAO, 1990). At the same time, many small-scale home visitation programs are impaired by the amount of time required of project managers to negotiate funding rather than improving services, contributing to staff training, or advancing other project goals. Second, the reliability of funding also helps to maintain the commitment of program personnel and ensure that the services provided are of the quality needed to advance abuse prevention purposes. In Hawaii, for example, the statewide success of Healthy Start has occurred contemporaneously with a legislative commitment to sustained funding of this initiative. Finally, reliable funding is necessary to ensure and maintain the visibility of the program in the community, and thus to strengthen its ties with supportive natural networks in the neighborhoods of recipient families.

These conclusions have added weight because these characteristics can also be found in other home visitation programs with abuse prevention goals that have attracted national attention, even though their successes have not been as comprehensively evaluated as have the Elmira and Hawaii projects (see Bryant, 1993). For example, the Parents as Teachers program (originally pioneered in Missouri) provides home visits by a trained paraprofessional to families on a monthly basis throughout the first years of a child's life. Weekly visits are scheduled for higher-risk families (e.g., adolescent parents), and home visits are supplemented by group meetings emphasizing parent support and education. Funding comes from the state as well as local and private sources. Other programs on the Healthy Start model can be found in Florida, Rhode Island, and many other states.

Taken together, a balance of hope and caution is necessary when evaluating the apparent success of home visitation initiatives with abuse prevention goals. Although it is reasonable to be cautiously optimistic based on the Elmira and Hawaii projects, there is risk that too much hope and unduly ambitious goals will attend the design and implementation of similar projects in other jurisdictions (Weiss, 1993). As noted repeatedly, the personal and family problems leading to child maltreatment often have long-standing origins and cannot be easily remedied, and the complexity of these problems defies single-strategy solutions. Although home visitation can address many of the problems of abuse-prone families, especially those associated with the lack of social support, limited parenting skills, or isolation in the community, other problems associated with child maltreatment (such as poverty and substance abuse) cannot be addressed as easily by a home visitation strategy alone. As noted by a pair of experienced researchers:

> No single support strategy, whether interpersonal or financial, can address adequately the range of obstacles to healthy development that poor children and adults face. A variety of complementary strategies are needed. In that light, . . . home visiting is an attractive element of a broader package of family support strategies we should all be promoting. (Larner & Halpern, 1987, p. 7)

Intensive Family Preservation

Home visitation offers a potentially useful means of enlisting social support for abuse prevention that can be incorporated into a primary prevention program (if visitation is broadly implemented) or a secondary prevention strategy (if visitation is targeted more specifically to high-risk families). But what about parents who have already abused or neglected their offspring? In these cases, tertiary prevention goals focus on preventing the reabuse of children and, when reasonable and possible, restoring healthy family functioning and remediating the effects of abuse on offspring. Social support, broadly conceived and incorporated into a comprehensive intervention program, might prove as helpful in accomplishing tertiary prevention goals as primary or secondary prevention by providing parents with counseling, instruction, material resources, connections to community assistance, and monitoring of parenting behavior. Social support might also benefit the child victims of maltreatment by offering them emotional nurturance, developmental guidance, and other supportive assistance to help them cope with family dysfunction and its consequences.

Clearly, however, a different kind of approach is necessary to accomplish tertiary prevention goals because, by contrast with those who are offered home visitation, families that have been targeted by the courts and child protection agencies for special assistance are often in crisis and turmoil, beset by multiple problems of daunting complexity. In contrast to the variety of promising program models for primary abuse prevention, however, there are very few approaches to tertiary prevention that have been carefully tested and evaluated to determine their success in preventing the reabuse of children. We need to look elsewhere for ideas about how social support might be incorporated into a broader intervention strategy of tertiary prevention. In this briefer section, we consider one strategy called *intensive family preservation* (IFP). IFP programs provide a range of home-based services to troubled families, but do so in a manner that directly addresses the immediate and serious crises of family members and the need to restore family functioning to a minimally adequate level. Although the goals of IFP interventions, and of family preservation efforts in general, are controversial and extend significantly beyond the prevention of child maltreatment, they may offer ideas for program elements that should be included in any comprehensive tertiary prevention program entailing social support.

What Is Intensive Family Preservation?

Intensive family preservation services are meant for families who have reached their limits and are in danger of having a child removed from the home because of child maltreatment, intractable conflict within the home (sometimes resulting in a child running away from home, or

the parent refusing to allow a child to live at home), juvenile delinquency, or other serious problems. Intensive family preservation services often represent the family's last chance to keep the child at home.

IFP programs were developed in response to a constellation of
concerns about child welfare that has emerged during the past 25
years: the increasing population of children in "temporary" foster care
placements that often became enduring residences for many children;
a growing emphasis on "permanency planning" to reduce the incidence of open-ended foster care placements by applying well-defined
plans to return children to their original homes or to create adoptive
placements in a timely fashion; a recognition that many children and
youth are ill-served by therapeutic and correctional institutions created on their behalf, and can often be better assisted by services in the
community and at home; and a concern with fundamental values
about the family as the best and most reliable child-rearing environment for most children (Forsythe, 1992; Wells, in press; Wells & Biegel,
1992). IFP programs are designed to reduce the likelihood of out-of-
home placement of children from troubled families by providing the
family with intensive, home-based services of various kinds for a
limited period to help restore effective parenting and more healthy
parent-child interaction, while also strengthening the family's ties to
other supportive services in the community that can provide longer
term assistance.

However, IFP programs must be viewed in the context of current
public debate about the value of family preservation efforts (cf. Gelles,
1993). Children are sometimes victimized rather than aided by the
heroic, persistent, and long-term efforts of the child protection system
to reunify a family that has become shattered for many reasons. As
we have noted earlier, the problems that contribute to child maltreatment are not easily remedied, and children are sometimes better
served by caseworkers' efforts to remove them from a dangerously
dysfunctional home than to heal an intractably broken family. Consequently, family preservation efforts will be effective for some families,
but not all, and considerable skill is required to determine which is
true for any particular family that has come to the attention of child
protection caseworkers. Moreover, IFP approaches are neither a quick
nor an easy solution for the families that might benefit from reunifi-
cation efforts; in many respects, they provide only a foundation for
longer term assistance, and are likely to be ineffective without the
concerted commitment of resources and personnel to long-term fam-

ily support. Thus, even though current interest in family preservation is a response to past problems of child protection in the United States, like any new strategy, it has its own challenges and shortcomings, and its potential benefits can be easily overestimated.

IFP programs are currently operating in about 30 states, and these programs vary in their design and orientation (Forsythe, 1992; Wells, in press). However, they share some common attributes. First, family preservation services are short-term, intensive, crisis-intervention services delivered in the family's home. In contrast to the home visitation programs summarized earlier, they are specifically limited to short periods (typically 1 to 3 months) for several reasons. According to IFP planners, a short, intensive period encourages family members to focus on remedying the problems that have brought them to a crisis, as well as providing incentives to work hard on accomplishing specific goals for change. A short intervention period also reflects an expectation that changes in family functioning can occur fairly quickly to resolve present crises, and it limits the family's dependence on the caseworker and also reduces the caseworker's exhaustion. Moreover, time-limited IFP services enable caseworkers to focus their energies on only a few families at a time while maintaining the cost-effectiveness of their services (Kinney & Dittmar, in press).

By offering these services in the home, moreover, IFP programs have the same advantages as home visitation: Home-based services are less reliant on family members' willingness and capacity to travel elsewhere to receive these services; they reduce resistance to assistance; and they enable caseworkers to obtain a more insightful, accurate picture of the living circumstances of family members that may contribute to their difficulties. Caseworkers are "on-site" when confrontations, conflicts, and other critical encounters occur between parents and offspring. In addition, these services are concentrated: The caseworker may work with the family for 5 to 20 hours weekly, flexibly scheduled at the family home, beginning within a day or two after the family's referral to the program. This is supplemented by telephone conversations and a variety of 24-hour on-call procedures that enable family members to obtain immediate contact with the caseworker as emergencies may develop. In a sense, the caseworker becomes a significant part of the family ecology for a temporary period to provide on-site, crisis-oriented aid.

A second feature of IFP is the array of services that is offered to families, which may include intensive counseling for all family members; helping family members to obtain welfare, a job, housing, food, financial aid, child care, or other necessities; parent education that includes teaching basic communication strategies, child-management techniques, nutrition, and appropriate developmental expectations; assistance with obtaining medical or health care; marital therapy; assistance with transportation; advocacy and legal aid; and other services depending on the family's needs and resources. In addition, the caseworker may provide referrals to neighborhood or community agencies that can provide other forms of assistance, such as a local food bank, social service agencies, schools, or Alcoholics Anonymous.

A third feature of IFP programs is the caseworker's training and supervision. Well-designed IFP programs have an extensive training regimen that provides the caseworker with the variety of counseling, crisis intervention, parent education, and other skills that are necessary to work with troubled client families. This initial training is supplemented by in-service training sessions that are intended to reinforce and strengthen these skills, extensive supervision by more experienced caseworkers, as well as group and on-call consultations to provide assistance with difficult family problems. Because IFP services are intensive by definition, caseworkers receive extensive training and support for their work.

Homebuilders as a Model

The first of the IFP programs to achieve national recognition was the Homebuilders program, which originated in Tacoma, Washington, in 1974 (Kinney & Dittmar, in press; Kinney, Haapala, Booth, & Leavitt, 1990; Pecora, Fraser, & Haapala, 1991). The Homebuilders program was designed for families with a child who was at risk of imminent placement out of his or her home. In addition, to be eligible to participate, at least one family member must express a desire to keep the family together, and no family member can refuse the option that the family remain intact.

The Homebuilders program exemplifies the IFP approach described above. Client families are to be seen by their caseworker within 24 hours after the family has been referred to the program. After that, they are seen as often as needed, for as long as needed, within the 4- to 6-week period of assistance. Caseworkers typically average between 8 and 10 hours weekly in face-to-face encounters with families, together with additional amounts of phone contact, with the amounts varying from week to week depending on the family's needs and progress. Emergency sessions are also arranged as needed. Family meetings with the caseworker are scheduled at the convenience of family members. In addition, caseworkers give families their home phone numbers, as well as the phone number of their supervisor and a electronic pager number, to ensure 24-hour access.

Characteristic of an IFP approach, Homebuilders caseworkers provide a wide range of services during their meetings with recipient families, typically tailored to the family's specific needs and the goals for intervention. Counseling, family therapy, parent education, and other kinds of emotional support, together with "concrete" assistance in the form of food and housing assistance, advocacy with welfare or employment agencies, and referrals to community resources are included. Caseworkers may also work directly with children, either in the home or elsewhere.

In the Homebuilders program, caseworkers see no more than two families at a time, which is intended to enable caseworkers to devote as much time as needed to client families, ensure flexibility in scheduling and access, and reduce the caseworker's proneness to exhaustion. Small caseloads also enable workers to devote time to service delivery issues outside of their direct encounters with family members (such as arranging for a doctor's appointment or negotiating a landlord dispute) as well as allowing adequate time for supervision and consultation. Homebuilders caseworkers receive extensive training upon their hiring (including starting a program of 21 training modules addressing many issues, including behavior management skills, anger self-control, and termination issues), ongoing in-service training throughout their first year of service, and considerable supervision and support as they work with families. New staff visit client families and develop individualized case plans together with their supervisors, for example, and all staff participate in weekly meetings with other caseworkers and their supervisors. Individual and emergency consultation with supervisors and/or more experienced caseworkers is also encouraged.

The Homebuilders designers are clear that their program is intended to accomplish limited goals: In their view, the goal is not to create "perfect families," but to teach family members the skills to stay together without further intensive help (Kinney et al., 1990). This means that at the end of assistance from Homebuilders, family members may need additional services. Instead of providing comprehensive assistance, Homebuilders is designed to function as a crisis intervention program to enable families to surmount the immediate difficulties that have led to a child's possible removal from the home, and to equip families to benefit from more traditional kinds of services after the crisis is over. It is for this reason, in part, that efforts to strengthen family members' connections to community agencies, neighborhood resources, and informal social networks are made.

The originators of the Homebuilders model argue that the collective impact of these program components is more than the sum of their parts:

> All these aspects of the model—the rapid response to referrals, the accessibility of workers at home during evenings and weekends, the time available for families, the location of services, the staffing pattern, the low caseloads, and the brief duration of services—produce a much more powerful intervention than one that utilizes only one or two of these components. . . . We believe that most families deserve strong, effective support in attempting to learn productive ways to cope with overwhelming problems before children are placed outside the home. (Kinney et al., 1990, p. 53)

Homebuilders has shown some success in accomplishing its immediate goal of preventing the removal of children from the home. In initial evaluation research, more than 90% of the families remained intact during the period of intervention, and when families were monitored a year after services ended, between 65% and 75% of families avoided the out-of-home placement of offspring (Kinney et al., 1990; Pecora et al., 1991). Unfortunately, other criteria of program effectiveness have been assessed more informally. In terms of client satisfaction and caseworkers' assessments of family functioning, for example, the families who have received Homebuilders services have improved during the period of assistance (Forsythe, 1992; Kinney & Dittmar, in press; Kinney et al., 1990). Positive effects on family members' relationships with members of their informal social networks have also been noted (Kinney & Dittmar, in press). Apart from anecdotal reports, however, there is no systematic evidence concerning the impact of Homebuilders on child maltreatment (cf. Forsythe, 1992).

Reasons for Caution

Although these encouraging results concerning the prevention of out-of-home placement have evoked national attention, the broader impact of IFP programs—and their relevance to the tertiary prevention of abuse—remain to be explored. Further evaluation studies are necessary, moreover, because as with home visitation, the benefits of IFP programs have not been consistently demonstrated, even for programs modeled on the Homebuilders approach (Pecora, 1991; Rossi, 1992; Wells & Biegel, 1992). Indeed, some IFP programs have failed to show that participation averted the out-of-home placement of children in client families when they were compared with control families (who received no intensive assistance) during the period of intervention, and longer term follow-up studies have shown that even when program effects are noted, they are not long-lasting. To be sure, some of the evaluation studies have been beset by methodological problems, such as difficulties in assessing which children are "at risk of imminent placement," problems in establishing suitable comparison groups, and other difficulties that could undermine their portrayal of program effectiveness (Pecora, 1991). Even so, these findings from other IFP programs are disconcerting, especially in contrast to the Homebuilders results. Moreover, cost-benefit studies based on these estimates of program effectiveness raise doubts about whether the investment in IFP programs yields a net savings to the public agencies that might sponsor them (Pecora, 1991).

Furthermore, thoughtful analysts of IFP programs question whether their success is suitably measured by the proportion of families in the program that manage to avoid having a child placed out of home during the period of treatment (Pecora, 1991; Rossi, 1992; Wells & Biegel, 1992). Not only is the placement criterion subject to a variety of influences that are independent of program effectiveness (after all, during treatment, children are unlikely to be removed from the home to give the intervention a chance to succeed), but some children may be hurt rather than helped by caseworker efforts to keep them with their families, especially if they remain at risk for further abuse. Furthermore, this avowedly minimalist criterion of averting placement fails to address whether family functioning is effectively improved by the caseworker's efforts, even though children remain at home. In the words of two observers:

> Even though intensive family preservation services are in-
> tended for children whose safety can be assured with the
> provision of services, there are no empirical data to document
> whether the children served are safe from abuse, neglect, and
> other forms of serious maltreatment, or for how long; whether
> the emotional problems that triggered their referral to a place-
> ment service are resolved; whether these children remain
> uninvolved in delinquent behavior; or whether the postpone-
> ment of entry into out-of-home placement that occurs for
> some children is desirable. (Wells & Biegel, 1992, p. 25)

These researchers note that it is also yet to be determined whether
IFP services are suitable for all families with children at risk for
out-of-home placement or, if not, for which families these services
are most appropriate.

Finally, it is important to be appropriately skeptical about the
capacity of local social service agencies to provide the kinds of comprehensive services to troubled families that are needed not only to
avoid out-of-home placement, but to accomplish tertiary abuse prevention goals. Because abuse-prone families are multiproblem families, the services that they require for effective family preservation are
almost certainly multifaceted, long term, and consequently expensive. One intensive examination of the services that were available in
one California county, and their effectiveness in preventing the reabuse of children within their families, concluded that existing services were woefully inadequate to the problems of troubled parents
and the children in their homes (Wald, Carlsmith, & Leiderman, 1988).

In the end, there is reason to believe that the constellation of
supportive services offered by a caseworker in an IFP program—
especially within the Homebuilders model—can provide immediate
short-term, crisis-oriented assistance to some troubled families, some
of whom have abused or neglected offspring. But it is also apparent
that after intervention has ended, these families remain vulnerable
and continue to need support and assistance to address a multiplicity
of problems besides preventing the removal of children from the
home. Parents may show continuing problems in caring for their
offspring that warrant additional services, or even the subsequent
removal of the child. In this respect, Homebuilders or any other IFP
program is probably not, in itself, a sufficiently comprehensive or
long-term intervention to provide effective assistance to these fami-

lies, especially when tertiary abuse prevention is concerned. In a sense, although a 1- or 2-month intensive intervention may help families to get back on their feet, it cannot be expected to inoculate them against continuing difficulties given the diversity of the financial, legal, personal, and social problems that are often part of their life experience. When the goal is abuse prevention, a more comprehensive program of social support and ancillary services is required. Many aspects of the IFP strategy—such as the provision of intensive, home-based services by a highly trained caseworker; the caseworker's availability on an on-call basis; the diverse constellation of services provided to troubled families, small caseloads; and an ecologically based approach—can be useful components of a more enduring, comprehensive, tertiary abuse prevention approach.

Searching for the Constituents of Effective Program Design

It should be clear that much is known, and much is not known, about how to design effective social support programs to prevent child maltreatment. On the positive side of the ledger, the results of studies evaluating the effectiveness of home visitation and IFP programs provide helpful suggestions for what might be the constituents of effective program design. Each strategy offers home-based services, for example, that reduce recipient reactance, transportation difficulties, and other obstacles, making each approach truly neighborhood based. In doing so, visitors and caseworkers can more effectively obtain a sense of the living circumstances, demands, and stresses of family members, as well as monitor parental behavior in its everyday context. Moreover, in the home, the worker can instruct and model effective techniques of child management that are more likely to be adopted because they are learned in the contexts in which they can be applied. They can also enlist the assistance of extended kin, neighbors, and friends who may be at home when the formal helper is there. Each strategy also uses a variety of procedures to reduce the burnout of the workers who provide assistance, whether by limiting caseloads, providing extensive training and supervision, or offering other means of support. In this respect, each program "supports the supporters" to ensure that they can provide the kinds of assistance that recipient families need.

Each strategy also offers a variety of forms of assistance to recipient families that are tailored to each family's unique needs and resources. Most important, a combination of "relational" services (related to counseling, education, and nurturance) and "concrete" services (related to advocacy and obtaining needed resources) is implemented. Each strategy seeks to ensure that workers alone are not responsible for assistance by striving to integrate the family into broader community resources and agencies that can provide longer term and more comprehensive aid. Indeed, doing so is a core feature of each program in recognition of the limits of what can be achieved by either temporary home visitation or short-term, crisis-oriented family preservation services. Related to this, each strategy tries to accomplish meaningful, but limited, intervention goals for client families. Many of these constituents of likely success are, of course, consistent with the formulations of Chapter 4 concerning the predictors of effective social support efforts for troubled families.

But the diversity of home visitation and IFP initiatives, and their very mixed success, suggest that much more must be learned about the factors that predict effective assistance involving social support interventions. It is quite likely, for example, that differences in client populations are important: Home visitation or family preservation programs that address the needs of families that are especially prone to child neglect—often in the context of socioeconomic distress—should probably be different from those that serve families that are physically or sexually abusive, or are at risk of being so. Likewise, cultural and regional variations should probably assume an important role in program design and implementation because of differences in family values, their perceived needs, and perceptions of the appropriate roles of formal and informal helpers in different cultural and subcultural groups. In addition, the communities in which assistance is offered can also shape the effectiveness of services. Some impoverished inner-city settings are dangerous not only to families but also to caseworkers, and some communities are so impoverished of resources that referrals to agencies and helpers outside the home become functionally impossible (cf. Barth, 1991). In short, flexibility in program design is necessary to enable abuse prevention programs to adapt to the particular needs and resources of the families and neighborhoods in which they are implemented.

The duration of services that is necessary to ensure the effectiveness of supportive interventions also merits further exploration. In evaluating the relative effectiveness of various home visitation initiatives, for example, the duration of visitation was identified as an important constituent of success: Longer lasting visitation produced more robust benefits for recipient families. In the case of Homebuilders, however, the emphasis is on short-term, crisis-oriented assistance, but with the recognition that the multiple needs of client families cannot be satisfied in such a short period and that follow-up services are usually necessary. It is likely, of course, that the most suitable duration of supportive assistance must be evaluated in relation to program goals and the severity of the family's problems, but this remains to be elucidated by research. A related issue for follow-up study, especially in the case of IFP programs, concerns how to enable and prepare families to make an effective transition from the services provided by an in-home, crisis-oriented caseworker to more traditional services offered in more traditional ways. It is possible that one of the important predictors of long-term success of an IFP intervention is whether family members become well-integrated into a range of other supportive services after the caseworker has finished his or her work with the family, or instead fail to benefit from these alternative means of support.

Finally, both programs exemplify the potential effectiveness of integrating formal helpers into the natural social networks of troubled families. In the case of home visitation, highly trained visitors, sometimes with specialized skills, were used in the Elmira and Hawaii programs to incorporate kin and friends into their supportive efforts, and similarly well-trained caseworkers are part of the Homebuilders initiative to work within the family ecology as advocates, mediators, and mobilizers of others' aid. It is possible that the kinds of skills required for effective secondary and tertiary abuse prevention programs make the enlistment of formal helpers from outside the family especially necessary, given the range of problems that family members experience. Recognizing the importance of formal helpers to these prevention efforts raises questions about the potential value of abuse prevention strategies that rely exclusively on mobilizing the assistance of informal helpers who are part of the natural social networks of troubled families. As we have seen in Chapter 4, doing so entails fairly complex considerations pertaining to their network roles and relationships that can complicate the effectiveness of such informal, neighborhood-based interventions if they are not buttressed by the work of formal, quasi-professional helpers.

On the other hand, it is arguable that the effectiveness of home visitation and IFP programs, where it has been demonstrated, has been fostered by the effective combination of formal and informal helping through the visitor's/caseworker's concerted efforts. Certainly, the program models that have been surveyed here underscore the need to integrate formal and informal assistance, especially in the context of interventions that are limited in duration or frequency. Thus, the important issue is not, perhaps, from where supportive interventions originate, but how the integration of formal and informal aid can best be achieved. We will consider this issue further in the next chapter.

These considerations underscore that identifying the constituents of effective program design is still ongoing, requiring a thoughtful interweaving of the results of research concerning social networks and social support with the lessons of intervention efforts described in this chapter. In the final chapter of this book, we will strive to "reweave the strands" of research and practice to formulate a set of conclusions and directions for further research.

7

Reweaving the Strands
Integrating Research, Practice, and Policy

One might be tempted to feel pessimistic after reflecting on the issues surveyed in this book concerning social support and the prevention of child maltreatment. In contrast to a conventional, and somewhat simplistic, view that social isolation is a global characteristic of abusive families that is partly responsible for their treatment of offspring, and that efforts enhance their support through formal and informal helpers will reduce abuse potential, it appears that the relations between isolation, support, and maltreatment are considerably more complex. Social networks may be sources of stress as well as support, for example, and the affirmation afforded by network associates may not only fail to reduce abuse potential, but may actually enhance it. Even when social support is offered, it may not be accepted because of the complexity of recipient reactions to assistance and the needs and roles of helpers, and it may also be ineffective in reducing abuse potential. Added to these considerations is the fact that the portrayal of the social isolation of maltreating families from research studies is breathtakingly shallow, with little evidence for the comprehensive insularity commonly believed to be true of them, and instead a picture emerges of diverse social needs that reflects the heterogeneity of the population of maltreating families. In all, research knowledge of the links between social insularity and abuse, and of the functioning of social support in troubled families, makes "more research is needed" the most confident conclusion that can be offered. Finally, the preceding chapter's review of abuse prevention strategies that involve social support may also inspire pessimism because it is hard to find unequivocal support for any coherent strategy—whether one entailing home visitation, intensive family preservation, or modifications of these strategies—that has consistent, demonstrated success in preventing abuse in high-risk populations. Although there are promising intervention approaches, there is no clear recipe for enlisting social support to prevent maltreatment.

Pessimism might be a natural response to the conclusions of the preceding chapters, but it would be inappropriate. Our disappointment in finding that maltreating families do not necessarily suffer from comprehensive social isolation only reflects the simplicity of our expectations and the subtlety and diversity of their challenges and problems. Our surprise at discovering how multidimensional are the factors predicting the impact of social support is coupled with an acknowledgment that these reflect the everyday complexities of natural social networks. Dismay at finding few causal links between social isolation and proneness to child abuse is diminished by recognizing the diverse needs of these multiproblem families, and social support can be helpful in addressing only some of them. And, as noted in the preceding chapter, the discouraging picture of the efficacy of abuse prevention strategies entailing social support must be balanced with hopeful findings coming from a few key demonstration projects, together with lessons from these projects concerning the importance of ecologically based interventions entailing well-trained staff, home-based services, the integration of formal and informal assistance, and long-term follow-up of client families.

In fact, much has been learned about social support and the prevention of child maltreatment that, although not providing definitive answers to initial questions and raising other queries that were not anticipated, provides a substantive foundation for further research, program design, and policy redirection. The task of this chapter is to reweave the strands of the issues, queries, and findings of the preceding chapters to offer a set of integrated, albeit provisional, conclusions that can guide further work in this field.

The Coordination of Formal and Informal Support Sources Is Important to a Coherent Abuse Prevention Strategy

Current interest in enlisting social support to prevent child maltreatment is proceeding in at least two directions. On one hand, the

U.S. Advisory Board on Child Abuse and Neglect (1990, 1991, 1993a, 1993b) has urged the development of strategies that enlist informal helpers in the neighborhoods of troubled families to provide broadly based assistance to reduce the isolation of abuse-prone families. By strengthening the assistance provided by these natural helpers, perhaps in the context of programs that foster neighborhood integrity and community identification, the board hopes that their affirmation, counseling, information provision, monitoring, and socializing of parental behavior will help to reduce risk to children. Government programs intended to combat child maltreatment would, under the advisory board's scheme, become reoriented toward strengthening community-based services, especially those oriented toward prevention and treatment.

On the other hand, some of the most ambitious and successful abuse prevention programs introduce well-trained formal helpers into the lives of abuse-prone families, either in the context of a home visitation program that provides a variety of supportive services to accomplish secondary prevention goals, or in the context of an intensive family preservation program that offers crisis intervention to indirectly advance tertiary prevention. The lessons of program evaluation studies of these projects suggest that formal helpers may be uniquely capable of offering the kind of specialized, intensive, and multifaceted aid that multiproblem recipient families need, especially if programs are designed to provide caseworkers and home visitors with the support they need to cope with the demands of their roles.

The efforts of both informal and formal helpers are important. As the U.S. Advisory Board has recognized, only by integrating troubled families into the informal supportive networks and other resources of their neighborhoods can they obtain the ongoing, long-term assistance that is most likely to enhance family functioning and reduce family strain. As we have seen, this is also recognized by the originators of the most successful home visitation and intensive family preservation programs; one of the crucial tasks of the home visitor or caseworker is to enfranchise extended family, neighbors, and friends into their efforts to improve the functioning of high-risk parents, and to act as mediators, advocates, and referral agents to link family members to community resources and agencies that can provide ongoing assistance. In each case, the limitations inherent in the formal agent's temporary role in family life are acknowledged by seeking to provide a foundation for longer term, informal assistance from the community.

Yet for reasons discussed in Chapters 3 and 4, reliance on informal helpers alone may be inadequate because of limitations in their capabilities, conflicts inherent in their roles, and the burdens of their own needs that are less likely to beset formal helpers. Neighbors, kin, and friends may strive to be emotionally supportive, but in doing so fail to monitor, challenge, or change abusive parental behavior; they may be deterred from assisting troubled families because of the poor social skills, resistance, or unrelenting neediness of the recipients of their aid; they may be preoccupied with the same economic, ecological, and personal problems of the family members they are in a position to assist, and prone to becoming exhausted by seeking to aid others in the context of their own life stresses; and they may not have knowledge of or access to other resources that troubled families need to function more effectively. Formal helpers are also susceptible to these challenges in providing aid, but because of the supervision and support they receive in their roles, as well as their training and background, they are less likely to be undermined by them. Informal helpers are, in short, essential but potentially unreliable support agents. Formal helpers are more skilled and may be more effective, but their aid is temporary.

Both are needed. By advancing strategies that focus on the coordination of formal and informal support agents, program planners have the best chance of developing an effective abuse prevention strategy. It is important to recognize that the coordination of formal and informal helpers is not necessarily easy or straightforward. As noted in Chapter 4, it requires that formal helpers recognize and appreciate the unique contributions that informal helpers can offer to troubled families, and respect the values and perspectives they share. Coordination may be undermined when informal network members seek to hide the detection of maltreatment by family members they care about, or by conflict between the values embraced by formal and informal helpers (recall from Chapter 6, for example, that conflict between the home visitor and family members sometimes occurred in the Elmira project). It seems clear, however, that the most effective abuse prevention strategy entailing social support will resist relying exclusively on either informal, neighborhood-based helpers or formal helpers from private or government agencies, but, recognizing the unique contributions each can offer to troubled families, seek to coordinate and integrate their contributions in a comprehensive, coherent intervention.

Strategies for Enlisting Informal Social Support Must Incorporate Both Neighborhood and Nonneighborhood Social Networks

Several conclusions from Chapters 2 and 3 suggest that a program of social support intervention, especially one emphasizing informal social networks, must extend significantly beyond neighborhoods to encompass extended kin; workplace social networks; friends who live outside local neighborhoods; associates through churches, unions, and other broader community groups; school-based associates; and other potentially valuable social resources to parents and their offspring.

First, research on social networks indicates that neighborhood associations do not constitute the majority of the relationships on which individuals commonly rely for social support. Most supportive social relationships are nonneighborhood based because of the extent to which natural networks encompass nonlocal extended kin, workplace or school associates who live elsewhere, friends who live in other neighborhoods, and other nonneighborhood people who are contacted regularly for visits or phone calls.

Second, neighborhood-based relationships are characterized by greater turnover than are other relationships (such as with extended kin and long-term friends), and thus may be a less consistent and more unstable source of supportive ties. This may be particularly true in impoverished and/or dangerous neighborhoods characterized by residential mobility and distrust, but where the need for local social support is greatest.

Third, in lower-income populations (where economic stress enhances abuse potential), social networks are smaller but are more kin based and less neighborhood focused, suggesting that neighborhood-based relationships may not be among the most salient or potent sources of potential support to them (although there are important variations in this conclusion based on ethnic group membership).

Fourth, maltreating families may be particularly unlikely to rely on neighborhood-based support systems because of the processes of insularity, stigma, and "social distancing" that are especially likely to occur in relationships with neighbors, who are more prone (according to Polansky's research) to identify maltreating parents and their offspring as "different" owing to the lack of reciprocity in mutual help-giving, social incompetence and indifference, and other indicators of problems and dysfunction. It is possible, perhaps likely, that these stigmatizing influences are more characteristic of neighborhood associations than of relations with extended kin, workplace friendships, or other associates because of the more limited bases for relationships formed with neighbors. Finally, consistent with this view, the neighborhoods in which high-risk families are likely to reside are themselves "needy neighborhoods" in which a lack of economic resources, high mobility in and out of the neighborhood, a lack of broader civic commitment, and the financial and personal stresses of its residents are likely to exhaust the supportive resources on which maltreating families might rely.

To be sure, there are some important advantages to an emphasis on developing informal supportive relationships for high-risk families that are neighborhood based. Neighborhood support networks help to create a more positive social ecology in which various prevention goals related to child maltreatment can be advanced because high-risk parents and their offspring are benefiting from supportive relationships with many people within their residential milieu. In a sense, neighborhood-based strategies that are combined with efforts to strengthen (sometimes reconstitute) neighborhoods are more comprehensive: They can potentially address the needs of many high-risk families living within a single geographical area. If it is possible to strengthen the "needy neighborhoods" in which many high-risk families reside, it could ultimately promise greater success than could more piecemeal efforts over a broader geographical net to strengthen nonlocal social support on a family-by-family basis. Furthermore, neighborhood-based supportive relationships do not rely on the additional resources (such as transportation, telephone, and other means of access) that sometimes hamper the efforts of impoverished families to maintain relationships with network members who live at greater distances.

Besides their easy access, many of the other benefits of informal support systems—their congruence with local norms and the variability of support functions, for example (Gottlieb, 1983)—are more easily accomplished within neighborhood-based support systems than in more extended, supportive network ties. In their insightful analysis of natural helpers, Collins and Pancoast (1976) emphasized that because of their informal roles and their connections to the values and norms of the community, neighborhood-based natural helpers can provide multifaceted forms of support that may be more accessible, meaningful, and stable than formal assistance agents can provide.

However, the benefits of neighborhood support are likely to be constrained by the inherent neediness and structural problems of the neighborhoods in which many abuse-prone families live, which is why a strategy of neighborhood social support is inextricably linked, in many cases, with efforts to strengthen or reconstitute the neighborhood itself. Furthermore, social support efforts that focus primarily on neighborhood relationships risk missing some of the more important, and potentially more powerful, social network relationships that high-risk families experience as more meaningful sources of assistance. Although relationships with extended kin can be characterized by conflict and intergenerational animosity, for example, and may not consistently advance abuse prevention goals, they are also consolidated by cultural definition and formal ties that provide greater stability to the supportive functions they can assume. Furthermore, several studies suggest that the lack of supportive ties with extended kin distinguish maltreating families more than their lack of ties to friends or neighbors, suggesting that their "social isolation" may be especially important when it is intergenerational rather than interresidential.

Along with extended kin, long-term friendships (which may or may not be neighborhood based) and workplace associations provide relationships that are knit together by common interests and concerns and have potentially greater stability than do neighborhood ties. To be sure, for economically stressed families, workplace associations may also be characterized by insularity and impersonality, especially in the kinds of service industry jobs that lower-income parents are likely to have. Nevertheless, they may provide a potentially important intervention avenue. For children, whose primary social networks are more likely to be neighborhood based because of peer relationships and school-based associations, interventions that foster friendships with individuals outside the local community may provide children with much-needed alternative role models and exposure to new perspectives that are valuable for purposes of prevention and developmental remediation.

Taken together, therefore, the notion of enlisting informal social support networks for preventing child maltreatment is certainly a good idea, but limiting this proposal to neighborhood-based social networks may unduly and unnecessarily constrain the range of potential supportive agents in the lives of maltreating parents and offspring. In this regard, the goals of the U.S. Advisory Board on Child Abuse and Neglect (1990, 1991, 1993a, 1993b) for strengthening informal support systems for high-risk families might be broadened use-fully beyond the neighborhood.

The provocative research of Garbarino and Polansky has, of course, provided a far richer portrayal of these neighborhoods than had previously existed. As earlier noted, however, both research initiatives have been limited by a failure to examine nonneighborhood-based social support that may provide the families they studied with alter-native sources of emotional sustenance, instrumental assistance, so-cial monitoring, and other resources. It would be valuable, therefore, if future researchers would extend these provocative studies to pro-vide a fuller portrayal of the broader social networks of maltreating families and the potential network resources that exist both outside and within their neighborhoods on which they can rely.

Different Maltreatment Subpopulations Have Different Social Support Needs

The importance of distinguishing among different forms of mal-treatment—while acknowledging that many families exhibit multiple kinds of maltreatment—is underscored by research on the social isolation of these families. Although strong generalizations are not supportable, it appears that when researchers attribute social isolation to a parent's deficits in social skills or competence, they are typically most concerned with populations in which child neglect is preemi-nent. Neglectful parents are also more likely to report loneliness or disappointment in close relationships and lack a sense of support from others around them. It appears, therefore, that a subset of mal-treating parents—predominantly, but not exclusively, neglectful fami-lies—experience limited personal competence in establishing and maintaining successful social relationships outside the family and with extended kin. Some researchers have suggested, in fact, that the child-rearing problems that these parents experience are generaliza-tions of their broader difficulties in maintaining coherent and suppor-tive social relationships (Burgess & Youngblade, 1988): These are "neglected" parents who are neglectful of fundamental social ties, as well as of their offspring.

There is other research evidence, far less substantial, that suggests that another form of social isolation derives instead from anger and conflict between maltreating parents and social network members, especially extended family. In this case, insularity derives from animosity and suspicion, and it appears that this is more likely to be true of physically abusive families than neglectful ones. It should be emphasized, however, that this is not a well-documented empirical picture and requires follow-up research. Finally, with respect to emotionally maltreating or sexually abusive parents, there is far less research evidence concerning the nature of their social isolation or, indeed, whether they are insulated at all. In her intensive intervention program, Daro (1988) found that all maltreatment subpopulations were comparably characterized by social isolation, but hers is the only study to make this comprehensive assessment. Even if this is verified, it may nevertheless be true that the causes and correlates of the social isolation of different subpopulations of maltreating parents are meaningfully different and are associated with different constellations of problems contributing to their abuse or neglect of offspring. Clearly, this merits further research exploration.

In addition to distinguishing among varieties of maltreatment, it is important to note that the social support needs of maltreating parents are also defined by other problems that may accompany child abuse or neglect. Parents who experience oppressive poverty may lack strong connections to others because they live in dangerous housing projects; they must move repeatedly; or their relations with others in their neighborhoods and communities are stressful, distrustful, and/or exploitative. Thus, their social isolation occurs for different reasons than for other families who experience greater economic well-being. Parents with a substance abuse problem may experience social isolation because of its impact on their capacity to hold a job, support a family, and even to function competently, and thus the reasons for their isolation differ from those of parents who do not have alcohol or drug-related problems, even though each are abusive. Young, adolescent parents may exhibit social insularity because of troubled relations with their families of origin, or because of school drop-out, and thus they differ from other parents as well. Therefore, it is essential that the heterogeneity of the causes of social isolation is recognized so that diverse interventive strategies will be well-suited to the constellation of needs that different family members experience.

Adding further complexity to this portrayal of the diverse support needs of abusive families is that the seriousness of their maltreatment of offspring—that is, its frequency and persistence over time and the harm it creates in children—also varies and helps to define the needs of these families for supportive assistance. For some families, economic aid and referrals to job-training and employment programs are likely to be sufficient to restore and remedy a temporarily dysfunctional pattern of family interaction, especially one where neglect owes to economic distress. For other families, long-term efforts involving many different kinds of interventions (e.g., substance abuse programs, family therapy, social skills training) may be necessary when abuse is long term, arises from many parental problems, and is integrated into long-standing patterns of family conflict. Therefore, in a sense, the support needs of maltreating families are individualized, based not only on the form of abuse but also its severity and the seriousness of the accompanying life circumstances of the family, as well as the network resources on which family members can rely.

In considering alternative intervention strategies to address these multifaceted needs, program planners should wisely consider the various functions of social support summarized in Chapter 3. Because "social support" is itself a heterogeneous phenomenon, the provision of it to different maltreating subpopulations is likely to entail very different things. Neglectful families may require diverse, multifaceted forms of social support that provide emotional affirmation, skill acquisition, counseling, and access to information and resources that can assist them financially, vocationally, and in obtaining housing and food, as well as in putting sometimes chaotic lives in order. Abusive families may require social support that primarily provides therapeutic counseling, especially in the context of parent education and other guided interventions that help to establish and reinforce new patterns of child management. Social support qua social control is important for all maltreatment subpopulations, especially in the context of tertiary prevention, but it may be especially critical for physically abusive and sexually abusive families in which child maltreatment is often integrated into broader patterns of family victimization and concealment. Needless to say, the forms of social support that are most valuable for the offspring of maltreating parents are different from those needed by perpetrators, and will depend on the age of the child, the kind of maltreatment, and whether the child is at home or in an out-of-home placement. Interventions that offer counseling and other forms of therapeutic guidance, as well as developmental remediation through therapeutic day care, peer social skills training, special educational assistance, or other programs, may be especially important for these children.

Program planners must also consider thoughtfully the avenues of social support that are likely to be most effective, especially if an important component of their intervention strategy includes enlisting informal social networks. The heterogeneity of the needs, capabilities, and backgrounds of abuse-prone families, in other words, mandates careful consideration of the resources of their social networks on which they can rely for supportive assistance. As we have seen, for example, some abusive families enjoy emotionally supportive relationships with network associates (especially in the extended family) who fail to challenge—and may actually reinforce—abusive parenting practices (Korbin, 1989, 1991). Other families report that their network associates provide broad affirmation of, but little tangible assistance with, parenting or child care concerns that are their sources of greatest stress (cf. Lovell & Hawkins, 1988). For some abuse-prone parents, peers provide valuable assistance, whereas extended family members are sources of stress and dissension; for others, the reverse may be true. In sum, carefully crafted social support interventions entailing informal helpers require individualized mapping of the social networks of recipients, assessing their perspectives concerning the strengths and weaknesses of those to whom they can turn for assistance.

Moreover, thoughtfully designed interventions will seek to accomplish much more than merely enhancing network size or social embeddedness—which are, as we have seen, relatively insensitive indicators of supportive assistance from network associates. Instead, more finely tuned interventions will strive, for example, to enhance the recipient's awareness of, access to, or reliance on individuals who offer the greatest potential aid while also seeking to enhance the supportive assistance of these people. Or it may seek to strengthen the recipients' social skills, reduce their reactance or defensiveness, or enhance their awareness of the need for supportive assistance to increase their acceptance of network aid. Or it may strive to support the natural helpers in the family's ecology to better equip them to provide assistance. In sum, an emphasis on enlisting informal networks in social support requires a careful analysis of the family's existing social connections to identify potential agents of aid, and strategies for enhancing support, that are likely to vary on a family-by-family basis because of the heterogeneity of abuse-prone families.

Finally, there is a suggestion in several research studies, unsubstantiated at present, that one secure, supportive social relationship may be all that is necessary to promote more adequate functioning in troubled parents. From the perspective of this "sufficiency model," a parent's capacity to rely on at least one supportive network member may make the difference between stress-reactive child abuse and the absence of abuse in the family history. Although this provocative idea requires further study, it suggests that the goals of social support interventions need not necessarily be expansive to accomplish valuable results in the lives of high-risk families, and further underscores the potential error of focusing on sheer network size as an intervention target.

The challenge, therefore, is to recognize that because social support is multifaceted and the needs of maltreating families are heterogeneous, different kinds of supportive interventions should be fostered for different maltreatment subpopulations. Incorporated within this task, however, is the corollary recognition that these families have other needs besides social support and that social support cannot meet all the needs of abuse-prone families.

Social Support Alone Is Unlikely to Be an Effective Preventive Intervention

If maltreating families are multiproblem families, and if their social isolation derives from a variety of associated socioeconomic, ecological, familial, and personal difficulties, then social support interventions must be integrated with other services to provide effective preventive assistance. As suggested earlier, social support programs should be integrated with social skills training for some maltreating families, with intensive therapy for some or with detoxification and substance abuse treatment programs for others. For adolescent parents, social support that integrates day care with educational assistance from the school system may be most beneficial, together with career planning or counseling concerning further education. For children who are in foster care because of abuse or neglect, integrating social support into their foster care placements and drawing on their preexisting support networks in the school and neighborhood of origin is necessary (cf. Lewis & Fraser, 1987).

The operative concept to underscore is *integrated* (cf. Miller & Whittaker, 1988; Tracy & Whittaker, 1987). Social support that exists independently or at the periphery of other kinds of assistance may not be as effective because it is not tied to other valued resources. On the other hand, when social support is an intrinsic component of other forms of support, its impact may be enhanced. One of the features of everyday assistance by informal helpers is that emotional support and counseling occurs in the context of other, more tangible kinds of aid, whether in the exchange of baby-sitting, food items, labor, or financial assistance. When formal helpers are involved, their impact can also be enhanced when they are conduits of other resources to recipients. One of the reasons, for example, for the success of Hawaii's Healthy Start program is that the assistance provided to high-risk families is multifaceted, entailing both "relational" and "concrete" forms of assistance from which parents can benefit. It is quite likely that positive recipient reactions to these programs derive, primarily or in part, from the range of aid they receive. Other examples of integrated social support programs include Gaudin's Social Network Intervention Project, which combines strategies to enhance informal network support for neglectful families with the assistance of regular volunteer aides, the enlistment of neighborhood helpers, and social skills training (Gaudin et al., 1990-1991); Childhaven's efforts to combine quasi-therapeutic full-time day care services with practical parent education, casework support, parent support, family therapy groups, and social agency referrals (Durkin, 1986; Miller & Whittaker, 1988); and Powell's (1979, 1987, 1988) cooperative child care resource centers for high-risk urban families, which combines regular child care with the development of mutual-aid support groups among parents, together with community referrals. In each case, the integration of social support (broadly defined) with other services means that the program as a whole is internally consistent and mutually reinforcing.

Integrating assistance in this manner is not necessarily easy. When government agencies are involved, for example, institutional boundaries and turf battles can make it difficult to coordinate the efforts of an abuse prevention program originating in a department of social services with the maternal and child health programs coming from a department of health, even though each can benefit recipient families by their integration. Further institutional boundaries are encountered when educational, welfare, and legal assistance must be enlisted. When private agencies are concerned, funding constraints may undermine efforts to provide recipient families with multifaceted forms of aid, whereas coordination with other agencies may be limited by differing goals, agendas, and timetables. These are formidable obstacles, but do not qualify the conclusion that because social support interventions can address only some of the needs of abuse-prone families, the integration of social support programs with other forms of assistance to high-risk families is likely to have an impact that is greater than the sum of their parts.

Coordinating Social Support Efforts With Preexisting Programs Serving High-Risk Families Opens New Avenues for Effective Assistance

As indicated by the preceding analysis, fostering social support alone is unlikely to be an effective preventive intervention unless it is combined with other services that benefit high-risk families. This suggests that grafting the efforts of formal or informal helpers into programs that serve these families might be especially helpful because of how parents already recognize the benefits of the accompanying services. Moreover, the stigma that might be attached to carefully targeted social support interventions for maltreating families would be undermined by their integration with social service programs that either assist high-risk families under a general entitlement model, provide services to broadly defined needy families, or offer universal benefits.

Public Assistance

Under welfare reform of the late 1980s, for example, the federal government has assumed an expanded role in supporting child care services to welfare recipients and enlisting the states in enhancing and regulating the quality of these services, although welfare reform initiatives of the 104th Congress may substantially change this role. The Family Support Act approved by Congress in 1988 requires participation in job training programs for welfare recipients, but provides the parents of young children with a child care subsidy to ensure the adequate care of offspring, and maintains this subsidy for 1 year after welfare eligibility has ended. The child care subsidy may be used to purchase care from relatives as well as from unrelated caregivers. Moreover, the act also enlists states more directly in the provision of child care services and the enhancement of their quality than has previously been true, recognizing the links between child care quality and children's development (e.g., Phillips, Howes, & Whitebook, 1992).

Given the strong association between socioeconomic distress and child maltreatment, multiple avenues exist for using the provisions of welfare reform to enhance the detection of child maltreatment (through state-regulated training of child care workers in subsidized care settings) and offering treatment to abuse-prone parents, as well as for assisting children who are the victims of maltreatment. Special quasi-therapeutic day care services can be created for the offspring of parents who have been adjudicated for child abuse or neglect, or for other low-income, high-risk parents, to assist children in the context of programs that also seek to improve parenting behavior. Incentives can be incorporated into the job training components of welfare reform to enhance the involvement of welfare recipients with their offspring and to foster their ties to the community, such as by including them as paid aides in the neighborhood child care settings where their offspring are located, offering allied programs that foster time-management and other personal skills as well as job-related capabilities, or through more systematic parent-training efforts. Moreover, welfare reform provisions can be used to place welfare recipients in service jobs within their local communities, and thus further integrate them with community agents and resources.

Other public assistance programs can also include social support components for high-risk families. The Women, Infants, and Children (WIC) program has long been recognized as an important avenue for enhancing the nutritional adequacy of lower-income families, and the benefits it provides are, on the whole, nonstigmatizing to recipients. It is possible that WIC could be used as an avenue for identifying and accessing high-risk families for additional services, such as child care support or informal parent or neighborhood networking. The Early Periodic Screening, Diagnosis, and Treatment (EPSDT) program could be modified to include interventions specifically targeted toward lower-income families that would enhance its role in the early detection of child maltreatment.

Schools

Schools are another social institution that can provide social support for maltreating families. As the success of Head Start has shown, incorporating parent involvement into early childhood education provides broad benefits for parents and offspring alike. Similarly, enfranchising high-risk families into the curricular and extracurricular activities of children at their schools might provide one avenue for reducing the social insularity of these families by strengthening their links to community resources and agents. Moreover, children's involvement in extracurricular activities (including after-school programs) is one means of keeping low-achieving and needy children tied to the school, and thus to reliable sources of social support. Therefore, schools are perhaps one of the most important community-based social institutions to which social support efforts can be linked and, in impoverished or isolated (e.g., rural) communities, may be one of the most reliable social institutions available to needy families.

Schools can be helpful in many potential ways. Just as the availability of affordable, high-quality (and, on occasion, quasi-therapeutic) child care services can provide support to maltreated children and also assist their parents by reducing child care demands, the availability of after-school programs at schools in high-risk neighborhoods can mutually benefit children and their parents. Reliable after-school care reduces the stresses of juggling late-afternoon child care and work responsibilities that many parents experience, and it removes children from the domestic demands and stresses that can contribute to abuse. After-school programs can also potentially provide the kinds of social and educational assistance to maltreated and other needy children that may be more difficult to provide in structured, curricular contexts. After-school programs can be appealing to children if they are oriented around the activities and interests that children find attractive and engaging, such as sports, music, hobbies, and social activities (Medrich et al., 1982). Partly because they are local and school based, they do not depend on parents' active efforts to facilitate children's involvement, and this surmounts one of the obstacles to program participation for some children (O'Donnell & Steuve, 1983). Activities can be easily structured to foster the kinds of social skills and successful peer relations that maltreated children often lack, and can also be designed to enhance self-esteem and perceptions of self-competence through the use of noncompetitive, mastery-oriented activities and supplementary educational projects. Moreover, the adult directors of these activities are more likely to be perceived by children as potential sources of social support because of their informal roles; teachers, by contrast, are not regarded by children as supportive figures, and the same may also be true of school counselors and administrators (Furman &

Buhrmester, 1985, 1992; Reid et al., 1989). The beneficial peer associations fostered by after-school programs may extend into children's other social activities, potentially fostering the development of extended peer support networks for maltreated children (Hirsch & Dubois, 1989). This may become especially important in preadolescence when peer networks become more independent of the family system (Berndt, 1989).

Schools can also be helpful as forums for peer counseling and peer tutoring programs for maltreated children with academic and personal difficulties. There is considerable research evidence that peer tutoring programs not only foster intellectual skills, but that they are also sources of mutual support that can enhance self-esteem and self-confidence (Asp & Garbarino, 1983). Peer counseling, in turn, might be an effective avenue for strengthening social support among age-mates. Moreover, the fact that counselors and tutors themselves reap considerable benefits from peer counseling and peer tutoring programs means that assistance is experienced as mutual, and this can contribute to strengthening supportive peer networks for targeted children and can help to reduce the social isolation that maltreated children may experience at school, as well as the stigma that may derive from receiving unreciprocated assistance from friends.

There are a variety of other ways that schools can provide social support to children with special needs: through special academic/counseling/parenting programs for teen parents who face the challenges of child rearing in the context of their own developmental needs; through academic curricula focused on health, parenting, and self-esteem; through information about community and recreational agencies that can provide additional sources of social support; and through opportunities to develop relationships with nonkin adults who are alternative models of healthy behavioral functioning (cf. Asp & Garbarino, 1983; Vondra, 1990). Finally, schools can be supportive resources for parents as well, especially if parents can become enlisted into adult neighborhood networks through their association with their child's academic and extracurricular activities. However, doing so requires considerable efforts by school personnel to enfranchise and welcome parents—especially marginal, lower-income parents—into the academic environment (Cochran & Riley, 1988). This is a difficult task, especially for school personnel who are often overtaxed by their other responsibilities. Moreover, the same kind of social distancing that can occur among the neighbors of troubled families can also characterize their encounters with school personnel, especially if the latter are not prepared for the special challenges posed by these families.

This portrayal of schools as sources of social support to high-risk families resembles Zigler's (1989) proposal for a "School of the 21st Century," which is also intended, in part, to involve schools as centers of neighborhood social support. In Zigler's proposal, neighborhood schools would be reformed as community resource centers where quality child care could be obtained, referrals to other agencies providing health care and other assistance could be made, home-based family support and parent education programs would be housed and coordinated, and a registration center for neighborhood family day care providers would be administered. Provided the necessary funding, staffing, and other resources, Zigler argues that such schools would function more effectively by providing and coordinating supportive services to families in the community, fostering attention to children's developmental needs before they enter kindergarten, and addressing the special needs of troubled families before their problems have become severe. Others have suggested that schools should become locations for neighborhood family resource centers that provide community referrals and networking, sponsor parent education and informal family support groups, coordinate resource sharing (e.g., a toy- or book-lending library), and sponsor other activities. In Chapter 6, several examples of school-based social support programs for parents were outlined (see also Bryant, 1993; Garbarino & Kostelny, 1994).

These proposals are built on the assumption that schools have the capacity, as well as being uniquely suited, to assume a central role in neighborhood-based social support systems. In a contemporary social context of growing criticism of schools for failing at their basic educational tasks, and a history of efforts to incorporate broadly defined goals into the mission of local school systems without enhanced funding or other resources, there may be good reasons for questioning this assumption. Certainly, it is foolish to expect schools to assume centralized community support functions without thoughtful consideration of how such school-based programs should be designed, the background and training of the personnel to staff them, the implications of these programs for the school's identity within the community, the consequences of integrating these programs into institutions with a primary educational mandate, and the space and other resources necessary for their effective operation. Moreover, the relation between these community services and the basic educational function of the school, as well as with other community agencies, remain to be elucidated.

However, schools are uniquely suited to become neighborhood resources of social support, especially in distressed neighborhoods where other institutional resources may be drained or deficient, and therefore the role of schools merits thoughtful consideration in the development of a neighborhood-based strategy of social support to abuse-prone families. Moreover, overburdened school personnel need not assume exclusive, or major, responsibility for the administration of such support services. Increasingly, school systems are engaging in partnership models involving outside agencies that, in collaboration with school personnel, design and direct cooperative programs for needy children and their families. Many of the school-based programs outlined in Chapter 6 and elsewhere rely on such a partnership approach. School-based programs to enhance social support to high-risk families should use such partnership programs as their model.

Other Community Institutions

Other social institutions may also become social support resources for high-risk families. Churches and other religious institutions have social support as a central goal, and they usually sponsor or support a variety of services that can assist high-risk families, including community food pantries, subsidized counseling services, outreach to local mission projects, clothing and food drives for neighborhood groups, soup kitchens, family assistance projects, and related activities. These are usually very helpful endeavors, especially when they reflect ongoing associations between religious communities and the neighborhoods they serve, as is often true with some African American churches (Pinderhughes, 1982). However, religious institutions sometimes may be regarded skeptically by maltreating families (cf. Giovannoni & Billingsley, 1970), whose lack of community involvement is likely to extend to religious activities as well. Consequently, initiatives that are intended to assist abuse-prone families must emphasize reaching out to high-risk families in their homes and neighborhoods. This is a challenging task because it requires considerable commitment from members of the religious community, who are as prone to social distancing from troubled families as are neighborhood residents. The development of cooperative ventures in needy neighborhoods, such as building projects fashioned after Habitat for Humanity and other programs, might provide one avenue for this kind of cooperative assistance.

Efforts to enlist community and recreational centers as neighborhood social support resources face similar problems. Because many mothers do not schedule and facilitate their children's involvement in neighborhood recreational activities (O'Donnell & Steuve, 1983)—perhaps as a result of their own lack of planning and participation in community groups—their children are frequently denied access to community activities from which they might benefit. Thus, community and recreational programs must either organize and coordinate local neighborhood activities to which children (and parents) can achieve easy access, or they must supplement their activities with transportation to and from the sites for needy families.

Besides enhancing access to high-risk families, there is another benefit to the efforts of churches, community organizations, and recreational groups to organize outreach activities in the neighborhoods where these families live. Insofar as many people engage in social distancing from high-risk families, encouraging them to become involved in community projects that provide direct assistance to needy neighborhoods is likely to reduce denigrating stereotypes, enhance their awareness and understanding of the conditions in which these families live, foster a sense that productive change can occur and, taken together, undermine social distancing. In a sense, the social insularity of advantaged families in the community can be undermined by encouraging them to participate in such outreach projects.

Altogether, there are many potential advantages to grafting social support resources onto preexisting programs from which high-risk families already benefit. Although integrating assistance in this manner requires thoughtful consideration of how expanding roles might alter the nature of these programs—whether they involve local schools, churches, community, or public assistance programs—in most cases, social support is a complementary task to those already assumed by these institutions and agencies. The equally important challenge is designing supportive programs that exploit the unique roles of these institutions in the communities in which they are embedded, compensate for their potential problems in providing social support (e.g., problems with access, conflicting institutional commitments and goals, etc.), and provide the needed resources to make support programs function effectively. These are formidable, but surmountable, challenges.

The Coordination of Supportive Assistance to Parents and Children Within High-Risk Families Is Essential to Helping Each

Because family life entails overlapping and integrated social connections, social support provided to one family member may have complex consequences for the rest of the family. As indicated in Chapter 2, support for parents may yield beneficial consequences for offspring, but in different circumstances may exacerbate their problems, such as when extended kin justify, ignore, or rationalize abusive behavior they witness in an effort to be emotionally affirming to the parent. Assistance to offspring that is intended to help them may do so, but may also provoke negative reactions from other family members when accepting such support places other family members in a humiliating or denigrating light, threatens prevailing modes of family interaction, or exposes the child to challenging new values, perspectives, and ideas. Consequently, the designers of social support interventions for abuse-prone families must thoughtfully consider how social support has direct and indirect consequences for different family members and, if possible, create interventions that simultaneously benefit both parents and their offspring.

The research on abuse-prone families indicates, for example, that child care and child-rearing demands are among the greatest stresses of family life from which relief is sought among extended kin, neighbors, friends, and other network associates. As a consequence, supportive programs that address child care needs can mutually benefit parents and offspring. The availability of high-quality child care services for specially targeted high-risk families could enhance the healthy functioning of infants and children and provide them with alternative attachment figures for emotional support (cf. Howes & Hamilton, 1992; Howes, Rodning, Galluzzo, & Meyers, 1988). Such services would also reduce the reliance of high-risk families on informal care from extended kin (which may add stress to relationships with extended family members); neighborhood family day care arrangements (which may be of poor quality); or ad hoc arrangements with live-in companions, friends, or neighbors (which may be of uncertain reliability and quality, and may actually subject children to further potential abuse). Parents would benefit from such arrangements by having a reliable source of satisfactory care available for offspring, and their links to community networks might also be strengthened through their contacts with caregivers, parent support groups, and other activities integrated into the child care program (Long, 1983). The same benefits can also be obtained through other kinds of child care assistance, such as through school-based after-school programs, drop-in and in-home respite care, cooperative neighborhood child care groups (cf. Powell, 1987, 1988), and other resources.

In a less direct (but potentially more influential) manner, troubled parents and their offspring are both likely to benefit from supportive interventions that strengthen the family's economic well-being (through public assistance, vocational training, and/or job placement services), enhance educational access for parents as well as offspring, reduce the danger of their neighborhoods through police involvement and community activism, foster access to recreational resources in the community (through transportation assistance as well as the establishment of neighborhood centers), and other interventions that provide shared family benefits.

Formal helpers can also enhance the integration of social support to parents and offspring, especially when they offer supportive assistance at home rather than at a clinic or other institutional setting. By providing parent education as well as counseling to family members, for example, Homebuilders caseworkers seek to address the conflicts that exist in the constellation of relationships that family members share so that children and their parents are able to remain together. In doing so at home, the caseworker's awareness of the impact of the physical ecology of the home and neighborhood, the everyday patterns of interaction with friends and neighbors, the stresses of the family's daily routine, and their impact on each family member becomes an important component of counseling. Perhaps most important, parent education and family therapy occur in situ—involving the everyday transactions of family members at home—rather than in the rarefied atmosphere of an office or clinic where parents are consulted independently of their offspring. This enhances the interco-ordination of assistance to each family member, the opportunity to consider each person's viewpoint on the family's problems, and the development of new, more successful, modes of interaction from which each family member can benefit.

When children are in out-of-home placements, the coordination of the child's social network with those of the foster family and the child's family of origin can become especially complicated (Whittaker, 1983). Temporary foster care placements have the goals of providing relief for abuse victims while preserving relationships with the family of origin, and these goals may conflict. Possessiveness and competitiveness between family units and the generation of loyalty conflicts in the child can undermine the child's experience of support in out-of-home placements, even if (and, perhaps, especially when) the foster parent is a member of the extended family or neighborhood (Lewis & Fraser, 1987). Moreover, social support that existed in the child's original neighborhood may not be maintained in the foster home, or, conversely, new avenues of helpful assistance developed for children with the foster family may not be continued when the child is returned home. In these cases, the child protection caseworker has a unique responsibility for maintaining supportive network ties for maltreated children across care settings so that the benefits of social support are not lost in multiple transitions, and that supportive assistance from one family network does not create conflict for the child in the other family setting. An adult in the child's community may also assume this "brokering" function, especially if the foster home is in the same neighborhood as the child's family and that adult has a trusted role in the child's life (Thompson & Flood, in press).

As these examples suggest, the coordination of supportive interventions to parents and offspring is important to ensuring that the benefits of assistance are shared or, at the least, do not indirectly undermine the needs of other family members. On the other hand, well-integrated supportive services in a neighborhood context have the potential for providing multiple benefits for parents and offspring alike.

Social Support Is Sometimes Best Achieved by Targeting Support Providers Rather Than Recipients Alone

One of the most important lessons emerging from the research reviewed in this book is that it is crucial to provide assistance to those who are being asked to offer social support to troubled families. This is true for both formal and informal helpers because despite their differences in training, background, and roles in relation to troubled families, each encounters formidable obstacles to providing assistance that can be exhausting, and ultimately undermine their effectiveness.

The reasons for exhaustion have already been noted: High-risk parents are often disinterested in or resistant to receiving support that provides emotional affirmation but also challenges their treatment of offspring; they are unlikely to reciprocate the support they receive and may instead make unrelenting and unreasonable demands on their helpers; their needs may be experienced as overwhelming to those who seek to assist them; their capacities to maintain supportive relationships may be limited because of poor social skills or other problems; and the neighborhoods in which they live may promote feelings of despair, suspicion, hostility, or hopelessness in helpers as well as recipients. Taken together, these factors can make providing social support a draining experience for formal and informal helpers alike.

Perhaps unsurprisingly, therefore, the most successful home visitation and intensive family preservation programs enlisted well-prepared professionals who received considerable training, extensive supervision, and support throughout the period they worked with abuse-prone families. In the Elmira home visitation project, visitors worked in teams to provide mutual aid; Hawaii's Healthy Start home visitors have an extensive training program prior to their first contacts with recipient families; and the Homebuilders project has a detailed curriculum spanning the caseworker's first year with the program, together with extensive consultation with experienced supervisors and on-call emergency assistance to aid in coping with difficult family problems. Moreover, caseloads are restricted in each program to further prevent worker burnout. In general, an appreciation of the unique difficulties in assisting multiproblem families is reflected in the extensive support provided to the formal helpers in these three interventions.

When informal helpers are enlisted as primary or ancillary support agents from the community, moreover, there are additional challenges to "supporting the supporters." First, it may be hard to find potential helpers with "freedom from drain" (Collins & Pancoast, 1976)—that is, individuals who are not themselves overwhelmed by the stresses of the socioeconomic, ecological, and personal circumstances they share with their neighbors—in the high-risk neighborhoods in which maltreating families can be found. Indeed, providing social support may impose so many added demands that helpers will eventually find it too overwhelming to do so. Second, because child abuse and neglect elicits such strong disapproval in our culture, it also may be difficult to find informal helpers who are willing to become supportively involved with parents who maltreat their children (especially when sexual abuse is alleged). This is especially likely if these parents have other undesirable characteristics, such as their marginality in the community, other disapproved behavior (such as alcoholism or spouse abuse) that makes them undesirable friends, or a failure to reciprocate help-giving, which makes them unrewarding targets of help. Finally, it is worth remembering that, especially in high-risk, distressed neighborhoods, natural helpers may not always be the best informal support agents to provide aid to maltreating families because the values they reinforce may not necessarily advance abuse prevention goals. While providing emotional affirmation, they may nevertheless promote child-rearing values that add, rather than diminish, risk to offspring.

These concerns, together with the necessity of integrating various sources of supportive assistance to abuse-prone families, suggest again that an effective preventive strategy entails not only the direct assistance of formal helpers but also their efforts to support and socialize the efforts of informal helpers in the family's natural network. Support of informal helpers might occur through their participation in the formal agent's activities with family members (such as the involvement of extended kin during home visits, or the participation of a neighbor in a caseworker's advocacy efforts on behalf of the family), as well as other kinds of education, counseling, and guided assistance. Enlisting a neighbor or grandparent in providing child care assistance for a stressed single mother, for example, might be especially helpful in the context of a caseworker's guidance concerning the developmental needs of the grandchild and the value of respite care for single parents. Organizing mutual support groups of natural helpers may also provide a much-needed source of guidance for those providing assistance to troubled families. In addition, the value of parent education for high-risk parents might be extended to providing informal instruction to others in the parent's natural network concerning children's needs and capabilities, the value of alternative approaches to child management, and the development of nonpunitive modes of child care. In a sense, by altering the child-rearing values of the family's network associates, a formal helper can add further catalysts for change to a high-risk parent's social ecology.

Finally, it is important to remember that formal and natural networks do not exhaust the range of support agents who can be enlisted to assist abuse-prone parents and their offspring. As indicated earlier, the anonymity entailed in many informal social encounters—ranging from casual conversations at a bar to counseling on a crisis line—may permit far more candid disclosure and effective assistance than the kinds of information that can be exchanged with ongoing social network members. Similarly, assistance in the context of self-help groups such as Parents Anonymous can be valuable precisely because the individuals to whom one discloses problems are similarly afflicted, and because the counseling they provide does not necessarily occur in the context of continuing, everyday social relationships (although, by mutual consent, they may expand their associations beyond the scope of the self-help group). In these circumstances, "supporting the supporters" is easier because the assistance they offer is not in the context of ongoing relationships—and indeed, their help derives some of its effectiveness from this fact. On the other hand, it is important to remember that because it is independent of ongoing social ties, this kind of assistance can be easily ignored or rejected by the recipient. Thus, the anonymity of certain social encounters may foster helpful self-disclosure and candor, but this may not effectively reduce abuse potential in troubled parents.

Considering the Complexity of Recipient Reactions to Aid Will Enhance the Efficacy of Social Support Interventions

Providing assistance to needy families can be a perplexing experience when, instead of gratitude, recipients respond with resentment, denigration of the aid, rejection of the benefactor, and/or an unwillingness to receive further assistance. Such reactions often contribute to the despair experienced by natural and formal helpers and undermines their motivation to provide future aid. However, the extensive literature on recipient reactions to aid, reviewed in Chapter 4, indicates that such reactions are not only normative but rational responses to the experience of helplessness, vulnerability, failure, dependency, and/or indebtedness that may derive from receiving assistance from others. Accepting aid often implies personal failure, invokes expectations of reciprocity that may be impossible to fulfill, and evokes fears of exploitation or stigmatization, especially in vulnerable or needy recipients, that accompany the feelings of gratitude and relief that are also a normative response to accepting aid. In short, receiving assistance is a complex experience, involving a mingling of positive and negative perceptions of the benefactor, the assistance, the recipient, and the circumstances in which help is offered and received.

Social support is distinguished from other kinds of assistance because it is meant to be an ongoing, rather than one-time, resource to troubled families. These complex recipient reactions to aid suggest that the manner in which social support is provided may be as important as the kind of assistance in predicting their willingness to accept future support. To ensure that troubled families will continue to accept the support offered them, social support interventions should include several features that will reduce perceptions of stigma, vulnerability, or failure.

First, interventions should offer recipients the opportunity to reciprocate the assistance they have received by providing help to others in ways that are consistent with the adult's skills, resources, and motivation. Although some adults may not take the opportunity to do so, such an offer provides a means of restoring equity in the mutual obligations entailed in a help-giving relationship, and can also contribute to self-esteem in recipients. Social support programs should identify a range of neighborhood-based projects to which recipient adults can contribute, including home-based assistance to older populations (e.g., Meals on Wheels programs), nonprofessional local housing construction projects (e.g., Habitat for Humanity homes), community-based child care and recreational programs, and related activities. Program options should also include providing assistance, as appropriate, to other high-risk parents in the context of a tertiary peer-support program (such as Parents Anonymous) or a secondary prevention program (such as Welcome Baby, another home visitation initiative for high-risk young mothers). A recipient's participation in programs like these not only satisfies cultural reciprocity obligations entailed in receiving assistance, but also contributes to the positive integration of recipient families into the neighborhood and community and may contribute to undermining unfavorable stereotypes of recipients by members of the larger community.

Second, recipient families should be convinced of their need for supportive assistance, rather than participating in a social support program for obligatory reasons (such as a prerequisite for material aid). Informal support is effective in part because it is freely given and freely received based on self-perceived need, and this helps to reduce perceptions of failure or dependency in a natural helping relationship. Some of the better-designed formal support programs, such as Healthy Start, integrate the provision of social support into other forms of assistance that recipients regard positively and are unlikely to see as stigmatizing or denigrating, and, as Hawaii's Healthy Start evaluation data indicate, they willingly accept these services.

To be sure, the potential benefits of a well-designed supportive intervention, together with the multiple needs of troubled families, may make it tempting to provide very strong incentives to participate, especially when children are likely to benefit when parents do so. Moreover, where tertiary prevention goals are concerned, some degree of coercion is probably inevitable, such as when client families participate in an intensive family preservation program because it is their last chance to avoid having a child removed from the home. However, even in these circumstances, it is important to help recipients appreciate how they can benefit from the services that are being provided to enhance their willingness to participate, their commitment to program goals, and the effectiveness of the assistance they are provided. If this is not done, the resentment and humiliation that derives from coerced enrollment may result in perfunctory participation with little hope for effective change.

Third, social support should be offered in the context of interventions that are as widely targeted as possible and that do not identify recipients as necessarily dysfunctional or needy. One of the more humiliating features of current public welfare policies is the stigmatization of recipient populations by delivery modes and eligibility requirements that denigrate them in public contexts. But when benefits are universalized, or are available to a wide range of individuals with various needs and backgrounds, accepting social and material support does not necessarily confer undesirable status. One of the attractive features of informal social support networks in neighborhoods and communities is that they are undiscriminating: All individuals enjoy social assistance from others whether they are at risk or not, and thus accepting support from neighborhood associates does not designate recipients as different from others. To the extent that formal social support interventions can emulate the nonstigmatizing features of these informal support networks, they will contribute to an enhanced willingness of needy parents and families to benefit from the services they offer.

Fourth, social support should be provided in a context of mutual respect; that is, support should not be accepted at an unnecessary cost to personal privacy, autonomy, or self-reliance. One of the explicit messages of Homebuilders caseworkers to client families, for example, is an expectation that meaningful and significant change in family functioning can occur over a short time with the parent's concerted effort—which is, in a sense, an empowerment approach. And insofar as the design of formal and informal support programs is intended to enhance the recipient's acceptance of support as an ongoing resource, efforts to preserve the recipient's self-esteem by portraying assistance as an outcome of mutual respect (rather than a bestowal), the benefactor's intentions as partly self-interested (rather than entirely altruistic), and the recipient's needs as extrinsically instigated (rather than due to personal inadequacy or failure) will also advance the goal of effecting meaningful change in family functioning. Furthermore, the acceptance of support should not entail greater intrusions on personal privacy than is necessary to achieve program goals, even if the purpose of social support is to curtail the risk of child maltreatment, because threats to privacy can lead to an unwillingness to receive further aid. In a sense, respect for recipients is a basic corrective to the features of help-giving that recipients experience as most denigrating.

To be sure, managing recipient reactions to aid is not only the responsibility of program designers. One of the goals of the supportive efforts of a caseworker, home visitor, or other formal or informal helper is to enhance a recipient's acceptance of assistance by fostering an awareness of the benefits of supportive assistance, teaching strategies for accepting criticism without avoiding or terminating interactions with others, increasing communication skills, encouraging the reciprocity of assistance, and fostering other social skills that make helping relationships mutually beneficial (Tracy, Whittaker, Boylan, Neitman, & Overstreet, in press). In this respect, the helper's task is not only to provide aid in the most nonthreatening manner possible, but to socialize recipients to accept assistance in a nondefensive, constructive way that will create further opportunities for helping.

Effective Social Support Interventions Can Involve Simple as Well as Complex Strategies

Throughout this discussion, the complexities and uncertainties in the design of effective social support programs in neighborhoods, the extended family, the workplace, and other social ecologies have been emphasized. The tension throughout this discussion has been to underscore the multidimensional considerations entailed in the use of social support for the prevention of child maltreatment while also identifying helpful avenues for potential intervention.

However, there are also some fairly simple, straightforward intervention strategies that can potentially enhance the social support available to abuse-prone families. If a high proportion of socioeconomically distressed, high-risk families are socially isolated, in part because they have no access to a telephone (cf. Deccio et al., 1991), subsidizing phone service may be a straightforward intervention with surprising benefits. If anonymous self-disclosure sometimes benefits socially isolated parents or offspring by providing nonrisky means of discussing personal problems, enhancing access to crisis hotline (and "warm-line") services may be valuable (cf. Peterson, 1990). If limited access to transportation contributes to impoverished community associations, incorporating free transportation to and from recreational, educational, and parenting activities may be an important key to intervention success—or, for that matter, lowering the cost and accessibility of public transportation for economically distressed individuals or communities. If there is limited popular awareness of the needs of socioeconomically distressed families or the community resources that exist to address those needs, grocery-bag inserts and milk-carton displays can help to remedy this problem. If child neglect derives, in part, from the inability of impoverished families to heat their apartments or afford child care while parents work, subsidizing these activities through an emergency fund may be an important (and remarkably cost-effective) ingredient of social support that keeps these families out of further trouble with child protection agencies (cf. Horowitz & Wintermute, 1978; Pelton, 1994).

In the end, of course, for most maltreating families, access to well-paying, affirming employment may be the most valuable social support intervention of all. A job at a reasonable wage reduces poverty, heightens access to work-related social networks that might assume a supportive role in a parent's life, enhances self-esteem, strengthens residential stability and integration into a community, and provides material benefits to the family. The availability of jobs at reasonable wages also benefits neighborhoods by curbing the downward spiral of many high-risk communities and strengthening the economic base for community planning. If one singular intervention were to be recommended to curb child maltreatment, adequate employment for lower-income families would be the answer.

Much More Research Is Needed

This phrase is the default conclusion of most research reviews in the behavioral sciences, but in this case reflects the enormous gaps in the literature surveyed in this book. In many ways, the success of efforts to develop effective social support interventions for abuse-prone families hinges on the development of essential new knowledge germane to this goal.

First, we need to know much more about the characteristics of different maltreatment subpopulations and their social support (and other) needs. Despite the fact that different forms of maltreatment overlap considerably, characterizing the population of maltreating adults and their victims heterogeneously rather than homogeneously enables us to think of social support as a resource that must be carefully tailored to the specific needs of troubled families. Not only the different forms of maltreatment but also the different constellations of needs of these families dictate different kinds of supportive interventions on their behalf, as well as different kinds of ancillary services with which support is integrated. Second, we need considerably greater information about the nature of the social networks of troubled and untroubled families, and how the structural and affiliational features of these networks contribute to perceptions of available social support in potential recipients and enacted support in the experience of high-risk families. This is critical to understanding which aspects of individual and family social networks are the most important targets for social support interventions and which potential network resources formal helpers can enlist in their efforts.

Third, we must know much more about the factors influencing the efficacy of potential social support interventions, including the stresses that exhaust support providers, the overlapping (and sometimes incompatible) consequences of support provided to different members of the family, and the characteristics of social networks that contribute to their supportive and stressful roles in the lives of individuals and families. As this review has clarified, basic theoretical and limited empirical work currently exists concerning these factors in untroubled families, but there remains little understanding of how these factors influence the efficacy of support interventions in abuse-prone families, and this constitutes a pressing research need. Fourth, we need well-evaluated, thoughtfully designed demonstration projects exploring various avenues for heightening natural support in the lives of maltreating families, and how these can be tied to formal supportive services. These four research goals are among many that have been identified in this research review, but they constitute a basic, and ambitious, research agenda.

Above all of these goals, however, is the need for greater knowledge of the social isolation of maltreating families: Current research evidence is simply too shallow to permit confident conclusions about the meaning of their social isolation, its relevance to child abuse and neglect, and the resources of their social networks. This is particularly striking in light of the rich conceptual portrayal of social networks and social integration that exists in current literatures in family sociology and community psychology, and which has been applied only haphazardly to research on the social isolation of maltreating families. Existing studies provide an inconsistent portrayal of maltreating families as differing from others in each aspect of their social networks except their limited social embeddedness, which is among the least sensitive indexes of social integration. Findings are clearly not definitive about whether high-risk families experience satisfaction with their support agents (and which of them they perceive to be most helpful), how often they report receiving tangible assistance from these network associates, and how they perceive the resources that may exist within their neighborhoods and larger communities. At the same time, there exist provocative empirical analyses of social isolation from researchers such as Garbarino and Polansky that highlight a number of important hypotheses meriting further investigation. Any effort to address the social support needs of maltreating families must rely on detailed information concerning their social isolation. At present, much still remains to be understood.

Social Support in the Context of Child Welfare Reform

In several important ways, a concern with social support as an abuse-preventive strategy runs counter to the prevailing orientations of the child protection system in this country. By contrast with the system's predominant concern with identifying, intervening, and prosecuting suspected offenders, the approaches discussed in this book are concerned with the primary and secondary prevention of maltreatment, and restoring troubled families to healthy functioning as part of a comprehensive abuse prevention strategy. In contrast to the system's predominantly coercive role in the lives of families where abuse or neglect is suspected or has occurred, a social support approach emphasizes the system's assisting, enabling involvement with needy parents as well as those who are guilty of maltreatment. In contrast to the system's currently limited, overstretched resources for addressing the multidimensional problems of child abuse and neglect, the approach outlined here does not necessarily entail greater funding or personnel (although it may), but emphasizes the redirection of existing resources toward prevention as well as enhanced efforts to coordinate intervention strategies with the services provided by other public and private agencies concerned with troubled families. In contrast to the system's predominant emphasis on families that have already been victimized by child maltreatment, the emphasis of this discussion has equally attended to the needs of abuse-prone families in which children have not yet been harmed.

Can the social support strategies outlined in this book fit into the prevailing orientation of the child protection system? Obviously they can, given the extent to which several promising abuse prevention programs entailing social support (especially those emphasizing home visitation) are being implemented in child welfare systems across the country, and that are showing signs of limited but hopeful success (but see Pelton, 1992, for a different view). And given that much of the impetus for examining the potential value of social support strategies comes from within, not just outside, the child protection system, there is reason for hope that such strategies can be usefully incorporated into contemporary approaches to child protection.

At the same time, however, growing interest in abuse prevention (of which social support strategies are one aspect) derives from increasing concern about the capacity of the contemporary child protection system to address the multifaceted problems associated with child abuse and neglect, for reasons outlined in Chapter 1. Prevention has become the focus of proposals for reform of child welfare because, among other reasons, of the belief that once the problems of troubled families have reached a point that an abused child has come to the attention of child protection authorities, these problems have often become so intractable and resistant to change (at least within the capabilities of the system to promote change) that intervention is often too late to substantially help the family. Prevention efforts targeted to high-risk families are one means of trying to address these problems before they have become so severe. In this respect, a focus on prevention reflects a broad recognition both of the seriousness of the problems contributing to child maltreatment (requiring assistance to troubled families before a child has become abused) and of the limitations of the current child welfare system for effectively addressing these problems once serious abuse has occurred. The proactive, rather than reactive, emphasis of abuse prevention efforts is a sharp contrast to the contemporary climate of child protection.

If social support is part of a broadly based interest in abuse prevention, it is worth pondering what kind of a reformed child protection system would have social support at the center of its preventive efforts. One avenue for reform consists of the proposals of the U.S. Advisory Board on Child Abuse and Neglect (1990, 1991, 1993a, 1993b) that would lead to the creation of a child-centered, neighborhood-based child protection system. These proposals have been considered throughout this book because they provide one impetus for exploring the potential value of enlisting informal community helpers in a comprehensive abuse prevention strategy. The U.S. Advisory Board has also offered broader proposals for system reform that entail the coordination of multiple federal agencies that have an interest in abuse prevention, together with local and state-wide efforts to develop grass-roots, community-tailored abuse prevention strategies. The overall import of the advisory board's proposals would be the re-creation of a child protection system emphasizing prevention and treatment, neighborhood support, and children's needs.

Another approach to child welfare reform has been proposed by Leroy Pelton (1989, 1990, 1991, 1992), who is concerned with the manner in which local child protection caseworkers provide assistance to the troubled families they encounter while investigating complaints of abuse or neglect. To Pelton, one significant problem is that caseworkers have two incompatible roles in relation to the family: On one hand, they are investigators who must recommend to legal authorities whether civil or criminal action against parents is necessary, and on the other hand, they are social workers who seek to offer assistance and support to troubled parents and to assist their children. Pelton has proposed divorcing the caseworker's investigative and support functions, and assigning the task of substantiating abuse allegations to specially trained law enforcement officials who have the skills and expertise to conduct effective investigations. This enables the child protection caseworker to be a more unequivocal support agent for parents and children who can mediate between the family and police investigators, inform the family about the progress of the investigation, advocate on behalf of the family to legal and social service agencies, help to obtain various kinds of material assistance for the family as needed, and concertedly advance family preservation efforts in the context of the abuse investigation.

The reformed caseworker's role would occur, according to Pelton, in the context of a reformed child protection system with an emphasis on prevention, not just prosecution, of child maltreatment. Such a child protection agency would be devoted exclusively to family support, abuse prevention, and family preservation efforts that can be offered to a broad range of families: not only those who have come to the attention of legal authorities because of abuse allegations, but also abuse-prone families who have been identified through professional referrals, as well as foster families and families who obtain these services through self-referral. (Pelton and others have noted that it is a sad fact of the contemporary climate of public policy that it is easier for family members to obtain needed social services after they have maltreated offspring rather than before, when those services might help to reduce the stresses and difficulties that can lead to abuse or neglect.) This reformed agency would provide and coordinate material assistance such as emergency caretaking and homemaker services; housing assistance; help in eliminating household health and safety hazards; emergency cash assistance; provision of toys, cribs, and playpens to needy families; enlisting visiting health aides; coordinating transportation assistance; fostering parent skills training; and enhancing access to welfare assistance, substance abuse programs, and other services. In this manner, the prevention of child maltreatment would be at least as important to a comprehensive public strategy for combating child abuse as would be the prosecution of offenders.

These proposals by Pelton, the U.S. Advisory Board on Child Abuse and Neglect, and others (e.g., Thompson & Flood, in press) together emphasize what might be called *preventive family preservation;* that is, by providing broadly based supportive assistance to families who are at greatest risk of abusing or neglecting their offspring, they seek to strengthen families before the emergency interventions that accompany abuse allegations are necessary, and thus, it is hoped, stem the cascade of problems that can become intractable by the time a child has been hurt or neglected. These are not preventive strategies alone, but preventions designed to enhance family preservation by recognizing the importance of families to children and to their development, and the value of strengthening troubled families to avoid out-of-home placement of their offspring.

This leads, finally, to another characteristic of the reformed child welfare system in which abuse prevention strategies entailing social support would be central. In such a reformed system, the needs of the children would assume far greater attention than they do under the present system (Thompson & Flood, in press). It is dismaying that children do not receive greater services in a system that is ostensibly designed for their benefit, although perhaps it is unsurprising. After all, the goal of abuse prevention is to reduce an adult's propensity to hurt, neglect, or otherwise harm children, and this requires an emphasis on parental attitudes and practices. Moreover, child maltreatment is not just a "child problem" because designing interventions to prevent abuse potentially entails reconstructing neighborhoods, enlisting effective substance abuse strategies, combating poverty, and other issues that consider the broader ecological context of abuse and neglect.

But a child protection system must be designed with the needs, perspectives, and interests of children in mind if it is to be a truly supportive system. Thompson and Flood (in press) have considered in detail what such a child-oriented child protection system might look like. They have proposed, for example, that children should receive their own supportive assistance throughout all phases of casework, which, depending on the child's age, might include a special advocate for the child appointed from within or outside the child protection agency who provides information that is adjusted to the child's level of understanding, emotional assistance, and advocacy, and who accompanies the child to interviews, counseling sessions, and, if necessary, courtroom appearances. They have argued that in most cases, parents should become better enfranchised in case planning and decision making, even if the child is removed out of the home, to ease the child's transition and respect the child's continuing attachments to family members even when the family has become dangerous for them. They have advocated including members of the child's natural networks from the neighborhood and community in casework to provide additional support to children throughout these procedures. They have proposed that children who are victimized by abuse or neglect become the focus of an individualized treatment plan that takes into account the type of maltreatment, the child's age and developmental capacities, the family ecology, and the particular resources and vulnerabilities of the child and the family as a whole. Such a treatment plan would seek to address the impact of abuse on the child's developmental functioning, drawing on a flexible range of integrated services within decategorized funding programs. Finally, they have proposed that the effectiveness of such a reformed child protection system would be measured, at least in part, by the continuing well-being of children who have been assisted by the system.

Like other proposals throughout this volume, these offer an ambitious agenda for child welfare reform. But it is arguable that ambitious proposals for reform are, perhaps, most necessary in the present climate of child and family policy in the United States. There is nothing simple or straightforward about the social circumstances of maltreating families or the problems that contribute to child abuse or neglect. Quite clearly, an enduring multistrategy approach is required to address the needs and challenges of these families.

References

Aber, J. L., & Cicchetti, D. (1984). The socio-emotional development of maltreated children: An empirical and theoretical analysis. In H. E. Fitzgerald, B. M. Lester, & M. W. Yogman (Eds.), *Theory and research in behavioral pediatrics* (Vol. 2, pp. 147-205). New York: Plenum.

Asp, E., & Garbarino, J. (1983). Social support networks and the schools. In J. Whittaker & J. Garbarino (Eds.), *Social support networks: Informal helping in the human services* (pp. 251-297). New York: Aldine.

Barrera, M. (1981). Social support in the adjustment of pregnant adolescents: Assessment issues. In B. Gottlieb (Ed.), *Social networks and social support* (pp. 69-96). Beverly Hills, CA: Sage.

Barrera, M. (1986). Distinctions between social support concepts, measures, and models. *American Journal of Community Psychology, 14*, 413-445.

Barth, R. P. (1991). An experimental evaluation of in-home child abuse prevention services. *Child Abuse & Neglect, 15*, 363-375.

Belle, D. (1982). Social ties and social support. In D. Belle (Ed.), *Lives in stress* (pp. 133-144). Beverly Hills, CA: Sage.

Belle, D. (Ed.). (1989). *Children's social networks and social supports.* New York: John Wiley.

Belsky, J. (1980). Child maltreatment: An ecological integration. *American Psychologist, 35*, 320-335.

Belsky, J., Robins, E., & Gamble, W. (1984). The determinants of parental competence: Toward a contextual theory. In M. Lewis (Ed.), *Beyond the dyad* (pp. 251-279). New York: Plenum.

Belsky, J., & Vondra, J. (1989). Lessons from child abuse: The determinants of parenting. In D. Cicchetti & V. Carlson (Eds.), *Child maltreatment* (pp. 153-202). Cambridge, UK: Cambridge University Press.

Berndt, T. J. (1989). Obtaining support from friends during childhood and adolescence. In D. Belle (Ed.), *Children's social networks and social supports* (pp. 308-331). New York: John Wiley.

Blyth, D. A., Hill, J. P., & Thiel, K. S. (1982). Early adolescents' significant others: Grade and gender differences in perceived relationships with familial and nonfamilial adults and young people. *Journal of Youth and Adolescence, 11*, 425-450.

Blyth, D. A., & Traeger, C. (1988). Adolescent self-esteem and perceived relationships with parents and peers. In S. Salzinger, J. Antrobus, & M. Hammer (Eds.), *Social networks of children, adolescents, and college students* (pp. 171-194). Hillsdale, NJ: Lawrence Erlbaum.

Breakey, G., & Pratt, B. (1991). Healthy growth for Hawaii's "Healthy Start": Toward a systematic statewide approach to the prevention of child abuse and neglect. *Zero to Three (Bulletin of the National Center for Clinical Infant Programs), 11*, 16-22.

Bronfenbrenner, U. (1977). *The ecology of human development.* Cambridge, MA: Harvard University Press.

Bronfenbrenner, U. (1986). Ecology of the family as a context for human development: Research perspectives. *Developmental Psychology, 22*, 723-742.

Bronfenbrenner, U. (1989). Ecological systems theory. In R. Vasta (Ed.), *Annals of child development* (Vol. 6, pp. 187-249). Greenwich, CT: JAI.

Bronfenbrenner, U., & Crouter, A. C. (1983). The evolution of environmental models in developmental research. In P. H. Mussen (Ed.), *Handbook of child psychology, Vol. 1. History, theory, and methods* (pp. 357-414). New York: John Wiley.

Brownell, A., & Shumaker, S. A. (1984). Social support: An introduction to a complex phenomenon. *Journal of Social Issues, 40*, 1-9.

Bryant, B. K. (1985). The neighborhood walk: Sources of support in middle childhood. *Monographs of the Society for Research in Child Development, 50* (Serial no. 210).

Bryant, H. D., Billingsley, A., Kerry, G. A., Leefman, W. V., Merrill, E. J., Senecal, G. R., & Walsh, B. A. (1963). Physical abuse of children: An agency study. *Child Welfare, 42*, 125-130.

Bryant, P. (1993). *Availability of existing statewide parent education and support programs, and the need for these programs nationwide* (Working Paper No. 861). Chicago: National Committee to Prevent Child Abuse.

Burgess, R. L., & Youngblade, L. M. (1988). Social incompetence and the intergenerational transmission of abusive parental practices. In G. T. Hotaling, D. Finkelhor, J. T. Kirkpatrick, & M. A. Straus (Eds.), *Family abuse and its consequences: New directions in family violence research* (pp. 38-60). Newbury Park, CA: Sage.

Cassel, J. (1974a). An epidemiological perspective of psychosocial factors in disease etiology. *American Journal of Public Health, 64,* 1040-1043.

Cassel, J. (1974b). Psychosocial processes and "stress": Theoretical formulations. *International Journal of Health Services, 4,* 471-482.

Cassel, J. (1976). The contribution of the social environment to host resistance. *American Journal of Epidemiology, 102,* 107-123.

Cazenave, N. A., & Straus, M. A. (1979). Race, class, network embeddedness and family violence: A search for potent support systems. *Journal of Comparative Family Studies, 10,* 281-300.

Cicchetti, D. (1990). The organization and coherence of socioemotional, cognitive, and representational development: Illustrations through a developmental psychopathology perspective on Down syndrome and child maltreatment. In R. A. Thompson (Ed.), *Socioemotional development* (Nebraska Symposium on Motivation, Vol. 36, pp. 259-366). Lincoln: University of Nebraska Press.

Cobb, S. (1976). Social support as a moderator of life stress. *Psychosomatic Medicine, 38,* 300-314.

Cochran, M. (1990a). Personal networks in the ecology of human development. In M. Cochran, M. Larner, D. Riley, L. Gunnarsson, & C. R. Henderson (Eds.), *Extending families: The social networks of parents and their children* (pp. 3-32). Cambridge, UK: Cambridge University Press.

Cochran, M. (1990b). The network as an environment for human development. In M. Cochran, M. Larner, D. Riley, L. Gunnarsson, & C. R. Henderson (Eds.), *Extending families: The social networks of parents and their children* (pp. 265-276). Cambridge, UK: Cambridge University Press.

Cochran, M. (1990c). Environmental factors constraining network development. In M. Cochran, M. Larner, D. Riley, L. Gunnarsson, & C. R. Henderson (Eds.), *Extending families: The social networks of parents and their children* (pp. 277-296). Cambridge, UK: Cambridge University Press.

Cochran, M. M., & Brassard, J. A. (1979). Child development and personal social networks. *Child Development, 50,* 601-616.

Cochran, M., Gunnarsson, L., Grabe, S., & Lewis, J. (1990). The social networks of coupled mothers in four cultures. In M. Cochran, M. Larner, D. Riley, L. Gunnarsson, & C. R. Henderson (Eds.), *Extending families: The social networks of parents and their children* (pp. 86-104). Cambridge, UK: Cambridge University Press.

Cochran, M., & Henderson, C. R. (1990). Illustrations. In M. Cochran, M. Larner, D. Riley, L. Gunnarsson, & C. R. Henderson (Eds.), *Extending families: The social networks of parents and their children* (pp. 58-64). Cambridge, UK: Cambridge University Press.

Cochran, M., Larner, M., Riley, D., Gunnarsson, L., & Henderson, C. R. (Eds.). (1990). *Extending families: The social networks of parents and their children.* Cambridge, UK: Cambridge University Press.

Cochran, M., & Riley, D. (1988). Mother's reports of children's personal networks: Antecedents, concomitants, and consequences. In S. Salzinger, J. Antrobus, & M. Hammer (Eds.), *Social networks of children, adolescents, and college students* (pp. 113-147). Hillsdale, NJ: Lawrence Erlbaum.

Cochran, M., & Riley, D. (1990). The social networks of six-year-olds: Context, content, and consequence. In M. Cochran, M. Larner, D. Riley, L. Gunnarsson, & C. R. Henderson (Eds.), *Extending families: The social networks of parents and their children* (pp. 154-177). Cambridge, UK: Cambridge University Press.

Cohen, S., & Wills, T. A. (1985). Stress, social support, and the buffering hypothesis. *Psychological Bulletin, 98,* 310-357.

Colletta, N. D. (1979). Support systems after divorce: Incidence and impact. *Journal of Marriage and the Family, 41,* 837-846.

Collins, A. H., & Pancoast, D. L. (1976). *Natural helping networks: A strategy for prevention.* Washington, DC: National Association of Social Workers.

Conger, R. D., Conger, K. J., Elder, G. H., Jr., Lorenz, F. O., Simons, R. L., & Whitbeck, L. B. (1992). A family process model of economic hardship and adjustment of early adolescent boys. *Child Development, 63,* 526-541.

Conger, R., Elder, G., Lorenz, F., Conger, K., Simons, R., Whitbeck, L., Huck, S., & Melby, J. (1990). Linking economic hardship to marital quality and instability. *Journal of Marriage and the Family, 52,* 643-656.

Coohey, C. (1993). *Child abuse and neglect: Reexamining the social isolation construct.* Unpublished manuscript, University of Chicago.

Coohey, C. (1994). *A network analytic approach to the study of child physical abuse and neglect.* Unpublished manuscript, University of Chicago.

Corse, S. J., Schmid, K., & Trickett, P. K. (1990). Social network characteristics of mothers in abusing and nonabusing families and their relationships to parenting beliefs. *Journal of Community Psychology, 18,* 44-59.

Cotterell, J. L. (1986). Work and community influences on the quality of child rearing. *Child Development, 57,* 362-374.

Coulton, C. J., Korbin, J., Su, M., & Chow, J. (in press). Community level factors and child maltreatment rates. *Child Development.*

Crittenden, P. M. (1985). Social networks, quality of child rearing, and child development. *Child Development, 56,* 1299-1313.

Crnic, K. A., Greenberg, M. T., Ragozin, A. S., Robinson, N. M., & Basham, R. B. (1983). Effects of stress and social support on mothers and premature and full-term infants. *Child Development, 54,* 209-217.

Crnic, K. A., Greenberg, M. T., Robinson, N. M., & Ragozin, A. S. (1984). Maternal stress and social support: Effects on the mother-infant relationship from birth to 18 months. *American Journal of Orthopsychiatry, 54,* 224-235.

Cross, W. E. (1990). Race and ethnicity: Effects on social networks. In M. Cochran, M. Larner, D. Riley, L. Gunnarsson, & C. R. Henderson (Eds.), *Extending families: The social networks of parents and their children* (pp. 67-85). Cambridge, UK: Cambridge University Press.

Cutrona, C. E. (1984). Social support and stress in the transition to parenthood. *Journal of Abnormal Psychology, 93,* 378-390.

Daro, D. (1988). *Confronting child abuse.* New York: Free Press.

Daro, D. (1993). Child maltreatment research: Implications for program design. In D. Cicchetti & S. Toth (Eds.), *Child abuse, child development and social policy* (pp. 311-367). Norwood, NJ: Ablex.

Davis, P. W. (1991). Stranger intervention into child punishment in public places. *Social Problems, 38,* 227-246.

Deccio, G., Horner, B., & Wilson, D. (1991). *High-risk neighborhoods and high-risk families: Replication research related to the human ecology of child maltreatment.* Unpublished manuscript, Eastern Washington University.

Dubow, E. F., Tisak, J., Causey, D., Hryshko, A., & Reid, G. (1991). A two-year longitudinal study of stressful life events, social support, and social problem-solving skills: Contributions to children's behavioral and academic adjustment. *Child Development, 62,* 583-599.

Dubowitz, H. (1989). Prevention of child maltreatment: What is known. *Pediatrics, 83,* 570-577.

Durkin, R. (1986). The use of therapeutic day care to resolve the legal dilemma of protecting the rights of both children and parents in equivocal cases of abuse and neglect. *Child Care Quarterly, 15,* 138-140.

Egeland, B., & Brunquell, D. (1979). An at-risk approach to the study of child abuse: Some preliminary findings. *Journal of the American Academy of Child Psychiatry, 18,* 219-235.

Egeland, B., & Sroufe, L. A. (1981). Developmental sequelae of maltreatment in infancy. In R. Rizley & D. Cicchetti (Eds.), *Developmental perspectives on child maltreatment* (pp. 7-92). San Francisco: Jossey-Bass.

Egeland, B., Sroufe, L. A., & Erickson, M. (1983). The developmental consequence of different patterns of maltreatment. *Child Abuse & Neglect, 7,* 459-469.

Eisenberg, N. (1983). Developmental aspects of recipients' reactions to aid. In J. D. Fisher, A. Nadler, & B. M. DePaulo (Eds.), *New directions in helping, Vol. 1. Recipient reactions to aid* (pp. 189-222). New York: Academic Press.

Elmer, E. (1967). *Children in jeopardy.* Pittsburgh: University of Pittsburgh Press.

Elmer, E. (1977). *Fragile families, troubled children.* Pittsburgh: University of Pittsburgh Press.

Erickson, M. F., Egeland, B., & Pianta, R. (1989). The effects of maltreatment on the development of young children. In D. Cicchetti & V. Carlson

(Eds.), *Child maltreatment* (pp. 647-684). Cambridge, UK: Cambridge University Press.

Featherman, D. L. (1983). Life-span perspectives in social science research. In P. B. Baltes & O. G. Brim (Eds.), *Life-span development and behavior* (Vol. 5, pp. 1-57). New York: Academic Press.

Feiring, C., & Lewis, M. (1988). The child's social network from three to six years: The effects of age, sex, and socioeconomic status. In S. Salzinger, J. Antrobus, & M. Hammer (Eds.), *Social networks of children, adolescents, and college students* (pp. 93-112). Hillsdale, NJ: Lawrence Erlbaum.

Feiring, C., & Lewis, M. (1989). The social networks of girls and boys from early through middle childhood. In D. Belle (Ed.), *Children's social networks and social supports* (pp. 119-150). New York: John Wiley.

Ferleger, N., Glenwick, D. S., Gaines, R. R. W., & Green, A. H. (1988). Identifying correlates of reabuse in maltreating families. *Child Abuse & Neglect, 12,* 41-49.

Fischer, C. S. (1982). *To dwell among friends: Personal networks in town and city.* Chicago: University of Chicago Press.

Fisher, J. D., Nadler, A., & Witcher-Alagna, S. (1982). Recipient reactions to aid. *Psychological Bulletin, 91,* 27-54.

Forsythe, P. (1992). Homebuilders and family preservation. *Children and Youth Services Review, 14,* 37-47.

Froland, C., Pancoast, D. L., Chapman, N. J., & Kimboko, P. J. (1981). Linking formal and informal support systems. In B. H. Gottlieb (Ed.), *Social networks and social support* (pp. 259-275). Beverly Hills, CA: Sage.

Fuddy, L. (1994). *Outcomes for the Hawai'i Healthy Start program.* Unpublished manuscript, Maternal and Child Health Branch, Department of Health, State of Hawaii.

Furman, W., & Buhrmester, D. (1985). Children's perceptions of the personal relationships in their social networks. *Developmental Psychology, 21,* 1016-1024.

Furman, W., & Buhrmester, D. (1992). Age and sex differences in perceptions of networks of personal relationships. *Child Development, 63,* 103-115.

Furstenberg, F. F., Jr. (1993). How families manage risk and opportunity in dangerous neighborhoods. In W. Wilson (Ed.), *Sociology and the public agenda* (pp. 231-258). Newbury Park, CA: Sage.

Garbarino, J. (1976). A preliminary study of some ecological correlates of child abuse: The impact of socioeconomic stress on mothers. *Child Development, 47,* 178-185.

Garbarino, J. (1977a). The price of privacy in the social dynamics of child abuse. *Child Welfare, 56,* 565-575.

Garbarino, J. (1977b). The human ecology of child maltreatment: A conceptual model for research. *Journal of Marriage and the Family, 39,* 721-735.

Garbarino, J. (1980). What kind of society permits child abuse? *Infant Mental Health Journal, 1,* 270-280.

Garbarino, J. (1989). Troubled youth, troubled families: The dynamics of adolescent maltreatment. In D. Cicchetti & V. Carlson (Eds.), *Child maltreatment* (pp. 685-706). Cambridge, UK: Cambridge University Press.

Garbarino, J., Burston, N., Raber, S., Russell, R., & Crouter, A. C. (1978). The social maps of children approaching adolescence: Studying the ecology of youth development. *Journal of Youth and Adolescence, 7,* 417-428.

Garbarino, J., & Crouter, A. (1978). Defining the community context of parent-child relations: The correlates of child maltreatment. *Child Development, 49,* 604-616.

Garbarino, J., & Gilliam, G. (1980). *Understanding abusive families.* Lexington, MA: D. C. Heath.

Garbarino, J., & Kostelny, K. (1991). *Child maltreatment as a community problem.* Unpublished manuscript, Erikson Institute for Advanced Study in Child Development, Chicago.

Garbarino, J., & Kostelny, K. (1994). Neighborhood-based programs. In G. B. Melton & F. D. Barry (Eds.), *Protecting children from abuse and neglect: Foundations for a new national strategy* (pp. 304-352). New York: Guilford.

Garbarino, J., & Sherman, D. (1980a). High-risk neighborhoods and high-risk families: The human ecology of child maltreatment. *Child Development, 51,* 188-198.

Garbarino, J., & Sherman, D. (1980b). Identifying high-risk neighborhoods. In J. Garbarino & S. H. Stocking (Eds.), *Protecting children from abuse and neglect* (pp. 94-108). San Francisco: Jossey-Bass.

Gaudin, J. M., & Polansky, N. A. (1986). Social distancing of the neglectful family: Sex, race, and social class influences. *Child and Youth Services Review, 8,* 1-12.

Gaudin, J. M., & Pollane, L. (1983). Social networks, stress and child abuse. *Child and Youth Services Review, 5,* 91-102.

Gaudin, J. M., Wodarski, J. S., Arkinson, M. K., & Avery, L. S. (1990-1991). Remedying child neglect: Effectiveness of social network interventions. *Journal of Applied Social Sciences, 15,* 97-123.

Gelles, R. J. (1973). Child abuse as psychopathology: A sociological critique and reformulation. *American Journal of Orthopsychiatry, 43,* 611-621.

Gelles, R. J. (1992). Poverty and violence toward children. *American Behavioral Scientist, 35,* 258-274.

Gelles, R. J. (1993). Family reunification/family preservation: Are children really being protected? *Journal of Interpersonal Violence, 8,* 557-562.

Gelles, R. J., & Cornell, C. P. (1990). *Intimate violence in families* (2nd ed.). Newbury Park, CA: Sage.

General Accounting Office. (1990). *Home visiting: A promising early intervention strategy for at-risk families* (GAO/HRD-90-83). Washington, DC: Government Printing Office.

General Accounting Office. (1992). *Child abuse: Prevention programs need greater emphasis* (GAO/HRD-92-99). Washington, DC: Government Printing Office.

Gil, D. G. (1970). *Violence against children: Physical child abuse in the United States.* Cambridge, MA: Harvard University Press.

Giovannoni, J. M., & Billingsley, A. (1970). Child neglect among the poor: A study of parental adequacy in families of three ethnic groups. *Child Welfare, 49,* 196-204.

Gottlieb, B. H. (1983). *Social support strategies.* Beverly Hills, CA: Sage.

Gottlieb, B. (1985). Theory into practice: Issues that surface in planning interventions which mobilize support. In I. G. Sarason & B. R. Sarason (Eds.), *Social support: Theory, research and applications* (pp. 417-437). The Hague, The Netherlands: Martinus Nijhoff.

Granovetter, M. (1973). The strength of weak ties. *American Journal of Sociology, 78,* 1360-1380.

Gray, J. D., Cutler, C. A., Dean, J. G., & Kempe, C. H. (1979). Prediction and prevention of child abuse and neglect. *Journal of Social Issues, 35,* 127-139.

Greenberg, M. S. (1980). A theory of indebtedness. In K. Gergen, M. S. Greenberg, & R. Willis (Eds.), *Social exchange: Advances in theory and research* (pp. 252-278). New York: Plenum.

Greenberg, M. S., & Westcott, D. R. (1983). Indebtedness as a mediator of reactions to aid. In J. D. Fisher, A. Nadler, & B. M. DePaulo (Eds.), *New directions in helping, Vol. 1. Recipient reactions to aid* (pp. 85-112). New York: Academic Press.

Gunnarsson, L., & Cochran, M. (1990). The support networks of single parents: Sweden and the United States. In M. Cochran, M. Larner, D. Riley, L. Gunnarsson, & C. R. Henderson (Eds.), *Extending families: The social networks of parents and their children* (pp. 105-116). Cambridge, UK: Cambridge University Press.

Halpern, R. (1984). Lack of effects for home-based early intervention? Some possible explanations. *American Journal of Orthopsychiatry, 54,* 33-42.

Hardy, J. B., & Streett, R. (1989). Family support and parenting education in the home: An effective extension of clinic-based preventive health care services for poor children. *Journal of Pediatrics, 115,* 927-931.

Hartup, W. W. (1983). Peer relations. In P. H. Mussen (Ed.), *Handbook of child psychology, Vol. 4. Socialization, personality, and social development* (4th ed., pp. 103-196). New York: John Wiley.

Hatfield, E., & Sprecher, S. (1983). Equity theory and recipient reactions to aid. In J. D. Fisher, A. Nadler, & B. M. DePaulo (Eds.), *New directions in helping, Vol. 1. Recipient reactions to aid* (pp. 113-141). New York: Academic Press.

Hawaii Department of Health. (1992). *Healthy Start: Hawaii's system of family support services.* Honolulu: Author.

Helfer, R. E. (1982). A review of the literature on the prevention of child abuse and neglect. *Child Abuse & Neglect, 6,* 251-261.

Heller, K. (1979). The effects of social support: Prevention and treatment implications. In A. P. Goldstein & F. H. Kanfer (Eds.), *Maximizing treatment gains* (pp. 353-382). New York: Academic Press.

Heller, K., & Swindle, R. W. (1983). Social networks, perceived social support, and coping with stress. In R. D. Felner, L. A. Jason, J. N. Moritsugu, & S. S. Farber (Eds.), *Preventive psychology: Theory, research, and practice* (pp. 87-103). New York: Pergamon.

Herrenkohl, R. C., Herrenkohl, E. C., & Egolf, B. P. (1983). Circumstances surrounding the occurrence of child maltreatment. *Journal of Consulting and Clinical Psychology, 51,* 424-431.

Herrenkohl, R. C., Herrenkohl, E. C., Egolf, B., & Seech, M. (1979). The repetition of child abuse: How frequently does it occur? *Child Abuse & Neglect, 3,* 67-72.

Hirsch, B. J., & DuBois, D. L. (1989). The school-nonschool ecology of early adolescent friendships. In D. Belle (Ed.), *Children's social networks and social supports* (pp. 260-274). New York: John Wiley.

Homel, R., Burns, A., & Goodnow, J. (1987). Parental social networks and child development. *Journal of Social and Personal Relationships, 4,* 159-177.

Horowitz, B., & Wintermute, W. (1978). Use of an emergency fund in protective services casework. *Child Welfare, 57,* 432-437.

House, J. H., Umberson, D., & Landis, K. R. (1988). Structures and processes of social support. In W. R. Scott & J. Blake (Eds.), *Annual review of sociology* (Vol. 14, pp. 293-318). Palo Alto, CA: Annual Reviews.

Howes, C., & Hamilton, C. E. (1992). Children's relationships with child care teachers: Stability and concordance with parental attachments. *Child Development, 63,* 867-878.

Howes, C., Rodning, C., Galluzzo, D., & Meyers, L. (1988). Attachment and child care: Relationships with mother and caregiver. *Early Childhood Research Quarterly, 3,* 403-416.

Hoyt, D., & Babchuk, N. (1983). Adult kinship networks: The selective formation of intimate ties with kin. *Social Forces, 62,* 84-101.

Hunter, R. S., & Kilstrom, N. (1979). Breaking the cycle in abusive families. *American Journal of Psychiatry, 136,* 1320-1322.

Jacobson, S. W., & Frye, K. F. (1991). Effect of maternal social support on attachment: Experimental evidence. *Child Development, 62,* 572-582.

Jennings, K. D., Stagg, V., & Connors, R. E. (1991). Social networks and mothers' interactions with their preschool children. *Child Development, 62,* 966-978.

Jensen, D. E., Prandoni, J. R., Hagenau, H. R., Wisdom, P. A., & Riley, E. A. (1977). Child abuse in a court referred, inner city population. *Journal of Clinical Child Psychology, 6,* 59-62.

Kamerman, S. B., & Kahn, A. J. (1993). Home health visiting in Europe. *The Future of Children, 3,* 39-52.

Kinney, J., & Dittmar, K. (in press). Homebuilders: Helping families help themselves. In I. Schwartz (Ed.), *Working with troubled children and their families in their own homes: Implications for policymakers and practitioners.* Lincoln: University of Nebraska Press.

Kinney, J., Haapala, D., Booth, C., & Leavitt, S. (1990). The Homebuilders model. In J. K. Whittaker, J. Kinney, E. M. Tracy, & C. Booth (Eds.), *Reaching high-risk families: Intensive family preservation in human services* (pp. 31-64). New York: Aldine de Gruyter.

Korbin, J. E. (1989). Fatal maltreatment by mothers: A proposed framework. *Child Abuse & Neglect, 13,* 481-489.

Korbin, J. E. (1991, November). *"Good mothers," "babykillers," and fatal child abuse.* Paper presented to the annual meeting of the American Anthropological Association, Chicago.

Korbin, J. E. (in press). Social networks and family violence in cross-cultural perspective. In G. B. Melton (Ed.), *The individual, the family, and social good: Personal fulfillment in times of change* (Nebraska Symposium on Motivation, Vol. 42). Lincoln: University of Nebraska Press.

Kotelchuck, M. (1982). Child abuse and neglect: Prediction and misclassification. In R. H. Starr (Ed.), *Child abuse prediction* (pp. 67-104). Cambridge, MA: Ballinger.

Ladd, G. W., Hart, C. H., Wadsworth, E. M., & Golter, B. S. (1988). Preschoolers' peer networks in nonschool settings: Relationship to family characteristics and school adjustment. In S. Salzinger, J. Antrobus, & M. Hammer (Eds.), *Social networks of children, adolescents, and college students* (pp. 61-92). Hillsdale, NJ: Lawrence Erlbaum.

Larner, M. (1990a). Changes in network resources and relationships over time. In M. Cochran, M. Larner, D. Riley, L. Gunnarsson, & C. R. Henderson (Eds.), *Extending families: The social networks of parents and their children* (pp. 181-204). Cambridge, UK: Cambridge University Press.

Larner, M. (1990b). Local residential mobility and its effects on social networks: A cross-cultural comparison. In M. Cochran, M. Larner, D. Riley, L. Gunnarsson, & C. R. Henderson (Eds.), *Extending families: The social networks of parents and their children* (pp. 205-229). Cambridge, UK: Cambridge University Press.

Larner, M., & Halpern, R. (1987). Lay home visiting programs: Strengths, tensions, and challenges. *Zero to Three (Bulletin of the National Center for Clinical Infant Programs), 8,* 1-7.

Lazarus, R., & Folkman, S. (1984). *Stress, appraisal and coping.* New York: Springer.

Leslie, L., & Grady, K. (1985). Changes in mothers' social networks and social support following divorce. *Journal of Marriage and the Family, 47,* 663-673.

Levitt, M. J., Guacci-Franco, N., & Levitt, J. L. (1993). Convoys of social support in childhood and early adolescence: Structure and function. *Developmental Psychology, 29,* 811-818.

Levitt, M., Weber, R., & Clark, M. (1986). Social network relationships as sources of maternal support and well-being. *Developmental Psychology, 22,* 310-316.

Lewis, M., Feiring, C., & Kotsonis, M. (1984). The social network of the young child: A developmental perspective. In M. Lewis (Ed.), *Beyond the dyad* (pp. 129-160). New York: Plenum.

Lewis, R. E., & Fraser, M. (1987). Blending informal and formal helping networks in foster care. *Child and Youth Services Review, 9,* 153-169.

Litwak, E., & Szelenyi, I. (1969). Primary group structures and their function: Kin, neighborhoods and friends. *American Sociological Review, 34,* 465-481.

Long, F. (1983). Social support networks in day care and early child development. In J. K. Whittaker & J. Garbarino (Eds.), *Social support networks* (pp. 189-217). New York: Aldine.

Lovell, M. L., & Hawkins, J. D. (1988). An evaluation of a group intervention to increase the personal social networks of abusive mothers. *Children and Youth Services Review, 10,* 175-188.

McAdoo, H. P. (1980). Black mothers and the extended family support network. In L. Rodgers-Rose (Ed.), *The black woman* (pp. 125-144). Beverly Hills, CA: Sage.

McCurdy, K., & Daro, D. (1994). Child maltreatment: A national survey of reports and fatalities. *Journal of Interpersonal Violence, 9,* 75-93.

Medrich, E. A., Roizen, J. A., Rubin, V., & Buckley, S. (1982). *The serious business of growing up: A study of children's lives outside school.* Berkeley: University of California Press.

Melson, G. F., Ladd, G. W., & Hsu, H.-C. (1993). Maternal support networks, maternal cognitions, and young children's social and cognitive development. *Child Development, 64,* 1401-1417.

Meyer, C. H. (1985). Social supports and social workers: Collaboration or conflict? *Social Work, 30,* 291.

Miller, J. L., & Whittaker, J. K. (1988). Social services and social support: Blended programs for families at risk for child maltreatment. *Child Welfare, 67,* 161-174.

Mitchell, R. E., & Trickett, E. J. (1980). Task force report: Social networks as mediators of social support: An analysis of the effects and determinants of social networks. *Community Mental Health Journal, 16,* 27-44.

National Commission on Children. (1991). *Beyond rhetoric: A new American agenda for children and families.* Washington, DC: Government Printing Office.

National Research Council. (1993). *Understanding child abuse and neglect.* Washington, DC: National Academy Press.

Newberger, E. H., Reed, R. B., Daniel, J. H., Hyde, J. N., Jr., & Kotelchuck, M. (1977). Pediatric social illness: Toward an etiologic classification. *Pediatrics, 60,* 178-185.

Nurse, S. M. (1964). Familial patterns of parents who abuse their children. *Smith College Studies in Social Work, 35,* 9-25.

Oates, R., Davis, A., Ryan, M., & Stewart, L. (1979). Risk factors associated with child abuse. *Child Abuse & Neglect, 3,* 547-553.

O'Donnell, L., & Steuve, A. (1983). Mothers as social agents: Structuring the community activities of school aged children. In H. Lopata & J. H. Pleck (Eds.), *Research on the interweave of social roles: Jobs and families, Vol. 3. Families and jobs* (pp. 113-129). Greenwich, CT: JAI.

Olds, D. L. (1988). The Prenatal/Early Infancy Project. In R. H. Price, E. L. Cowen, R. P. Lorion, & J. Ramos-McKay (Eds.), *14 ounces of prevention: A casework for practitioners* (pp. 9-23). Washington, DC: American Psychological Association.

Olds, D. L., & Henderson, C. R., Jr. (1989). The prevention of maltreatment. In D. Cicchetti & V. Carlson (Eds.), *Child maltreatment* (pp. 722-763). Cambridge, UK: Cambridge University Press.

Olds, D. L., Henderson, C. R., Jr., Chamberlin, R., & Tatelbaum, R. (1986). Preventing child abuse and neglect: A randomized trial of nurse home visitation. *Pediatrics, 78,* 65-78.

Olds, D. L., Henderson, C. R., Jr., Tatelbaum, R., & Chamberlin, R. (1986). Improving the delivery of prenatal care and outcomes of pregnancy: A randomized trial of nurse home visitation. *Pediatrics, 77,* 16-28.

Olds, D. L., & Kitzman, H. (1990). Can home visitation improve the health of women and children at environmental risk? *Pediatrics, 86,* 108-116.

Olds, D. L., & Kitzman, H. (1993). Review of research on home visiting for pregnant women and parents of young children. *The Future of Children, 3,* 53-92.

Ory, M. G., & Earp, J. A. L. (1980). Child maltreatment: An analysis of familial and institutional predictors. *Journal of Family Issues, 1,* 339-356.

Parke, R. D., & Bhavnagri, N. P. (1989). Parents as managers of children's peer relationships. In D. Belle (Ed.), *Children's social networks and social supports* (pp. 241-259). New York: John Wiley.

Parke, R. D., & Collmer, C. W. (1975). Child abuse: An interdisciplinary analysis. In E. M. Hetherington (Ed.), *Review of child development research* (Vol. 5, pp. 509-590). Chicago: University of Chicago Press.

Pecora, P. J. (1991). Family-based and intensive family preservation services: A select literature review. In M. W. Fraser, P. J. Pecora, & D. A. Haapala (Eds.), *Families in crisis: The impact of intensive family preservation services* (pp. 17-47). New York: Aldine.

Pecora, P. J., Fraser, M. W., & Haapala, D. A. (1991). Client outcomes and issues for program design. In K. Wells & D. E. Biegel (Eds.), *Family preservation services: Research and evaluation* (pp. 3-32). Newbury Park, CA: Sage.

Pelton, L. H. (1978). Child abuse and neglect: The myth of classlessness. *American Journal of Orthopsychiatry, 48,* 608-617.

Pelton, L. H. (1989). *For reasons of poverty: A critical analysis of the public child welfare system in the United States.* New York: Praeger.

Pelton, L. H. (1990). Resolving the crisis in child welfare: Simply expanding the present system is not enough. *Public Welfare, 48,* 19-45.

Pelton, L. H. (1991). Beyond permanency planning: Restructuring the public child welfare system. *Social Work, 36,* 337-343.

Pelton, L. H. (1992). A functional approach to reorganizing family and child welfare interventions. *Children and Youth Services Review, 14,* 289-303.

Pelton, L. H. (1994). The role of material factors in child abuse and neglect. In G. B. Melton & F. Barry (Eds.), *Safe neighborhoods: Foundations for a new national strategy on child abuse and neglect* (pp. 131-181). New York: Guilford.

Peterson, L. (1990). PhoneFriend: A developmental description of needs expressed by child callers to a community telephone support system for children. *Journal of Applied Developmental Psychology, 11,* 105-122.

Pettigrew, T. G. (1983). Seeking public assistance: A stigma analysis. In A. Nadler, J. D. Fisher, & B. M. DePaulo (Eds.), *New directions in helping, Vol. 3. Applied perspectives on help-seeking and -receiving* (pp. 273-292). New York: Academic Press.

Phillips, D. A., Howes, C., & Whitebook, M. (1992). The social policy context of child care: Effects on quality. *American Journal of Community Psychology, 20,* 25-51.

Pianta, R., Egeland, B., & Erickson, M. F. (1989). The antecedents of maltreatment: Results of the Mother-Child Interaction Research Project. In D. Cicchetti & V. Carlson (Eds.), *Child maltreatment* (pp. 203-253). Cambridge, UK: Cambridge University Press.

Pinderhughes, E. (1982). Afro-American families and the victim system. In M. McGoldrick, J. K. Pearce, & J. Giordano (Eds.), *Ethnicity and family therapy* (pp. 108-122). New York: Guilford.

Polansky, N. A., Ammons, P. W., & Gaudin, J. M. (1985). Loneliness and isolation in child neglect. *Social Casework, 66*, 38-47.

Polansky, N. A., Chalmers, M. A., Buttenwieser, E., & Williams, D. P. (1981). *Damaged parents: An anatomy of child neglect.* Chicago: University of Chicago Press.

Polansky, N. A., & Gaudin, J. M. (1983). Social distancing of the neglectful family. *Social Service Review, 57*, 196-208.

Polansky, N. A., Gaudin, J. M., Ammons, P. W., & David, K. B. (1985). The psychological ecology of the neglectful mother. *Child Abuse & Neglect, 9*, 265-275.

Popenoe, D. (1993). American family decline, 1960-1990: A review and appraisal. *Journal of Marriage and the Family, 55*, 527-555.

Powell, D. R. (1979). Family-environment relations and early childrearing: The role of social networks and neighborhoods. *Journal of Research and Development in Education, 13*, 1-11.

Powell, D. R. (1987). A neighborhood approach to parent support groups. *Journal of Community Psychology, 15*, 51-62.

Powell, D. R. (1988). Client characteristics and the design of community-based intervention programs. In A. R. Pence (Ed.), *Ecological research with children and families: From concepts to methodology* (pp. 122-142). New York: Teachers College Press.

President's Commission on Mental Health. (1978). *Task force report on community support systems.* Washington, DC: Government Printing Office.

Reid, M., Landesman, S., Treder, R., & Jaccard, J. (1989). "My family and friends": Six- to twelve-year-old children's perceptions of social support. *Child Development, 60*, 896-910.

Robertson, E. B., Elder, G. H., Jr., Skinner, M. L., & Conger, R. D. (1991). The costs and benefits of social support in families. *Journal of Marriage and the Family, 53*, 403-416.

Robertson, J. F. (1975). Interaction in three generation families, parents as mediators: Toward a theoretical perspective. *International Journal of Aging and Human Development, 6*, 103-110.

Rook, K. S., & Dooley, D. (1985). Applying social support research: Theoretical problems and future directions. *Journal of Social Issues, 41*, 5-28.

Rossi, P. H. (1992). Assessing family preservation programs. *Children and Youth Services Review, 14,* 77-97.

Salzinger, S., Antrobus, J., & Hammer, M. (Eds.). (1988). *Social networks of children, adolescents, and college students.* Hillsdale, NJ: Lawrence Erlbaum.

Salzinger, S., Feldman, R. S., Hammer, M., & Rosario, M. (1993). The effects of physical abuse on children's social relationships. *Child Development, 64,* 169-187.

Salzinger, S., Kaplan, S., & Artemyeff, C. (1983). Mothers' personal social networks and child maltreatment. *Journal of Abnormal Psychology, 92,* 68-76.

Sampson, R. J. (1992). Family management and child development: Insights from social disorganization theory. In J. McCord (Ed.), *Advances in criminological theory, Vol. 3. Facts, frameworks, and forecasts* (pp. 63-83). New Brunswick, NJ: Transaction Books.

Seagull, E. A. W. (1987). Social support and child maltreatment: A review of the evidence. *Child Abuse & Neglect, 11,* 41-52.

Select Committee on Children, Youth, and Families. (1987). *Abused children in America: Victims of official neglect.* Washington, DC: Government Printing Office.

Shinn, M., Lehmann, S., & Wong, N. W. (1984). Social interaction and social support. *Journal of Social Issues, 40,* 55-76.

Shumaker, S. A., & Brownell, A. (1984). Toward a theory of social support: Closing conceptual gaps. *Journal of Social Issues, 40,* 11-36.

Siegel, E., Bauman, K. E., Schaefer, E. S., Saunders, M. M., & Ingram, D. D. (1980). Hospital and home support during infancy: Impact on maternal attachment, child abuse and neglect, and health care utilization. *Pediatrics, 66,* 183-190.

Simons, R. L., Lorenz, F. O., Conger, R. D., & Wu, C.-I. (1992). Support from spouse as mediator and moderator of the disruptive influence of economic strain on parenting. *Child Development, 63,* 1282-1301.

Simons, R. L., Lorenz, F. O., Wu, C.-I., & Conger, R. D. (1993). Social network and marital support as mediators and moderators of the impact of stress and depression on parental behavior. *Developmental Psychology, 29,* 368-381.

Smith, J., & Adler, R. (1991). Chidren hospitalized with child abuse and neglect: A case-control study. *Child Abuse & Neglect, 15,* 437-445.

Smith, S. (1975). *The battered child syndrome.* London: Butterworth.

Smith, S. M., Hanson, R., & Noble, S. (1974). Social aspects of the battered baby syndrome. *British Journal of Psychiatry, 125,* 568-582.

Stack, C. (1974). *All our kin: Strategies for survival in a black community.* New York: Harper & Row.

Starr, R. H. (1982). A research-based approach to the prediction of child abuse. In R. H. Starr (Ed.), *Child abuse prediction* (pp. 105-134). Cambridge, MA: Ballinger.

Steinberg, L., Catalano, R., & Dooley, D. (1981). Economic antecedents of child abuse and neglect. *Child Development, 52,* 975-985.

Straus, M. A. (1980). Stress and physical abuse. *Child Abuse & Neglect, 4,* 75-88.

Straus, M. A., Gelles, R. J., & Steinmetz, S. (1980). *Behind closed doors: Violence in the American family.* Garden City, NY: Doubleday/Anchor.

Straus, M. A., & Kantor, G. K. (1987). Stress and child abuse. In R. E. Helfer & R. S. Kempe (Eds.), *The battered child* (4th ed., pp. 42-59). Chicago: University of Chicago Press.

Thompson, R. A., & Flood, M. F. (in press). Toward a child-oriented child protection system. In G. B. Melton (Ed.), *Toward a child-centered, neighborhood-based child protection system.* Lincoln: University of Nebraska Press.

Thompson, R. A., Scalora, M. J., Castrianno, L., & Limber, S. P. (1992). Grandparent visitation rights: Emergent psychological and psycho-legal issues. In D. Kagehiro & W. Laufer (Eds.), *Handbook of psychology and law* (pp. 292-317). New York: Springer-Verlag.

Thompson, R. A., & Wilcox, B. (in press). Child maltreatment research: Federal support and policy issues. *American Psychologist.*

Tinsley, B. R., & Parke, R. D. (1984). Grandparents as support and socialization agents. In M. Lewis (Ed.), *Beyond the dyad* (pp. 161-194). New York: Plenum.

Toro, P. A. (1982). Developmental effects of child abuse: A review. *Child Abuse & Neglect, 6,* 423-431.

Tracy, E. M. (1990). Identifying social support resources of at-risk families. *Social Work, 35,* 252-258.

Tracy, E. M., & Whittaker, J. K. (1987). The evidence base for social support interventions in child and family practice: Emerging issues for research and practice. *Child and Youth Services Review, 9,* 249-270.

Tracy, E. M., Whittaker, J. K., Boylan, F., Neitman, P., & Overstreet, E. (in press). Network interventions with high risk youth and families throughout the continuum of care. In I. Schwartz (Ed.), *Working with troubled children and their families in their own homes: Implications for policymakers and practitioners.* Lincoln: University of Nebraska Press.

Turner, R., & Avison, W. (1985). Assessing risk factors for problem parenting. *Journal of Marriage and the Family, 43,* 881-892.

Unger, D. G., & Powell, D. R. (1980). Supporting families under stress: The role of social networks. *Family Relations, 29,* 566-574.

Unger, D. G., & Wandersman, L. P. (1985). Social support and adolescent mothers: Action research contributions to theory and application. *Journal of Social Issues, 41,* 29-45.

U.S. Advisory Board on Child Abuse and Neglect. (1990). *Child abuse and neglect: Critical first steps to a national emergency.* Washington, DC: Government Printing Office.

U.S. Advisory Board on Child Abuse and Neglect. (1991). *Creating caring communities: Blueprint for an effective federal policy on child abuse and neglect.* Washington, DC: Government Printing Office.

U.S. Advisory Board on Child Abuse and Neglect. (1993a). *The continuing child protection emergency: A challenge to the nation.* Washington, DC: Government Printing Office.

U.S. Advisory Board on Child Abuse and Neglect. (1993b). *Neighbors helping neighbors: A new national strategy for the protection of children.* Washington, DC: Government Printing Office.

Vaux, A. (1985). Variations in social support associated with gender, ethnicity, and age. *Journal of Social Issues, 41,* 89-110.

Vaux, A. (1988). *Social support: Theory, research, and intervention.* New York: Praeger.

Vondra, J. I. (1990). The community context of child abuse and neglect. *Marriage and Family Review, 15,* 19-38.

Wahler, R. G. (1980). The insular mother: Her problems in parent-child treatment. *Journal of Applied Behavior Analysis, 13,* 207-219.

Wahler, R. G., & Hann, D. M. (1984). The communication patterns of troubled mothers: In search of a keystone in the generalization of parenting skills. *Education and Treatment of Children, 7,* 335-350.

Wald, M. S., Carlsmith, J. M., & Leiderman, P. H. (1988). *Protecting abused and neglected children.* Stanford, CA: Stanford University Press.

Wasik, B. H. (1993). Staffing issues for home visiting programs. *The Future of Children, 3,* 140-157.

Wasik, B. H., Bryant, D. M., & Lyons, C. M. (1990). *Home visiting.* Newbury Park, CA: Sage.

Weinraub, M., & Wolf, B. M. (1983). Effects of stress and social supports on mother-child interactions in single- and two-parent families. *Child Development, 54,* 1297-1311.

Weiss, H. B. (1993). Home visits: Necessary but not sufficient. *The Future of Children, 3,* 113-128.

Wekerle, C., & Wolfe, D. A. (in press). Prevention of child physical abuse and neglect: Promising new directions. *Clinical Psychology Review.*

Wells, K. (in press). Family preservation services in context: Origins, practices, and current issues. In I. Schwartz (Ed.), *Working with troubled children and their families in their own homes: Implications for policy-makers and practitioners.* Lincoln: University of Nebraska Press.

Wells, K., & Biegel, D. E. (1992). Intensive family preservation services research: Current status and future agenda. *Social Work Research & Abstracts, 28,* 21-27.

Whittaker, J. K. (1983). Social support networks in child welfare. In J. Whittaker & J. Garbarino (Eds.), *Social support networks: Informal helping in the human services* (pp. 167-187). New York: Aldine.

Whittaker, J. K., Schinke, S. P., & Gilchrist, L. D. (1986). The ecological paradigm in child, youth, and family services: Implications for policy and practice. *Social Service Review, 60,* 483-503.

Willis, D. J., Holden, E. W., & Rosenberg, M. (1992). *Prevention of child maltreatment: Developmental and ecological perspectives.* New York: John Wiley.

Wolock, I., & Horowitz, B. (1979). Child maltreatment and material deprivation among AFDC-recipient families. *Social Service Review, 53,* 175-194.

Young, G., & Gately, T. (1988). Neighborhood impoverishment and child maltreatment: An analysis from the ecological perspective. *Journal of Family Issues, 9,* 240-254.

Young, L. (1964). *Wednesday's children: A study of child neglect and abuse.* New York: McGraw-Hill.

Zellman, G. (1990). Child abuse reporting and failure to report among mandated reporters. *Journal of Interpersonal Violence, 5,* 1-11.

Zellman, G., & Anter, S. (1990). Mandated reporters and CPS: A study in frustration. *Public Welfare, 48,* 1-31.

Zigler, E. F. (1989). Addressing the nation's child care crisis: The school of the twenty-first century. *American Journal of Orthopsychiatry, 59,* 484-491.

Zuravin, S. J. (1986). Residential density and urban child maltreatment: An aggregate analysis. *Journal of Family Violence, 1,* 307-322.

Zuravin, S. J. (1989). The ecology of child abuse and neglect: Review of the literature and presentation of data. *Violence and Victims, 4,* 101-120.

Author Index

214

Subject Index

About the Author

Ross A. Thompson is a Professor of Psychology at the University of Nebraska—Lincoln, where he has also served as Associate Director of the university's Center on Children, Families and the Law. He received his Ph.D. in Developmental Psychology from the University of Michigan in 1981, where he was a Bush Fellow in Child Development and Social Policy. Since coming to Nebraska in 1981, he has been active both as a developmental scientist and a psycholegal scholar. As a developmental psychologist, his work has focused on infant-parent attachment and its later consequences, early emotional development and the growth of emotional regulation, and family relationships. He is Associate Editor of *Child Development* (the flagship journal of the Society for Research on Child Development) and has written the chapter on early socioemotional development for the next *Handbook of Child Psychology*. As a psycholegal scholar, he has written on child maltreatment, the effects of divorce and custody on children, grandparents' rights, infant day care, and research ethics. He lectures on children and the law at the university's College of Law and on family policy at the university's College of Human Resources and Family Sciences. Dr. Thompson has received the Boyd R. McCandless Young Scientist Award for Early Distinguished Achievement from the American Psychological Association (Division 7), the Meyer Elkin Award for an essay submitted to *Family and Conciliation Courts Review*, and has been a Senior NIMH Fellow in Law and Psychology at Stanford University. He is the editor of *Socioemotional Development* (Nebraska Symposium on Motivation) and a coauthor of *Infant-Mother Attachment*.